ON THE RECORD

On the Record

music journalists
on their lives, craft,
and careers

MIKE HILLEARY

UNIVERSITY OF MASSACHUSETTS PRESS
AMHERST AND BOSTON

ISBN 978-1-62534-538-7 (paper); 537-0 (hardcover)

Designed by adam b. bohannon
Set in Parkinson
Printed and bound by Books International, Inc.

Cover design by adam b. bohannon

LIBRARY OF CONGRESS CATALOGING-IN-PUBLICATION DATA

Names: Hilleary, Mike, interviewer.
Title: On the record : music journalists on their lives, craft, and careers
    / [interviews by] Mike Hilleary.
Description: Amherst : University of Massachusetts Press, 2020. |
Identifiers: LCCN 2020019220 | ISBN 9781625345370 (hardcover) | ISBN
    9781625345387 (paperback) | ISBN 9781625345394 (ebook) | ISBN
    9781625345400 (ebook)
Subjects: LCSH: Music journalists—Interviews. | Musical criticism.
Classification: LCC ML3785 .O6 2020 | DDC 070.4/4978—dc23
LC record available at https://lccn.loc.gov/2020019220

British Library Cataloguing-in-Publication Data
A catalog record for this book is available from the British Library.

To Kristin, Sam, and Noah

CONTENTS

acknowledgments
ix

introduction
1

bylines
5

CHAPTER ONE
The Music That Makes Us
25

CHAPTER TWO
Humble Beginnings
44

CHAPTER THREE
Interviews
92

CHAPTER FOUR
Criticism
131

CHAPTER FIVE
Print versus Digital
169

CHAPTER SIX
As an Industry, As a Career
188

CHAPTER SEVEN
What Music Does, and Why It Matters
224

What's the impulse behind art? It's saying in whatever language is the language of your work, "If I could move you as much as it moved me ... if I can move anyone a tenth as much as that moved me, if I can spark the same sense of mystery and awe and surprise as that sparked in me, well that's why I do what I do."

Greil Marcus
2013 commencement address
at New York's School of Visual Arts

Where do you get off? Where do you get sweet? I am dark and mysterious, and PISSED OFF! And I could be very dangerous to all of you! I am not sweet! And you should know that about me ... I am THE ENEMY!

William Miller
Almost Famous (2000)

ACKNOWLEDGMENTS

This book would not have been possible first and foremost without the time and willingness of its contributing interviewees. Thank you for responding to my e-mails, talking with me, and renewing my excitement for this project after every conversation.

Among those interviewed, a few must, of course, be singled out. Immense gratitude must go to Amanda Petrusich. Thank you for signing a copy of your book all those years ago and giving me the courage to try to make something that I could in turn sign for you one day. I must also thank you for being my first interview when I still didn't know what the hell this thing could ultimately be and how far it would go. You set the bar for every interview that followed. You are the patron saint of this undertaking, and I will continue to read everything you will ever write.

I must also express my appreciation and thanks to Jessica Hopper, who not only exposed and pushed me toward a host of diverse, talented voices worth interviewing for this book but also helped me navigate at critical points the logistical maze of book proposals, query letters, and contract legalese. Thank you for always being available to answer my silly questions and never making me feel like I wasn't worth your time.

Thank you to Chuck Klosterman and Rob Sheffield. Whoever said "Never meet your heroes" obviously never had a conversation with either one of you. Thank you for inspiring me with your words, for being so damn gracious and unbelievably approachable.

Thank you to Lizzy Goodman. Though compiling these quotes in some semblance of order was only a fraction of the work you must have done for *Meet Me in the Bathroom*, you are my kindred spirit.

Of course, thank you to Mark and Wendy Redfern, for giving me my first steady writing gig and the opportunity to not only interview some of my favorite musical artists over the years but to grow as a music journalist as well. I'll be on your masthead until the end.

Finally, this book would surely not have been possible without my editors, Matt Becker, Ivo Fravashi, and Rachael DeShano, as well as Courtney Andree and the staff of the University of Massachusetts Press. Thank you for believing in the idea of this book when it seemed like no one else did, for shaping and refining its content, and giving this undertaking a home. Thank you to my friends and family, and to anyone who has picked up a magazine or gone online and read my work. To my mother, Kathy, and my father, Richard, for your encouragement and your old record collections. To my mother-in-law, Jane, for being so adamant that there was a book inside me. Here's hoping there's a few more. To my brothers, Chris and Brad, for joining me at my first concerts. To my sisters-in-law, Kate and Sara, for having good taste in music. To my sons, Sam and Noah. This book might have been finished a bit faster if it wasn't for you two, but I will never complain about that fact. Not ever. Most importantly, thank you to my wife, Kristin. How a dyed-in-the-wool Parrothead and an indie music devotee fell in love I will never know; but then again, if it weren't for a song being played, I would never have walked up and met you. So yeah, music literally changed my life.

ON THE RECORD

INTRODUCTION

Listening to music is more often than not a solitary experience for me. While over the past several years I've become a bit more communal with what comes out of my music player—particularly when it comes to introducing a specific song or artist to my young children—for the most part my tendency has been to keep my listening habits to myself, funneling it all through a pair of headphones. I think I enjoy listening to music this way because it not only increases my ability to tune out the rest of the world—much to the chagrin of anyone trying to get my attention—it always makes me feel as though I'm holding on to an inconsequential secret. Nobody's going to get hurt if someone ultimately interrogates me for an answer, but there's still this strange, private satisfaction that I get to experience something I can keep for myself.

Even when I go to concerts, surrounded by throngs of people that are in attendance for the very same reason I am, I have an incredibly difficult time embracing the shared spectacle of the performance. I'm not the kind of person who will look over at the stranger next to me after a song ends to gauge whether their reaction and appreciation is equal to my own. It's as if I put on blinders. I focus on what's happening in front of me, as if it's just for me. Maybe that's being too self-serious or limiting of what it means to go to a concert, but after so many years going to shows on my own, it's just the way I take it all in and preserve my enjoyment of it.

My life as a writer is just as closed off. I don't have a writing partner. I don't sit around with a team of people pitching ideas and what-if scenarios as though I'm workshopping plot points for a television series. My writing is a private endeavor. I'm often in a separate room, most likely with a door closed. It requires silence. I can't even listen to the music I so regularly

1

turn to because even that stymies my ability to punch out few measly sentences on my laptop. It's just me, myself, and an uncontrollable reflex to fidget my legs up and down while I think of the next thing to type.

This self-administered seclusion only becomes more accentuated when you factor in my lifestyle as a freelance writer covering music. There is no newsroom for me to travel to and spend my day, which means my primary form of communication with my editors and colleagues is almost completely through e-mail, a method of correspondence that lends itself to very little interpersonal discussion or personality, and usually involves the phrase "just following up." If it weren't for the utility of social media, of following and friending people I write for or work alongside, I honestly wouldn't even have the slightest idea of what my coworkers look like or what they do in their off-hours. They would just be disembodied names that occasionally send me attached documents with track changes.

A couple of years ago this kind of vacuum-sealed state of being started to have a real effect on me. I had become, for lack of a better word, lonely. It's one thing to do a job. It's another to do a job without any real point of reference as to whether your experience aligns with anyone else's.

To make a complicated comparison, I saw myself as a small satellite drifting aimlessly in orbit around the expanse of music journalism, and after so many years of feeling alone, I felt the need to make some meaningful contact with whomever else was floating out in the void with me. I needed to connect, to actually talk to, identify with, and share a real conversation with others about this job, this life, and find out what being a music journalist meant to someone else, and hopefully in turn reestablish what it meant to me.

My naïve outreach amazingly got an unexpectedly high response rate. Some were freelancers like myself, regularly enduring a similar kind of grind of pitches, rejection letters, deadlines, and invoices. Others were editors and staff writers, individuals whose respected output and tenacity landed them the semisecurity of steady work. Others still were publication founders and editors-in-chief, captains of ships that do everything in their power to simultaneously rail against and adapt to the onslaught of an ever-evolving media landscape. Finally, there were the venerated authorities, the authors, critics, essayists, and storytellers that had become so influential in the field of music journalism that they made writing about music its own kind of art form.

When I first started this endeavor, I didn't really know what it was ultimately going to be. I had hopes that with the right number of people's involvement, my interrogations could eventually be published in some formal way. Until that time I was mostly just hoping to have some good conversations and maybe transcribe the results on my personal website as a series of blog posts. I was just enjoying the fact that people whose work I admired were messaging me back with equal enthusiasm, all for the sake of taking about music journalism. That connection that I was craving was taking shape. There were drawbacks, of course. After about two dozen interviews, the sensational high of talking with such hardworking and accomplished individuals also inadvertently began to warp the mirror I held up to myself and my own work. I fell into the trap of comparison, asking myself how on earth I could possibly measure up to what these people were able to do. It was a dangerous emotional position to be in, and one I thankfully righted myself out of. After some considerable reflection, I realized I needed to stop comparing myself to these other writers and simply start comparing myself to who I had once been. Was I a better writer, a better music journalist, than when I started this book? The answer was always yes. I was learning and absorbing so much from the conversations I had been having.

Just as I learned and changed through the process of making this book, it is my inevitable hope that any music journalist, whether a complete novice or an established veteran, or even someone who just enjoys reading music journalism, learns something from the transcripts that are included. I like to think of this book as a kind of massive roundtable discussion. I hope you find the answers and commentary within illuminating.

It should be noted that over the decades there have a number of famous digs at music journalism as a profession, as a calling. One of the more famous declarations famously came from Frank Zappa, who said, "Rock journalism is people who can't write interviewing people who can't talk for people who can't read." My personal favorite, however, will always be the maxim "Writing about music is like dancing about architecture." While this quote was connected to Elvis Costello for a time as a kind of repudiation or dismissal, I like to think of this quip in the context of its originator, comedian and musician Martin Mull, who was merely commenting on the ineffability of giving such an abstract form of expression a sense of clarity and context. Of course, it doesn't stop us from trying, from channeling our inner Bowie, who said it most succinctly: "Let's dance."

BYLINES

Hanif Abdurraqib is a poet, essayist, and cultural critic from Columbus, Ohio. He is the author of *The Crown Ain't Worth Much*, nominated for a Hurston-Wright Legacy Award; *They Can't Kill Us Until They Kill Us*, named a best book of 2017 by NPR, *Pitchfork*, *Oprah Magazine*, the *Chicago Tribune*, *Slate*, *Esquire*, *GQ*, and *Publishers Weekly*, among others; a book on A Tribe Called Quest titled *Go Ahead in the Rain;* a collection of poems *A Fortune for Your Disaster;* and a history of black performance in the United States *They Don't Dance No Mo'.* He is a Callaloo Creative Writing fellow, a poetry editor at *Muzzle Magazine*, and a member of the poetry collective Echo Hotel with poet/essayist Eve Ewing.

ESSENTIAL READS

They Can't Kill Us Until They Kill Us (Two Dollar Radio, 2017)
A Fortune for Your Disaster (Tin House, 2019)
"On Summer Crushing" (*Paris Review*, June 2019)

Nitsuh Abebe is a story editor at the *New York Times Magazine*. He used to be a contributor at *Pitchfork* and the pop critic at *New York* magazine.

ESSENTIAL READS

"Why Can't Beyoncé Have It All?" (*New York*, February 2013)
"Amy Winehouse's Intelligent Soul" (*Vulture*, July 2011)
"Making Plans for Daniel" (*Pitchfork*, March 2006)

Michael Azerrad is the author of *Come as You Are: The Story of Nirvana* and *Our Band Could Be Your Life: Scenes from the American Indie Underground, 1981–1991.* He has written for *Rolling Stone*, the *New York Times*, the *Wall Street Journal*, the *New Yorker*, and many other periodicals.

ESSENTIAL READS

*Our Band Could Be Your Life: Scenes from the Indie Underground,
1981-1991* (Little, Brown, 2001)
Come as You Are: The Story of Nirvana (Doubleday/Main Street, 1993)
"Nirvana: Inside the Heart and Mind of Kurt Cobain" (*Rolling Stone,*
April 1992)

Tom Breihan is the senior editor at Stereogum. He's been a staff writer at the *Village Voice,* where he wrote the *Status Ain't Hood* blog, and at *Pitchfork.* He's written for *GQ,* Grantland, The Ringer, Deadspin, and elsewhere. He writes the columns "The Number Ones" for Stereogum and "Age of Heroes" for The AV Club. He lives in Charlottesville, Virginia.

ESSENTIAL READS

"Avail Reunite in Richmond, and It's Pretty Close to Perfect"
(Stereogum, July 2019)
"The Number Ones: ABBA's 'Dancing Queen'" (Stereogum, October
2019)
"We Took The Mountain Goats' John Darnielle to His First Pro
Wrestling Show in 35 Years" (Stereogum, April 2015)

Gabriela Tully Claymore is a former managing editor of Stereogum. She's currently working toward her MFA at the University of Iowa's Nonfiction Writing Program.

ESSENTIAL READS

"Cat Power Has Returned, but for Chan Marshall Everything Is New"
(Stereogum, October 2018)
"*Dragging a Dead Deer up a Hill* Turns 10" (Stereogum, June 2018)
"The Lush Sound and Shattering Silence of *Phantom Thread*"
(Stereogum, February 2018)

Jim DeRogatis is an assistant professor at Columbia College Chicago, co-host of *Sound Opinions* on public radio, and the author of eleven books, including *Let It Blurt: The Life and Times of Lester Bangs, America's Greatest Rock Critic; Staring at Sound: The True Story of Oklahoma's Fab-*

ulous Flaming Lips; and his most recent work, *Soulless: The Case against R. Kelly.* He lives on the Northwest side of Chicago, and plays drums in the punk rock band VORTIS, which recently released the album *This Machine Kills Fascists.*

ESSENTIAL READS

> *Soulless: The Case against R. Kelly* (Abrams Press, 2019)
> "Charles Manson's Musical Ambitions" (*New Yorker,* August 2019)
> "A Postcard from Cleveland" (*Chicago Reader, New York Press,* and
>   *L.A. New Times,* 1996)

Stephen Deusner is a longtime freelance music journalist fascinated by regional forms of musical expression in America. He wrote his first album reviews for the *Memphis Flyer* in the early 2000s and currently writes for *Uncut* magazine, *Pitchfork,* Stereogum, the *Bluegrass Situation,* and *American Songwriter,* among other online and print magazines. He contributed to the 2011 *Poetics of American Song Lyrics* and is the author of a forthcoming book about the Drive-By Truckers and the nature of Southern identity.

ESSENTIAL READS

> "Party Off, Garth: The Short Life and Long Death of Chris Gaines"
>   (Stereogum, May 2016)
> Liner notes for The Glands' *I Can See My House from Here* (New West
>   Records, November 2018)
> "Joan Shelley: Tales from the Riverbank" (*Uncut,* September 2019)

Ryan Dombal is the features editor at *Pitchfork.*

ESSENTIAL READS

> "Marvin Gaye: *Here, My Dear*" (*Pitchfork,* July 2017)
> "True Myth: A Conversation with Sufjan Stevens" (*Pitchfork,* February
>   2015)
> "St. Vincent: Reckless Precision" (*Pitchfork,* February 2014)

Matt Fink is a freelance writer whose work has appeared in *Under the Radar, Paste,* the All Music Guide, and many others. He is currently a doctoral student at Kent State University, where he taught writing from 2010 to 2016.

ESSENTIAL READS

"MGMT: Fated to Confuse" (*Under the Radar,* August 2013)

"Controversy, Conspiracy, and the Constitution: A Conversation with Steve Earle" (*Paste,* Fall 2002)

"Father John Misty: The Saboteur" (*Under the Radar,* January 2016)

Larry Fitzmaurice has been writing professionally about music and popular culture for over a decade. He worked at *Pitchfork* as a senior editor for the first half of the 2010s and has since written for publications including *New York* magazine, *Vulture, Entertainment Weekly,* the *Guardian, GQ, Rolling Stone, SPIN,* and the *Fader.*

ESSENTIAL READS

"Rite of Passion" (*Pitchfork,* July 2012)

"Tame Impala, Chillwave, and Other Dispatches from the Vibe Generation" (Noisey, December 2015)

"The 1975 Have Nowhere to Grow but Up" (*Fader,* September 2019)

Hannah Giorgis is a culture writer at the *Atlantic.* Her work has appeared in publications including the *New York Times Magazine,* the *New Yorker,* the *Fader, Bon Appétit,* and *Pitchfork.* She lives in Brooklyn.

ESSENTIAL READS

"The Weeknd's East African Roots" (*Pitchfork,* June 2015)

"The 'African Giant' Challenging Musical Boundaries" (*Atlantic,* July 2019)

"Smino's Funky Raps Soothe the Soul" (*Atlantic,* November 2018)

Lizzy Goodman is a journalist and the author of *Meet Me in the Bathroom,* an oral history of music in New York City from 2001 to 2011. She lives in LA with her basset hound Jerry Orbach.

ESSENTIAL READS

"Kendrick Lamar, Hip-Hop's Newest Old-School Star" (*New York Times Magazine,* June 2014)

"Kim Gordon Sounds Off" (*Elle,* April 2013)

"Trent Reznor's Soundtrack to the Apocalypse" (*Village Voice,* July 2017)

Andy Greene is a senior writer at *Rolling Stone,* where he's been on staff for over fifteen years.

ESSENTIAL READS

"Radiohead's Rhapsody in Gloom: 'OK Computer' 20 Years Later" (*Rolling Stone,* May 2017)

"Bill Withers: The Soul Man Who Walked Away" (*Rolling Stone,* April 2015)

"Steve Perry Still Believes" (*Rolling Stone,* October 2018)

Jayson Greene is a contributing editor and former senior editor at *Pitchfork.* He is the author of the memoir *Once More We Saw Stars,* published by Knopf in 2019. His writing has appeared in the *New York Times, Vulture,* and *GQ,* among other publications. In 2017, his *Pitchfork* column "Overtones" was nominated for an American Society of Magazine Editors award in Columns and Commentary. He lives in Brooklyn with his wife and son.

ESSENTIAL READS

"Life, Death, and John Prine" (*Pitchfork,* April 2018)

"Keep the Things You Forgot: An Elliott Smith Oral History" (*Pitchfork,* October 2013)

"How Do We Live with Music Made by Problematic Artists?" (*Pitchfork,* January 2019)

Christian Hoard is the music editor at *Rolling Stone.* Previously, he wrote for *SPIN, Blender,* the *Village Voice,* and the *Michigan Daily.* He lives in Brooklyn with his wife and his dog, Fritz.

ESSENTIAL READS

"The Slow Climb: How the Mountain Goats' John Darnielle Became the Best Storyteller in Rock" (*Rolling Stone,* April 2015)

"Wu & A: RZA on Making Peace with Raekwon and the Future of Wu-Tang Clan" (*Rolling Stone,* November 2014)

"Show Tune Liberation" (*Village Voice,* January 2006)

Marc Hogan is a senior staff writer at *Pitchfork,* where he has been contributing since 2004.

ESSENTIAL READS

"The Record Industry Expects a Windfall. Where Will the Money Go?"
(*Pitchfork*, May 2019)

"Uncovering How Streaming Is Changing the Sound of Pop"
(*Pitchfork*, September 2017)

"This Is Not a Mixtape" (*Pitchfork*, February 2010)

Clover Hope is a New York–based writer and editor who's worked at *Billboard, Vibe, XXL,* and *Jezebel.* She's also written for *SPIN, GQ,* the *New York Times,* and the *Village Voice,* among other publications.

ESSENTIAL READS

"The Making and Unmaking of Iggy Azalea" (*Jezebel,* September 2017)

"Lemonade Is Beyoncé's Body and Blood" (*Jezebel,* April 2016)

"The 100 Problems of Kanye West" (*Village Voice,* January 2009)

Jessica Hopper is a Chicago-based author and music journalist.

ESSENTIAL READS

Night Moves (University of Texas Press, 2018)

The First Collection of Criticism by a Living Female Rock Critic
(Featherproof, 2015)

The Girls' Guide to Rocking (Workman, 2009)

Hua Hsu is a staff writer at the *New Yorker.* He is the author of *A Floating Chinaman: Fantasy and Failure across the Pacific.* He has also written for *Artforum,* Grantland, *Slate,* the *Village Voice,* and the *Wire* (UK). He teaches at Vassar College.

ESSENTIAL READS

"No Compromises" (*New Yorker,* March 2015)

"Bjork's Visions of an Enchanted Future" (*New Yorker,* December 2017)

"Stephen Cheng Released One Single That Sounded Like Nothing
Else. But Who Was He?" (*New Yorker,* August 2019)

Steven Hyden is the author of four books, including *Your Favorite Band Is Killing Me, Twilight of the Gods,* and, with Steve Gorman, *Hard to Handle:*

The Life and Death of the Black Crowes, This Isn't Happening: Radiohead's Kid A and the Beginning of the 21st Century. His work has also appeared in the *New York Times Magazine,* the *Washington Post, Billboard, Rolling Stone,* Grantland, The A.V. Club, *Uproxx,* and The Ringer.

ESSENTIAL READS

Your Favorite Band Is Killing Me (Little, Brown and Company, 2016)
Twilight of the Gods (HarperCollins, 2018)
Hard to Handle: The Life and Death of the Black Crowes: A Memoir, with Steve Gorman (Da Capo Press, 2019)

Josh Jackson is cofounder and editor in chief of *Paste* magazine, a website covering everything from music to books to craft beer. Under his leadership, *Paste* has won numerous awards and now attracts more than seven million visitors every month. Jackson has been a regular music and film critic for CNN Headline News and three Atlanta radio stations; he oversaw and cohosted four music podcasts for Coca-Cola; and he's written more than one thousand stories for various publications, including assignments on six continents.

ESSENTIAL READS

"Josh Ritter: Songs for Days of Doubt" (*Paste,* issue 21)
"Chris Thile: Life Is a Variety Show" (*Paste,* June 2018)
"Remembering Scott Hutchison of Frightened Rabbit" (*Paste,* May 2018)

Craig Jenkins is a Manhattan-based writer and pop music critic for *New York* magazine whose work has also appeared in *Pitchfork, Billboard, Complex,* and *SPIN.*

ESSENTIAL READS

"The Perfectionist: Mac Miller Is Finally Making the Music He's Always Wanted to Make" (*Vulture,* September 2018)
"How Will Rock and Roll Find Its Future?" (*Vulture,* December 2018)
"'Old Town Road' and When Genre Becomes a Prison" (*Vulture,* April 2019)

Maura Johnston is a writer and editor who teaches at Boston College.

ESSENTIAL READS

"'Since U Been Gone': The Crossover Pop Needed, the Anthem Rock
Deserved" (NPR, August 2018)

"We'll All Go Down Together: Billy Joel Says Goodbye to Nassau
Coliseum" (Deadspin, August 2015)

"How George Michael Transformed Pop Music" (*Time*, December 2016)

Ilana Kaplan is a writer and editor living in Brooklyn, New York. She is currently an editor at *Digiday* and previously worked for the *Independent*, the *Observer*, and *Paper*. For the past ten years, she's covered music and culture for publications including the *New York Times*, *Rolling Stone*, *Billboard*, NPR, *Vanity Fair*, *Pitchfork*, and *SPIN*.

ESSENTIAL READS

"Shocking Omissions: Rilo Kiley and the Alt-Pop Force of 'More
Adventurous'" (NPR, October 2017)

"Passion Pit's Michael Angelakos on His Fight to Make Mental Health
Care Accessible for Artists" (*Billboard*, July 2017)

"Jenny Lewis, Full of Confidence and Ballads, on Why She Isn't
Running Away Anymore" (*Los Angeles Times*, March 2019)

J. Edward Keyes is the editorial director for Bandcamp, and has been writing about music for over twenty years. His work has appeared in *Rolling Stone*, *SPIN*, *Pitchfork*, *Entertainment Weekly*, the *Village Voice*, and multiple other outlets. His piece "Where's the Party? 13 Hours with the Next Franz Ferdinand" was included in *Da Capo's Best Music Writing 2006*.

ESSENTIAL READS

"Will Moloney Is the Best Indie Rock Songwriter You've (Probably)
Never Heard Of" (*Bandcamp Daily*, November 2017)

"Charly Bliss: Fizzy Guitar-Pop That's Big, Bright, and Full of Feelings"
(*Bandcamp Daily*, April 2017)

"Protomartyr, *The Agent Intellect*" (*Pitchfork*, October 2015)

Chuck Klosterman is a writer and journalist living in Portland, Oregon. He has written for *SPIN*, the *New York Times Magazine*, *GQ*, *Esquire*, the *Guardian*, ESPN, *Billboard*, and the *Washington Post*. He is the author of eleven books, including *Fargo Rock City* and *Killing Yourself to Live*. He was awarded the ASCAP Foundation Deems Taylor Award for music criticism in 2002.

ESSENTIAL READS

Killing Yourself to Live (Scribner, 2005)

"The Life and Times of KISS" (Grantland, April 2014)

"Taylor Swift on 'Bad Blood,' Kanye West, and How People Interpret Her Lyrics (*GQ*, October 2015)

Ryan Leas is the features writer for Stereogum and the author of the 33 1/3 about LCD Soundsystem's *Sound of Silver*. He has also written for *Pitchfork*, Deadspin, *GQ*, and Noisey. Originally from Pennsylvania, he now lives in Brooklyn.

ESSENTIAL READS

Sound of Silver (Bloomsbury, 2016)

"Wasted Days: Strand of Oaks Finds Life Beyond Sex and Drugs" (Stereogum, February 2017)

"Empty Streets, Empty Nights: The Blue Nile's Elusive Masterpiece *Hats* at 30" (Stereogum, October 2019)

Joe Levy, executive editor of *Rolling Stone* from 1997 to 2007, has worked at *SPIN, Billboard, Details,* and the *Village Voice;* appeared frequently on MTV and VH1; and has been a special correspondent for *The Today Show*. His work has appeared in the *New York Times* and the *Wall Street Journal Magazine,* and his interviews include those with Bruce Springsteen, Paul McCartney, and U2.

ESSENTIAL READS

"The Beastie Boys Are Back in Town" (*Rolling Stone,* August 1998)

"Pavement: Put It All Down" (*Village Voice,* December 2004)

"Bruce Springsteen: The *Rolling Stone* Interview" (*Rolling Stone,* November 2007)

Emily J. Lordi is an associate professor of English at Vanderbilt University and a freelance critic whose work appears in such venues as the *New Yorker* and *Billboard*. She is the author of three books: *Black Res-*

onance (2013). *The Meaning of Soul* (2020). and a 33 1/3 book. *Donny Hathaway Live* (2016).

ESSENTIAL READS

"Black Magic. White Soul" (*New Inquiry*. November 2013)

Donny Hathaway Live (Bloomsbury. 2016)

"Toni Morrison and Nina Simone. United in Soul" (*New Yorker*. August 2019)

Jillian Mapes is a New York–based. Ohio-bred culture writer and editor. Since 2016. she has served as a senior editor at *Pitchfork*. working primarily on commentary and features. She previously held editorial positions at *Vulture/New York* magazine. *Billboard. Flavorwire*. CBS Radio. and the *Indianapolis Star.* Her byline has also appeared in *GQ. Rolling Stone.* the *Onion.* the *Hollywood Reporter. SPIN,* and more.

ESSENTIAL READS

"The Year 'Indie Rock' Meant Something Different" (*Pitchfork*. December 2017)

"Weezer: *Weezer (The Blue Album)*" (*Pitchfork*. February 2017)

"This Woman's Work: The Many Lives of Angel Olsen" (*Pitchfork*. August 2016)

David Marchese is a staff writer at the *New York Times Magazine.*

ESSENTIAL READS

"In Conversation: Eminem" (*Vulture*. December 2017)

"In Conversation: Erykah Badu" (*Vulture*. January 2018)

"Talk: Trey Anastasio" (*New York Times Magazine*. June 2019)

Eric T. Miller started *MAGNET* in 1993 as a twenty-one-year-old journalism student at Temple University and has been the magazine's only constant staffer throughout its history. He lives in Philadelphia and has seen Guided by Voices live many more times than you.

ESSENTIAL READS

"What I've Learned" (*MAGNET*. issue 150)

"Tom Petty: If I Had My Way. I'd Tear the Building Down" (*MAGNET*. issue 57)

"Guided By Voices: Robert Pollard, Who Are You?" (*MAGNET*, issue 23)

Puja Patel is the editor in chief of *Pitchfork*, the most trusted voice in music. Prior to joining *Pitchfork*, she was editor in chief of *SPIN* and senior editor at Deadspin, and spent the early years of her writing career as a columnist at MTV and the *Village Voice*. She has contributed music writing to *Rolling Stone*, the *Washington Post*, *VICE*, and the *Fader*, among others.

ESSENTIAL READS

"We Got That Ass! Inside the World of Jersey Club" (*SPIN*, March 2013)

"Kingston Ave. Dreaming: Dancehall, Hip Hop and New York City" (Red Bull Music Academy, April 2015)

"Future Is Now" (*SPIN*, April 2014)

Jenn Pelly is a contributing editor at *Pitchfork* and author of *The Raincoats*. Her writing has appeared in the *New York Times*, *Rolling Stone*, the *Guardian*, the *Wire*, NPR, and *Teen Vogue*. She is a cocurator of Basilica Soundscape and lives in New York.

ESSENTIAL READS

The Raincoats (Bloomsbury, 2017)

"Unraveling the Sexism of Emo's Third Wave" (*Pitchfork*, November 2017)

"Jenny Lewis Escapes the Void" (*Pitchfork*, March 2019)

Liz Pelly writes about music, culture, streaming, and the internet. She is a contributing editor at the *Baffler*, where she writes a column about how music is being reshaped by the platform economy. In 2018, she received a Reeperbahn Festival International Music Journalism Award for the year's best work of music journalism. She lives in New York.

ESSENTIAL READS

"The Problem with Muzak: Spotify's Bid to Remodel an Industry (*Baffler*, December 2017)

"Discover Weakly: Sexism on Spotify" (*Baffler*, June 2018)

"Streambait Pop: The Emergence of a Total Spotify Genre" (*Baffler*, December 2018)

Amanda Petrusich is a staff writer at the *New Yorker* and the author of three books about music. She is the recipient of a Guggenheim Fellowship in nonfiction and has been nominated for a Grammy Award. Her criticism and features have appeared in the *New York Times*, the *Oxford American, SPIN, Pitchfork, GQ, Esquire, Playboy*, the *Atlantic*, and the *Virginia Quarterly Review*. Her most recent book, *Do Not Sell at Any Price*, explored the obsessive world of 78-rpm record collectors. She is an assistant professor in the writing program at New York University's Gallatin School.

ESSENTIAL READS

"Cat Power: All This Light" (*Pitchfork*, August 2012)

Do Not Sell at Any Price: The Wild, Obsessive Hunt for the World's Rarest 78rpm Records (Scribner, 2014)

"Paisley Park: Prince's Lonely Palace" (*New Yorker*, June 2018)

Ann Powers is a critic and correspondent for NPR Music and the author of several books, including *Good Booty: Love and Sex, Black and White, Body and Soul in American Music*. She is currently writing a book about Joni Mitchell's music and cultural impact.

ESSENTIAL READS

"Turning the Tables," NPR Music series on recentering the popular music canon

Good Booty: Love and Sex, Black and White, Body and Soul in American Music (Dey Street Books, 2017)

Tori Amos: Piece by Piece (with the artist, Broadway Books, 2005)

Jack Rabid is the founder, editor, and publisher of thirty-nine-years of the New York music magazine the *Big Takeover*. His writing has appeared in *SPIN, Interview*, All Music Guide, eMusic, *The Trouser Press Record Guide, Creem*, the *Village Voice*, Amazon.com, *Ice, Rock 'n' Roll Globe, Maximum Rocknroll, Paper, Rockpool, Alternative Press, Musichound, Stereotype, East Village Eye, CDNow, Jam TV, Hit List, AMP, Seconds, Generation*, and more. He is the club/radio DJ and host of "The Big Takeover Show," and lives in Brooklyn with his wife, Mary, and their two grade school children.

ESSENTIAL READS

"Fighting Words: Tell Us What You Really Think, Johnny Rotten" (*SPIN*, September 2007)

Speech to the Institute of Contemporary Arts, "Figures of Speech" Dinner: On V. Vale and *Search and Destroy Magazine* (October 2007)

"Inflammable Material at 40: A Conversation with Stiff Little Fingers' Jake Burns on the Punk Classic's Anniversary, While Looking Back at Belfast during 'The Troubles'" (*Rock 'n' Roll Globe*, February 2019)

T. Cole Rachel is a writer, teacher, and ceramic cat collector who lives in Brooklyn. He creates poems, essays, and all manner of culture-related journalism. His work has appeared in *Interview*, the *Fader*, *Pitchfork*, *New York Times Magazine*, *Bon*, *Man of the World*, *OUT*, *Dossier*, *Maxim*, and Stereogum. He is a regular contributor to *Pitchfork* and has served as a contributing editor at both *V Magazine* and *Interview*, and as senior editor at the *Creative Independent*. His books include *Surviving the Moment of Impact* and *Bend, Don't Shatter*.

ESSENTIAL READS

Surviving the Moment of Impact (Soft Skull Press, 2002)

"Pop Sovereign: A Conversation with Madonna" (*Pitchfork*, March 2015)

"53 Miles West of Venus: The Enduringly Queer Legacy of the The B-52s" (*Pitchfork Review*, issue 5)

Ben Ratliff is the author of four books, including *Every Song Ever: Twenty Ways to Listen in an Age of Musical Plenty* (Farrar, Straus and Giroux, 2016); *The Jazz Ear: Conversations over Music* (Times Books, 2008); and *Coltrane: The Story of a Sound* (Farrar, Straus and Giroux, 2007). He was a pop and jazz critic at the *New York Times* from 1996 to 2016, and has written for other publications, including *Esquire*, the *New York Review of Books*, *Rolling Stone*, and *Pitchfork*. He teaches cultural criticism at New York University's Gallatin School of Individualized Study.

ESSENTIAL READS

"School's in Session. but Don't You Dare Take Notes" (*New York Times*, May 2011)

"Cecil Taylor, Pianist Who Defied Jazz Orthodoxy, Is Dead at 89" (*New York Times*, April 2018)

"We Are an Instrument" (*Affidavit*, July 2018)

Mark Redfern is the copublisher and senior editor of *Under the Radar*, a music print magazine and website he founded with his future wife, Wendy Lynch Redfern, in 2001. Born in London, his British father was a music photographer, and his American mother a travel writer and magazine editor. In Los Angeles, Mark met and fell in love with Wendy, an aspiring music photographer, and *Under the Radar* was hatched, at first as a black-and-white zine mostly written by Mark, but soon enough as a nationally distributed full-color print magazine, one that can lay claim to the first national interviews with Vampire Weekend and Fleet Foxes and the last ever interview with Elliott Smith. In 2012 the Redferns moved from Los Angeles to Lexington, Virginia. They continue to publish *Under the Radar* several times a year while maintaining its website daily and encouraging their daughter Rose's love of superheroes, David Bowie, CHVRCHES, and playing piano.

ESSENTIAL READS

The Protest Issue (*Under the Radar*, 2004, 2008, 2012, 2016)

Music vs. Comedy Issue (*Under the Radar*, 2011)

My Favorite Album Issue (*Under the Radar*, 2019)

Wendy Lynch Redfern was born in Cocoa Beach, Florida, where as a child she would watch nearby NASA launch rockets into space. In her midtwenties she moved to Los Angeles to pursue a career in music photography, which is when she met her future husband, Mark Redfern, an aspiring music journalist. Together in 2001 they launched *Under the Radar*, the nationally distributed print magazine and website. Wendy has laid out and designed every print issue, as well as being the copublisher with Mark. For *Under the Radar* Wendy has taken many iconic photos, including conducting the last ever photo shoot with Elliott Smith before his untimely passing. Her photos have also appeared in the pages of *Rolling Stone, NME, Vanity Fair,* and countless other magazines, books, and websites. She currently lives in Lexington, Virginia, with Mark and their daughter, Rose.

ESSENTIAL READS

Best of the Decade Issue (Under the Radar, 2009)

Wasted on the Youth Issue (Under the Radar, 2010)

10th Anniversary Issue (Under the Radar, 2011)

Mark Richardson has been writing about music, culture, and technology for more than twenty years and served as the editor in chief and executive editor of the online music magazine *Pitchfork* from 2011 to 2018. During his tenure as editor in chief, *Pitchfork* won a National Magazine Award for general excellence in digital media. He is the author of *Zaireeka,* a book in the 33 1/3 series about the Flaming Lips album of the same name. Mark has taught courses on music writing and arts criticism at the Craig Newmark Graduate School of Journalism at CUNY and Columbia College Chicago, and his work has appeared in publications that include the *Wall Street Journal, Billboard,* the *Village Voice,* and the *Washington City Paper.*

ESSENTIAL READS

Zaireeka (Continuum, 2010)

"Listening for Silence with the Headphones Off" (*Pitchfork,* August 2018)

"Back to the Stratosphere: How the Rarest Music in the World Comes Back" (The Ringer, February 2019)

Rob Sheffield is a columnist for *Rolling Stone,* where he has been writing about music, TV, and pop culture since 1997. He is the best-selling author of five books, including *Love Is a Mix Tape: Love and Loss, One Song at a Time; Talking to Girls about Duran Duran: One Young Man's Quest for True Love and a Cooler Haircut;* and *Turn Around Bright Eyes: The Rituals of Love and Karaoke.* His most recent books are *On Bowie* and *Dreaming The Beatles: The Love Story of One Band and the Whole World,* which won the 2017 Virgil Thomson Award for outstanding music criticism. He lives in Brooklyn and will probably ruin your karaoke evening with his version of "Damn I Wish I Was Your Lover."

ESSENTIAL READS

> *Love Is a Mix Tape: Love and Loss, One Song at a Time* (Crown, 2007)
> *Dreaming The Beatles: The Love Story of One Band and the Whole World* (Dey Street, 2017)
> "The Eternal Sunshine of Harry Styles" (*Rolling Stone*, September 2019)

Maria Sherman is a music and culture critic living in New York City. She is a senior writer at *Jezebel* and previously worked as a managing editor at Gizmodo Media Group, senior correspondent at Fuse TV, and contributor at BuzzFeed Music. She has written for NPR, *Vulture*, *SPIN*, *Rolling Stone*, and many others.

ESSENTIAL READS

> *Larger Than Life: A History of Boy Bands, NKTOB to BTS* (Black Dog and Leventhal, an imprint of Hachette, 2020)
> "Truly, Madly, Deeply: Exploring the Relationship between Fandom and Mental Health" (EMP Pop Con 2016, republished by Fuse TV)
> "Paramore's 'After Laughter' Is Something New, Built from Pieces of the Past" (NPR, May 2017)

Jes Skolnik is senior editor of *Bandcamp Daily*. Their work has been published in *Pitchfork*, the *New York Times*, and many other publications.

ESSENTIAL READS

> "The Power of Community: Team Dresch Return" (*Bandcamp Daily*, May 2019)
> "A History of Anti-Fascist Punk around the World in 9 Songs" (*Pitchfork*, March 2017)
> "Beyond Representation: In Music and Media, Gender Equality Will Take a Revolution" (NPR, August 2018)

Laura Snapes is the *Guardian*'s deputy music editor and a former editor at *Pitchfork*.

ESSENTIAL READS

"How Robyn Transformed Pop" (*Guardian*, September 2018)

"St. Vincent Is Telling You Everything" (Buzzfeed News, September 2017)

"Look What You Made Her Do: The Political Awakening of Taylor Swift" (*Guardian Weekend*, August 2019)

Brittany Spanos is a staff writer for *Rolling Stone* who focuses primarily on pop music, black American music history, and internet fandom. Her work has previously appeared in the *Village Voice*, *Cosmo*, *Rookie*, *SPIN*, *Pitchfork*, and more. Since starting at *Rolling Stone* as an online producer in 2015, she's written multiple cover stories (on Cardi B, Janelle Monáe, Lizzo) and has interviewed everyone from Stevie Nicks to 21 Savage. In 2016, Spanos was a consultant for the MTV Video Music Awards.

ESSENTIAL READS

"The Year of Cardi B" (*Rolling Stone*, October 2017)

"Janelle Monáe Frees Herself" (*Rolling Stone*, April 2018)

"*Silver Springs:* Inside Fleetwood Mac's Great Lost Break-Up Album" (*Rolling Stone*, August 2017)

Bonnie Stiernberg is a freelance writer based in Brooklyn by way of Chicago, covering music, television, and pop culture. She was formerly music editor at *Paste* magazine, and recently her work has appeared in *Billboard*, *Rolling Stone*, Noisey, *No Depression*, *Glamour*, GRAMMY.com, The Bluegrass Situation, and more.

ESSENTIAL READS

"The World According to Father John Misty" (*Paste Quarterly*, issue 1, March 2017)

"How to Get Old: Muscle Shoals after Its 50 Years of FAME" (*Paste*, July 2014)

"Sleater-Kinney Are Embracing Whatever Comes Next" (Grammy.com, August 2019)

Brandon Stosuy left *Pitchfork* to cofound The Creative Independent, where he is the site's editor in chief. He cofounded and cocurates the annual Basilica Soundscape festival in Hudson, New York, and is a music curator at the Broad Museum in Los Angeles. For the past several years he and the visual artist Matthew Barney have collaborated on a series of live events, objects, print publications, and a large anti-Trump countdown clock related to their performance space, REMAINS. Their most recent book, *ADAC*, was published by Dashwood in 2013. Stosuy's anthology, *Up Is Up, but So Is Down: New York's Downtown Literary Scene, 1974–1992*, was published by NYU Press in 2006. He's published two children's books, *Music Is* (2016) and *We Are Music* (2018), both with Simon & Schuster. His *Wayfinding Guided Journals* are being published in three volumes by Abrams.

ESSENTIAL READS

"A Blaze in the North American Sky" / "A Brief Oral History of U.S. Black Metal (*Believer*, July 2008)

"Sufjan Stevens: *Carrie & Lowell*" (*Pitchfork*, March 2015)

"How to Organize Your Own Music Festival" (*Pitchfork*, September 2016)

Carvell Wallace is a culture and music writer with bylines at *Pitchfork*, MTV, *GQ*, the *New Yorker*, *Esquire*, and others. He is a regular contributor to *Slate* and the *New York Times Magazine*, and cowrote *The Sixth Man* with Golden State Warriors forward Andre Iguodala. He is currently working on a book about cultural trauma.

ESSENTIAL READS

"Thelonious Monk: So Plain Only the Deaf Can Hear" (*Pitchfork*, April 2016)

"Prince Can't Die" (MTV News, April 2016)

"The Darkness and Beauty of Noname's *Telefone*" (MTV News, August 2016)

Christopher R. Weingarten is a former contributing editor at *Rolling Stone* and senior editor at *SPIN*. His work has been featured in the *New York Times*, the *Village Voice*, Stereogum, and more.

ESSENTIAL READS

It Takes a Nation of Millions to Hold Us Back (Bloomsbury, 2010)

"Run the Jewels: How 2014's Brashest Rap Duo Came Back from
   Oblivion" (*Rolling Stone*, October 2014)
"Artist of the Year: Death Grips" (*SPIN*, November 2012)

Carl Wilson is a freelance writer and editor based in Toronto. He's the author of *Let's Talk About Love: A Journey to the End of Taste*, a widely acclaimed book about class politics, aesthetic philosophy, and Céline Dion.
He has been *Slate*'s music critic since 2013, and has also written for the
New York Times, the *Globe and Mail*, *Billboard*, and many other publications, and has taught at the University of Victoria and the Flying Books
School in Toronto.

ESSENTIAL READS

Let's Talk About Love: Why Other People Have Such Bad Taste
   (Bloomsbury, 2007 and 2014)
"It's Too Late to Cancel Michael Jackson" (*Slate*, February 2019)
"The Band That Meant Too Much" (*Slate*, August 2019)

Lindsay Zoladz is a freelancer and former staff writer at The Ringer. She was
previously the pop music critic for *New York* magazine and an associate
editor at *Pitchfork*. She lives in Brooklyn.

ESSENTIAL READS

"Joni Mitchell: Fear of a Female Genius" (The Ringer, October 2017)
"Pretty When You Cry" (*Pitchfork*, June 2014)
"Leaving Britney Alone" (The Ringer, August 2016)

CHAPTER ONE

The Music That Makes Us

Memory is an amazing thing. It's interesting how the more time passes after an event, the less we remember of the specific details and the more we hold on to the event's emotional impact and resonance. Music is one of those few art forms that embeds itself in memory. You hear a song, you hear a record, and somehow you're right back where you were when you first heard it. It wrenches you there on a subconscious level. Even if you can't remember exactly what you were doing at the given moment and time the music entered your ears, you're brought back to the feeling.

Many people—particularly music journalists—feel this way in regard to memory and music. "How I remember a year or a month or a day is largely triggered by music," says Rob Sheffield. "If you ask me any date on the calendar, what I remember is what music I was into at the time and what my friends were listening to and what my loved ones were listening to. It's weird. It's just how my brain processes time. That's how my memory happens to work. You're stuck with the brain you've got." Lindsay Zoladz shares a similar sentiment: "It's so closely tied to people's emotions and memories, how an album that you loved from a certain year in your life can bring you back to that place. It really lends itself to that kind of personal narrative because people hold the music they love so close to them in their lives."

Maybe that's the reason we still get excited about discovering new music—whether it's committing yourself to a young artist or band's debut work or taking a long-overdue listen to an already established or acclaimed act's back catalog for the first time. That discovery becomes yet another place marker, a pushpin, for the events of your life to latch on to like a homing beacon.

The loudest, brightest beacon for many is that moment when that one artist or record or song suddenly became intimately focused against the art form's everyday omnipresence, when it became something more than just pleasing to the ears, but meaningful to experience. We reach this epiphany through a variety of similar but unique ways: being subjected to the music library of our parents, through the recommendations of a revered older sibling or friend. Nowadays even streaming service algorithms play their part in meaningful discovery. Everyone can trace to this kind of starting point. Music journalists simply look back at theirs with a different perspective, an origin story to something more.

Hanif Abdurraqib Music was always a background to things going on in the house. I've always imagined music, if nothing else, as a soundtrack to my daily movements. I was raised Muslim, and there's something very musical about the call to prayer. So I imagine that was an introduction to music, too, as an understanding of music as something holy. Then there was Whitney Houston's "I Wanna Dance with Somebody." That was definitely the first one I understood as a pop song I could relate to. I was young, and my mom was listening to it in the kitchen. And that's how I knew it was a good song.

Craig Jenkins Music has been my interest since I can remember. I've been told my favorite album when I was three years old was *Purple Rain*.

Lindsay Zoladz My first favorite song ever was Billy Joel's "We Didn't Start the Fire," which has since become my karaoke staple. I know every word to it. There's a video of me—I think I was three years old—and I had one of those tape-recorder karaoke things with the little face on it from Fisher Price, and I have the Billy Joel tape in there and I'm singing the song with my aunt, but obviously I don't know any of the words, so I'm making up words about things that I know about, which are mostly Ninja Turtles. I'm making up words to the tune of "We Didn't Start the Fire," that's just "Donatello, Raphael, Michelangelo . . ." I think that's my earliest musical memory. I remember loving that song. I think Billy Joel has publicly apologized for that song, which you shouldn't.

Michael Azerrad When I was a preschooler, my parents sent me to a Dalcroze class, also known as eurythmics. Yes, that's where Annie Lennox and Dave Stewart got the band name. Basically, it teaches you to feel music in your entire body and incorporates a deep sense of rhythm. That experience made a massive impact on me. I just have this all-over response to music; it's hardwired into me and will never go away. For one thing, it's surely why I became a drummer. . . . As far back as I can remember, my parents played all kinds of music on the home stereo: jazz, classical, folk, electronic music, ragtime, etcetera. I got exposed to a whole lot of stuff from very early on. But then my father read a *Newsweek* article about a new album by The Beatles called *Sgt. Pepper's Lonely Hearts Club Band*, and he picked it up at Sam Goody and brought that home. My parents, who were from the big band era, didn't listen to it more than once or twice, but I fell deeply in love with that record, commandeered it and played it over and over and over, obsessively, as kids do. I was just a little kid, so I didn't really have the ability to say something like, "This is what I want to do with my life," but after I heard that record I knew I'd found my place: I knew I was a rock person. Soon after that, I started a band with my friends down the street. We couldn't play at all, but we knew we had to be in a rock band.

Jillian Mapes My dad really loved The Beatles, and I was totally a Beatles kid. That's a certain kind of kid. And my brother and I used to dance around to—I can't believe this because the song is so horribly violent—"Maxwell's Silver Hammer." We used to dance around to it and act it out, banging the hammer on our heads. We had no idea, but it was definitely a fond memory growing up. It's such a base thing. It formed what I thought music was and what I thought taste was.

Gabriela Tully Claymore I think when I really started to come into my own taste I was in late elementary school. I don't know how but I discovered the Ramones. I just loved it because it was perfect music for me at that age. Really simple lyrics, kind of funny, and accessible. And then I was a totally typical middle schooler who thought she was really punk and cool, so I got really into Green Day. That was probably the first band that I was really obsessed with. And that's when I really started to look out for stuff that was new and be excited about it. I think middle school age is when most people are coming into their own tastes and seeking out new music.

Clover Hope We were an immigrant family and my dad was always playing '60s old-school Motown records in the house. Percy Sledge. Sam Cooke. That was kind of my first love of music. He had actual vinyls of all these albums, and it was a range: Michael Jackson, Madonna, and a lot of oldies. We're from Guyana—I was born there—so there was a lot of Caribbean music: reggae, soca, calypso. There was just always something playing in the background growing up. Then in the '90s, when I was a teenager, I transitioned into learning my own taste through my sister, who was listening to '90s R&B and rap. Xscape cassette tapes and all that.

Hannah Giorgis My parents are both immigrants. I grew up hearing my mom listen to a ton of Ethiopian music. Both my parents listened to a ton of it—my dad more so Ethiopian worship songs. My mom was a little more all over the place. But aside from that, which was a core part of my musical diet growing up, there was a ton of Michael Jackson, Whitney Houston, Anita Baker. Not a lot of Prince or even Janet [Jackson]— some of the artists who have a record of being a little bit more overtly sexual. That's again partly because of a sort of Ethiopian, Christian conservativism. But I also grew up in Orange County, and pop punk was a huge part of my tween and teen musical diet. I still have the biggest soft spot in my heart for Dashboard Confessional. I feel really lucky in a sense that I listened to a lot of stuff growing up. My aunt is a huge fan of country, and so that was always playing when she was around. And then I have an older half brother who really loved Tupac, so that was around all the time, too, and I started coming into rap the more I was hanging out with him. It just feels I've been lucky to have a fairly cross-genre, cross-national experience in that sense. And I think the other thing is that because my family is from Ethiopia, there are a lot of ties to Jamaica and the Caribbean in general with reggae and dancehall and more recently soca, which has been a pretty huge part of my musical intake, along with Afrobeat and a very diasporic pan-African musical palette, which is important to me, especially now that I understand it intellectually as well as viscerally.

Jack Rabid When I was a little boy I joined The Beatles fan club at age six, back when The Beatles were an actual band, as opposed to an icon. They were my favorite band in the whole world. They were everywhere, as ubiquitous as you could imagine. You heard them all day long, in gas stations, grocery stores, shopping centers, the car radio. And I'd always recognize them. It was a feedback loop. Between having most of their records and hearing them on the radio constantly, I knew every one of their songs. And from that base you can base an entire lifetime passion, because The Beatles were almost like twenty bands in one in their variety. From there I just stayed a rock music fan until punk came along. I still just listened to my Beatles records and whatever my older brothers owned, and the usual hits on the radio. Right up until about 1977–78. Then my friends got into David Bowie, and I resisted as long as I could, and I lost. I really tried hard, too. I was like, "I don't want to like that guy. He's a weirdo. He's a freak." When I realized that I was a fan, I was really disappointed in myself. I was like, "Oh god, what have I done?" But I just couldn't stop listening to the David Bowie best-of album *Changes*, one my friend insisted that I borrow from him. And once that dam burst, it was just like endless Stooges and Velvet Underground and Brian

Eno and New York Dolls and Iggy Pop. And then from there it was the Ramones and the Sex Pistols and The Clash, and all hell broke loose. Pretty soon, I had two hundred different punk rock albums by the time I was like seventeen. And the ones I didn't have, my friends did, and I taped them from them, and they taped mine. And I hadn't even left the suburbs yet. I was seventeen and listening to import albums like The Adverts or Johnny Thunders's Heartbreakers while I was reading my Shakespeare homework. I was hooked forever.

Jes Skolnik My parents are musicians. I grew up with music. I grew up in DC, and I started going to punk shows when I was very young because my parents had access to that world. It was not because I was a particularly cool kid. It was because my dad did sound at different shows. But he took me to my first when I was ten, and by that I mean the first show I asked to go to. And that show was Bikini Kill and The Nation of Ulysses. I didn't know these bands from anybody. I just picked up the flyer in the record store was like, "This is really cool." It was totally an accident. I really fell into it headfirst and was just like, "Oh shit." I was ten years old and was like, "This is what I want to be when I grow up. This is so cool." So I started going to riot grrrl meetings and got into riot grrrl and positive force, and I started writing zines and reviewing records. I was maybe twelve or thirteen when I started doing that. So I have been an amateur critic for a very long time, but it didn't really occur to me to professionalize that for really long time.

T. Cole Rachel I think for most people the music that you listen to when you're a teenager is always going to feel the most important just because you can listen to music in ways when you're a teenager that you really don't as an adult. I don't have time to listen to *Disintegration* twenty times in a row in my room as a grown person with a job, but when you're a teenager you have all the time in the world to do that, you know? You really kind of live inside that music, and I feel like the records that sort of come into your life during those years become so formative, if for no other reason than you just have all the time and energy to devote to them. I feel really lucky I was in high school going into college in the early '90s. Going to the first two or three years of Lollapalooza I saw Nirvana and Pavement and all those bands many, many times. I remember seeing Jane's Addiction in 1991 when I was not old enough to drive yet and just being like, "What is this?"

Chuck Klosterman I remember when music became important to me, which was about fifth grade. I listened to Top 40 music, like anybody else, and then my brother had come home from the army—I'm the youngest of seven kids, so I have siblings who are much older—and he had a handful of tapes. I remember one was Huey Lewis and the News' *Sports*, one was a Cars record. But he also had Motley Crew's *Shout at the Devil* and Ozzy Osbourne's *Speak of the Devil*, which is the live record that Ozzy made of old Black Sabbath songs with the guitarist from Night Ranger. And my brother also brought back a Walkman, which I had never seen before. I think in some ways I was into the Walkman almost as much as I was into the music—just the idea of wearing headphones and being able to walk around. But I started listening to the Motley Crew cassette and the Ozzy cassette and reading the liner notes inside of the cassettes. I don't know why it was such a transformative experience, but I guess it was just the idea that I felt like I'd found something I liked and that liking it was my own decision.

Hannah Giorgis There are two records that come to mind which are very different in genre. One is Usher's *8701*. I developed an attachment to that album. It made me understand that I can have a stake in an artist's work even if I'm not in my twenties. I was maybe ten or eleven. It felt important for me for reasons that were not just, "Oh, my older cousin plays it all the time." The other album was *Transatlanticism* by Death Cab for Cutie. I think it was the first time that as an immigrant growing up in Orange County I heard an album by a band that looked nothing like me, that had experiences wildly different from mine—just to pick a song— that title track having that sense of longing and that sense of crossing boundaries and crossing territory and moving toward something that's uncertain. I remember feeling like that was the first time I heard that conveyed so clearly, and it felt like a poem.

Puja Patel I grew up in such an interesting household for music. It wasn't in the background. I woke up to music playing every day. My mom would blast Bollywood music and then the American pop counterparts like Chaka Khan, Janet Jackson, Tina Turner, Whitney Houston. I would live my life through my mom's music in that way. And then my dad was into Fleetwood Mac and Bruce Springsteen. I grew up in a rural area outside of Baltimore. I came from immigrant parents where different music was playing in our house all the time. But I did not grow up with The Beatles or the Stones or Led Zeppelin. I was honestly super intimidated by those bands until I was much older, truly, because it felt like this very American sensibility around music that all the other kids understood immediately and I had no idea what was going on. Early listening is something that's very clearly passed down to you by your parents. But I had this cool neighbor who eventually went to the MICA art school and she was into Fiona Apple and No Doubt and Alanis Morissette. I think that angsty, independent, in-your-face women who also had this really strong, mysterious, feminist appeal to them influenced me as a kid. I was like, "That's a cool woman, that's the type of woman that I aspire to be one day." That went hand in hand with, like, Whitney Houston, who is just fun to me.

Josh Jackson I was a classic rock kid in high school, listening to the same thing that people ten years before me had been listening to, or even longer than that. I had been bemoaning the state of modern music as a fourteen-year-old. What really was a turning point for me was discovering a mixtape that my sister's boyfriend at the time had made for her. I listened to it one time and was like, "What is this?" It had a whole mix of stuff on there, from The Plimsouls, R.E.M., The Smiths. It was this whole new kind of music for me. And it was right as U2 was getting bigger, and right down the street in Athens R.E.M. was blowing up, and I just latched on to all of that. Rather than music being this sort of background thing that

I enjoyed, it became this thing I started to search out with new bands. *120 Minutes* on MTV was a huge influence on me. I would set the VCR to tape it every night and I'd watch it when I got home from school the next day, just discovering so many new bands that were on this cutting edge of modern rock, whatever you called it at the time.

Ryan Dombal I didn't come from a musical family or anything. One of my formative musical influences was my best friend's older brother. I'm an only child, so I had to get that older brother wisdom somewhere else. This is the early '90s, and he loved Guns N' Roses. Rumor had it he also jumped onstage during a Van Halen concert on Long Island, where I grew up—I wasn't there, and didn't see it, but it only added to the myth for me. I was just enthralled by music as a teenager. I would spend hours with friends watching videos, goofing on them, marveling at them. I would tape *120 Minutes* on VHS. I distinctly remember seeing The Verve's "Bitter Sweet Symphony" on that show, where the singer, Richard Ashcroft, just walks down a street and bumps into people, and thinking it was the coolest thing I had seen in my entire life. Growing up in the '90s, it was a really great time for music videos, and they really captured my imagination.

Jenn Pelly I didn't grow up in a particularly musical household, which sometimes surprises people because my twin sister is also a music journalist, and we have a younger sister who is a fashion stylist in the music industry. But we did grow up on Long Island, which in the early 2000s was a fairly musical place. There was an active underground for emo, pop-punk, hardcore, grindcore, ska, metal, indie. We got into all of that in middle school, around 2001. That was our introduction to music beyond Top 40. Music became this new compass for understanding how to be a person. We started going to shows all the time. It was the era of Myspace and LiveJournal and Kazaa, but I think going to shows and connecting in that way was hugely important. I still have a deep love for live music—it feels very central to my existence—and I think it stems from those early experiences.

Maura Johnston I grew up in a musical household. My grandmother was a singer. There was always music in my house, and I grew up at the perfect time to really start loving music. I turned five in 1980 and my cable company got MTV two years later. And so I just immersed in all of that. I mean, back then I still had to go to the grocery store near me to buy records, and then gradually graduating to the mall.

Stephen Deusner For me it was the video for R.E.M.'s "Talk about the Passion." When my small town got MTV for the first time, I remember staying up really late one night watching videos. I couldn't turn it off. In their off hours, their programming was stuff that wasn't the Top 40, and I remember catching that song. And I don't remember what about it caught my attention, but the next time we were in a big city that had a mall, I remember I had to look for the R.E.M. album. It was *Eponymous.* I listened to it and absorbed it and I remember thinking at one point, "I'm the only person in my town listening to this." Which may not have even been true, but it felt that way. To have ownership of something, to feel like, "This is mine and nobody else's." That meant a lot to me.

Eric T. Miller I was living in West Virginia and it was hard to really get new music, but we would go down to the department store and they'd put the new '45s out. I always liked that there'd be the radio song but then you get the B-side. I was always really into the B-sides stuff. The gateway drug was R.E.M. and *Fables of the Reconstruction.* I knew some of their stuff before, but that was the first record that I listened to back and forth all the time. And from there it was all the British stuff, like The Smiths and The Cure. My dad started to see how interested in music I was getting, so on the weekends he would drive me to different record stores. It just kept on escalating, just my music fandom.

Jenn Pelly Fiona Apple is probably my favorite songwriter. Hearing her records in high school, in the mid-2000s, was the first time I really felt like a musician was reflecting my own experience back to me. It was an emboldening, line-in-the-sand experience, as a fan and also as a writer.

Her lyrics were clearly feminist. I was a teenager, and I didn't have the vocabulary for this yet, but I was starting to consider the reality of being a journalist with a feminist agenda. In eleventh grade, the adviser of the school paper brought us on a field trip to the office of our local alt-weekly, the *Long Island Press*, and we had opportunities to contribute. It was inspiring to be around working journalists, especially investigative reporters for a nontraditional newspaper. I started freelancing for anyone who would let me. I figured it would be nearly impossible for me to sustain a life as a writer, so I really poured myself into it obsessively. I like thinking about the beginnings of things because we're always circling back to beginnings. Whether you're pitching a new publication or privately committing to pursuing a story idea, it's the same process of locating just enough confidence within yourself to actually do something. I thought about this a lot while I was working on my book about The Raincoats: I feel like you can really hear so many beginnings on that record.

Ben Ratliff I probably didn't notice music all that much until the late '70s, so I guess I would have been about ten years old. But I do remember in a short period of time hearing music from the 1950s, specifically Fats Domino and Chuck Berry, because we had the soundtrack to the movie *American Graffiti*, which was a weirdly popular record in the late '70s when you think about it. That music was only twenty years old then. It's the equivalent of a kid today listening to whatever came out in 1997, like Beck's *Odelay*, or Janet Jackson's *Velvet Rope*. Not so hard to imagine.

Mark Richardson In the midseventies my parents had Elton John's *Greatest Hits*, the one where he's got the white suit and big glasses and a cane and he's in the front of the piano. It's unbelievable. My parents were not huge music people, but they did have that album. And I remember that being played and the song "Daniel" in particular. There's something about the sound of the synths in "Daniel," a very particular quality to them. I don't know what kind of keyboard it is, but it sounds to me a little bit like steel drums or something. It has this kind of Caribbean feel to it to me. I love that song, and I love that whole album, but I do remember that being a very early instance where I really fixated on the emotional quality of a specific sound, and that the sound of the synths could really make me feel this kind of yearning and longing. Even aside from a song, just simply the sonic quality of that particular instrument in that mix, had a big effect on me.

Jim DeRogatis The first record I ever bought was The Blue Album, The Beatles' greatest hits collection. And, you know, I went to see Beatlemania on Broadway when I was really young, and it was so exciting to hear these songs brought to life. The first concert I actually went to was Jethro Tull at Madison Square Garden with an older cousin. I love the *Heavy Horses* album. But I think when I realized that there was more, that there was a tremendous power for catharsis and emotion that could be expressed in music as in no other art form, and that this was not out of my reach, was when I was at mass just before Christmas in the gym of Hudson Catholic Regional High School for Boys in Jersey City and there was a band playing—a group of incredibly cool long-haired seniors—and they played "Let It Be." And John Lennon had been shot to death on the street just across the river on December 9, 1980. And I love John Lennon, and here was this music that was live with eight hundred kids in a high school that impacted me. I could feel the bass drum pounding in my chest, and the guitar riff is soaring over the basketball hoops, and I cried. And you know, okay this is different than Jethro Tull at Madison Square Garden or Beatlemania or even the records I was listening to obsessively since age ten or eleven. I'm here now. We are here now. We are a community having this experience now and nothing could possibly be more powerful. Never mind that those assholes in the band chose a song by Paul McCartney to pay tribute to a stone cold atheist. "Imagine no religion." They got just about everything wrong, you know what I mean? It's a spiritual. "Mother Mary came to me." John Lennon no doubt puked when McCartney recorded that for fuck's sake. But it moved me. It was powerful.

Mark Redfern My dad was a music photographer, so I grew up going to music festivals as a kid—mainly jazz ones because that was what he was into. It was at various jazz festivals, mainly ones in France, where I got to meet the likes of Dizzy Gillespie, Art Blakey, George Benson, and Tony Bennett, all who my dad was friendly with, backstage or in hotel bars, when I was still in elementary school. I remember being in the photo pit with my dad and sister as he photographed James Brown at the Nice Jazz Festival in the South of France, and that night as I was trying to sleep in the hotel I experienced a ringing in my ear for the first time and it really freaked me out, until my sister explained to me that it was because we'd been a little too close to the speakers. My dad also shot The Beatles on the Magical Mystery Tour and other rock legends in the '60s and '70s, such as Jimi Hendrix, so he wasn't just about jazz. In fact, his first book of music photography was published by a company partly run by Pete Townshend of The Who, and there's a photo of me as a four- or five-year-old with my dad and Townshend at the book launch. I grew up in London with a British dad and an American mother, and when they divorced I moved with my mom to America at age seven, eventually settling in suburban New Jersey and becoming obsessed with Madonna, with posters of her splashed across my childhood bedroom. When we moved back to London for high school, my cool half brother, eleven years my elder, exposed me to Kate Bush, R.E.M., The Cure, and Cocteau Twins, and then cool '90s movie soundtracks like *Pump Up the Volume* and *Until the End of the World* also gave me first listens to hipper bands like the Pixies, Talking Heads, Depeche Mode, and Nick Cave. And then I really got into music in college in Los Angeles. I really got into all the Britpop—Pulp, Suede, Blur, etcetera—and shoegazing music the '90s—Lush, Ride, Slowdive. My love of Britpop was perhaps a way to reconnect to my British heritage, and when I'd go home to London for the summers, I would seek out all the singles for the B-sides and see as many shows and go to as many festivals as possible. My brother even convinced me to break into Glastonbury in 1995—security was more lax back then, although we accidentally snuck in next to the festival's police compound and somehow still made it in—

and we got to see The Verve, The Charlatans, Elastica, and others, but also got terrible sunburn because we forgot to pack sunblock.

Laura Snapes My first transformative record was the Spice Girls' debut album. It wasn't just music I heard in the car: it was a whole lifestyle, and lifeline, really, for a dorky seven-year-old who didn't have a ton of friends. They became the basis for the one true friendship I did have: we would write letters to the band, dress up as them, design outfits for them, sing their songs in the playground, learn their dances for performances in assembly. My obsession with them also got me into reading pop magazines like *Smash Hits* and *Top of the Pops*, which, obviously, had an enormous impact. Here was a whole clubhouse that I wanted to join. I always remember Geri saying that when she was a kid, she thought pop stars lived in a box and were only let out to be on TV, but that now she was a pop star, she understood the reality of it—that you're still a whole person. That really stuck with me, and even though I of course had a very juvenile conception of what a twenty-something woman's life was, it made me want to understand them as whole people.

Carvell Wallace When I was in sixth or seventh grade, I lived in a small town in Pennsylvania, and I had a cousin who lived in DC, and my cousin was always my plug for much more culturally advanced stuff because there wasn't a whole lot of stuff happening where I was. So when he would come visit, he'd always have these mixtapes, and he would be like, "Have you heard this? Have you heard that?" But he came one day and he had this tape of this rapper who was rapping these really stupid stories about funny things happening to him. But he had a little flow and he was kind of smart and the beats were funny. And it was Will Smith. This was before his album *He's the DJ, I'm the Rapper*. This was his early stuff before "Parents Just Don't Understand." And I remember listening to that music and feeling that even though I didn't love him and think he was great—I can't stress that enough, I did not love him and think he was great—I did recognize that there was something really interesting about what he was doing in relationship to the rest of rap. And I remember noticing that it meant something that he was do-ing this at the time, that it was contextualized, that what he was doing had some context. I didn't have words for these thoughts in seventh grade, but I just remember that feeling. And I'll never forget listening to those tapes that my cousin gave me because I was obsessed with them, because what he was doing with rap and storytelling was just different to what everyone else was doing. And I was somehow aware that that was something. A year or two later I heard *Straight Outta Compton*. You also had Slick Rick's *The Art of Storytelling* and Too Short's *Life Is . . . Too Short* all coming out. By this point I'd moved to the West Coast. And so all three of those albums really impacted me. I also had *Fear of a Black Planet* on heavy rotation. Those four albums really became important because they also were about a movement. They were about a moment. They weren't necessarily about the same movement, but they were about overlapping movements. And I think those were the early times of which I recognized a valuable cultural ex-pression through music that is a response to the world. *Straight Outta Compton* especially and *Fear of a Black Planet* were both works of art that were direct responses to things not happening in a studio. Those were responses to the world. And they made it clear. N.W.A.'s first line, "You are now about to witness the strength of street knowledge," that was a call, like, "We are going to disrupt our current understanding of what is valuable in society and we're going to give you a flip side narrative that you don't have, and we're doing it specifically because this narrative is missing, and the lack of that narrative is causing prob-lems for our people. Here. We're now presenting this." So I would say that between seventh and ninth grade I began to realize, "Oh music is about a response to the world."

Emily J. Lordi The first thing that comes to mind is Aretha Franklin's cov-er of Sam Cooke's "A Change Is Gonna Come." When she recorded it in 1967, it was a few years after Sam Cooke's death, and she has this frame that she adds to it, this little introductory frame that she attaches to the song where she says, "There's an old friend that I once heard say,

/ something that touched my heart." On the face of it that is her paying tribute to Sam Cooke and saying he's no longer with us. But when I thought about it in the context of 1967, I was thinking about the song as an act of mourning, not just for Sam Cooke but for all the other black leaders who had passed away by that time, political leaders like Malcolm X and Medgar Evers, as well as musical icons like Billie Holiday and Dinah Washington. There's so many losses that are that are sustained by '67. Aretha's album comes out in March, and Otis Redding and John Coltrane will die later that year, and of course King is assassinated the following spring. So Aretha is not necessarily intentionally trying to get all of that in her song, but the song, with that frame, can be read in that way. Her frame, which on the face of it, to be honest, I found sort of corny, but when I thought about it more, or thought about it differently—and this is something criticism and writing about music requires—you take another listen and the question becomes, "Okay, maybe I don't really like this, but what can I make of it? How can I listen again in a way that's more respectful, and that engages a wider context?" So that would be a moment where when I thought about the song in this other way, as an almost historical metacommentary on how many people, how many "old friends," had been lost. Which gave me a much more profound appreciation for it.

Lizzy Goodman I am a rock nerd, but like I didn't grow up being one of those people who knew everything about music. The obvious place to start is my parents, and particularly my father. My dad was a big Dylanhead, and a lot of Beatles and Rolling Stones and Bob Dylan played in our house. And also, strangely, Talking Heads. There'd be these weird bands that snuck in that only later I realized were really incongruous. I really thought The Beatles and Talking Heads were contemporaries of each other. They would play "Burning Down the House" and "Love Me Do." I knew about all the other bands that anyone else who went to high school in the '90s would know about. And I felt connected to them—I thought Eddie Vedder was the only person who understood me, and I would write letters to him in my journal—but I wasn't a music dork that spoke only that language and used that language to better understand myself. I was just a teenage kid who was into the bands that all my other friends were into. Of course, beneath the surface, I'd had this kind of intense education almost accidentally in the founding members of British and American rock 'n' roll through my parents. And so when I got to college there was this one guy that I met—he always get so mad when I talk about this—but freshman year when we moved in he was playing "Chimes of Freedom" by Bob Dylan at massive top volume in this quad. And as a pretentious eighteen-year-old, of course, I was like, "That person's going to be my friend." And it was this guy Mike who I'm still friends with. And Mike was cool. He had gone to boarding school on the East Coast, and he was a real music nerd. He just educated me. He taught me about Pavement and Aphex Twin and Stereolab and Belle and Sebastian and Guided by Voices, and American indie rock. Pavement became one of my favorite bands ever. I learned about the Pixies from him, who are probably my favorite band ever. Just all that stuff. Everything that's actually good that was getting made during the time that I could have been paying attention and just wasn't, that was when my real education started.

Jessica Hopper What I realized when I actually found punk rock was that I had been looking for the punk rock of things. I don't want to say "I was a child activist," but I didn't go to camp, my parents let me do what-the-fuck-ever because I was independent as a child, and starting in the fourth, fifth, sixth grade what I would do during the summer was volunteer at organizations and do phone banks and be on the phone for like a "No Nukes" campaign, or I was going to protests or rallies or whatever, and it was just what I did all the fucking time. And I knew there was music about it, but I had no idea how to find it or connect why I was lying down on a freeway on-ramp with a bunch of adults and weird teenagers, or walking around downtown Minneapolis in a gas mask—which the frequency with which I ran into my parents on their lunch hour has become a running family joke. But that was fundamentally who I was. I was like, lot of hope, lot of save-the-world, lot of living-in-fear-of-dying-in-a-nuclear-holocaust and what-would-happen-to-the-world-if-people-didn't-recycle. But around the time that was really a thing for me, really feeling a deep political consciousness, and nascent connection to the dire straits of the wider world, I started to get into music. I started to realize you could find those kinds of sentiments of care and anger and will for disruption in music. And that's all I could pinpoint it as. First it was a song here or there, and then I heard my first Tracy Chapman album where it was personal and political. When I got in ninth grade I was definitely at that point—I was a zero. I didn't have a thing I was into. And one day this kid came up, sat down next to me, and was like, "Are you a hippie or a punk? What are you?" And I was like, "I don't know. Either? Both?" I was like, "I've never heard of punk rock," and he made me a tape, and I was like, 'Oh, this is what I was looking for." But this was the thing. I didn't start on something like the Sex Pistols. It was the Boredoms, Bongwater, Pussy Galore, Big Black, Babes in Toyland, Sonic Youth, all that stuff. But I was like, "Oh shit." As soon as I heard it I was like, "No, this is it." And eventually I got into hip-hop and other stuff too, but it was like music was the thing I was looking for. I just didn't know about it. But as soon as I heard punk rock I went from zero to "This is my life," to expertise, to you hanging out at the record store, to going to every record store in town diligently trying to get all the information I could and trying to find all the fanzines I could—because I knew that was a really good way to find out about music—and I just started reading, just devouring, religiously living by music criticism and those source materials by the end of ninth grade. That was my fucking world.

Rob Sheffield As a little kid I would hang out at the library every chance I had. That's where I wanted to spend all my free time. And the public library in Milton, Massachusetts, had an LP section, so I would often have a stack of records and just be listening on the headphones, and a stack of books to flip through at the same time. It's funny. I remember being a little kid in the library and I was reading Lillian Roxon's *Rock Encyclopedia*—thank God that book was in my library when I was a little kid—and I remember reading her description of the Altamont Festival in 1969. I remember lifting my head from the book and just looking at the bookshelves around me and just marveling to myself, like, "Oh my god! That's what that verse in 'American Pie' is about." "Jumpin' Jack Flash sat on a candlestick." "No angel born in hell." I was like, "Oh my god. This song that I've loved since I could walk or talk, I finally understand it. There's this whole historical aspect about it." That kind of thing was mind-blowing and inspiring for me. It's funny, I wonder how much of it is having "American Pie" as one of my first favorite songs. That was the first actual record I owned that was a pop and rock and roll record and was a song on the radio. I heard it and was singing it on the radio, and one day my dad brought it home for me when he came home from work. That was the first '45 I owned. That was 1971, when I was five years old. It was the kind of thing to have '45s of long songs where the first half of the song was on side one and then the second half on side two. The way the story fit together and the way it was such an elaborate story, that stuck in my head. I could tell from the beginning that it had echoes of rock and roll because my parents grew up on '50s rock and roll, Elvis and doo-wop and stuff, and that's what they listened to. So I recognize lots of references to that in "American Pie." For me knowing that song and having that song stuck in my head is sort of like a skeleton of a musical and cultural memory and history. And then being able to, by reading and listening to more music and picking more things up, being able to sort of put flesh on that skeleton and try to dress it up a bit.

CHAPTER TWO

Humble Beginnings

Music journalism is a simple marriage of combined interests: a love of music and a love of writing. The love of music almost always comes first. Its access is easier, and its effects are much more immediate. An appreciation and love of writing takes more time, requiring a skill set that has to be taught and developed.

Perhaps this is why early in a music journalist's exploration of storytelling and criticism, when he or she reaches that point where they can't help but obsess over an artist or band's narrative arc, the behind-the-scenes makings of individual albums and songs, or the meaning and consequence of a lyric or melody, writing feels like taking off some imperceptible shackle. You're able to give what were likely inarticulate, internalized reflections some actual external thought and ownership. "Very early on, I adopted writing as a sense-making tool for me in my life," says Amanda Petrusich. "It was the way I made sense of things. It's still the way I make sense of things. Most of that stuff doesn't get published. They say that babies experience the world through their mouths first— just putting everything they find into their mouths. I was putting things into sentences. Trying to understand music, why it worked on me in the way that it did, why I loved it so much—writing about it was a way for me to unlock that mystery."

Turning what feels like a unique literary impulse into a functional and practical career path is a bit more difficult to unlock. Its beginnings are often without expectation, its steps forward often feeling accidental. All you know is you just want to write about music. What comes next depends on a whole host of variables.

Jenn Pelly I think I was drawn to writing at a young age, partially from being really shy. Even as a kid, it seemed hard to talk to people. Writing was a way of existing.

Laura Snapes I like having the space to work out what I think about something and come up with a coherent argument. I couldn't extemporize anything like that. I'm better on paper than in person.

Jayson Greene It's kind of a compulsion. Writing was one of the first things I ever really did. As a very little kid I would dictate stories to my mother before I could write them down myself. Recently my parents dug up an old paper I wrote in fourth grade. You had to write an essay about yourself, and mine said I wanted to be an "author." So I think that was really, really based in my personality. I was writing long, involved, multiple-chapter stories at my desk by hand in second grade. I also loved music, very naturally and obsessively. By the time I was old enough to think about a career, I already had this huge catalog of knowledge in my head, by virtue of interest and excitement. I had never thought about whether or not I was doing anything worthwhile in the larger sense, but it turns out that I accidentally was. I don't know how to really *be* without writing. I require writing to exist. I get peevish and angry and depressed if I don't write something almost every week.

Lizzy Goodman I have always felt a kind of low-grade panic-anxiety thing since as young as I can remember about all the things that I have to say about what I see and observe in the world. And it's just this deep anxiety about not being able to get them out. I've been writing in journals since I was literally five years old. The early ones, they're hilarious. They're barely legible because they're written by a child in crayon, but there I am, trying to talk about a pony that I saw that day. So it's very deep in me, this need to express—not just in a person-to-person way but in some formatted, structured, creative, discrete, creative way—what I see around me and what it means to me. Joan Didion famously talks about writing to understand what she thinks, and I relate to that.

Hannah Giorgis I love writing when it feels like putting a puzzle together. There's this project management instinct to me that's like "Here's this big unknown thing that I'm looking at. I know that I have these puzzle pieces here. Well, what if we line them up like this?" And that kind of playing around and almost visualizing in that way is really fun. That kind of space of discovery can feel really generative and really rewarding to be part of.

Jayson Greene I mean writing is reading and reading is writing. I don't separate the two of them. I don't really just read books. I read and annotate them, not literally with a pen but I have to write down what I'm thinking about the books and transcribe sentences. The relationship is very much a feedback loop. I think all those things to me encompass what it means to write. I think all those things are part of the job of writing.

Hanif Abdurraqib Writing is hard. Writing is difficult. Writing is just a difficult task.

Jessica Hopper It's the worst and the best.

Lizzy Goodman I was not a good writer for a really long time. And that is very debilitating and disillusioning and heartbreaking. I mean I sucked in a constructive way. But it really is powerful to be able to sit down and say what you mean. And I can't do it every day, and I don't take it for granted. It might leave me tomorrow. But for the moment I seem to be able to more often than not, with great cost to my own personal health, I'm able to sit down and tell you what I mean. And that is a great relief on an existential level. And that's important.

Amanda Petrusich The actual act of writing, of sitting down and making sense of something, of putting it into words, and then arranging those words in a way that I find beautiful, even if no one else does, even if no one else even reads it—I'm so happy doing that. I just love writing and reading so much. That, for me, is the best part of my job. Sitting down with all this stuff that you've gathered—information or impressions or notes or quotes or observations or whatever it is—and finding a way to synthesize that grist into a cohesive, coherent narrative that might mean something to somebody else, or point something out that they had not previously considered. It's such a privilege, and I love doing it so much.

Hua Hsu I always think of writing as an asymptote, like two lines that approach each other but never ever meet. All writing is an attempt to approach a sensation in your mind. As far as the larger ideas that are scaffolding a piece, whether they're drawn from history or theory or something I feel or some suspicion I have about the world, that stuff's usually a fun puzzle to work out in my head.

Lizzy Goodman Someone said to me recently when they had to start writing something, "I'm not like you. I don't like doing this." And I was like, "Are you crazy? I don't like doing this. Nobody likes it. Before I sit down in front of any blank page I will literally do anything else and deal with that." And yet...

Gabriela Tully Claymore It's cool when you feel like you get this sense of greater understanding from a piece of art by creating your own out of it.

Lindsay Zoladz I wasn't someone who set out to be a music writer specifically, but I've always been interested in writing and always wanted to be a writer and always was interested in music and was a really big fan. I think I didn't realize until after I started writing that those two things intersected with me.

Rob Sheffield Well I have always written about music since I was a kid. It's something that I always liked to write about and of all the other things that I like to write about I've always loved to drop music into it. I've always been responding to the world around me largely through music and no matter what I've been writing, music has been a part of it.

Hanif Abdurraqib As a kid I was writing journals to myself about music albums and songs I loved, trying to articulate my love of those things to audiences that were largely myself. I think that's how I learned to articulate and talk about music and be open and critical about it.

Amanda Petrusich For me, music journalism combined the two things that I really loved, reading and records. As a kid, I remember devouring *SPIN* magazine and *Rolling Stone* and just thinking, "I can't believe people get to do *this* for a living." It just seemed so impossibly cool.

Jillian Mapes I was totally one of those kids who—I don't know what it was, I just always wanted to do this. I had a subscription to *Rolling Stone* from like twelve years old and was just like, "Yup, I wanna do this."

Maria Sherman I knew from an early age that I wanted to write, and I knew I wanted to write about music. It came really naturally to me. I was a big magazine person. I grew up primarily on military bases in Germany. I was a bit of an army brat. My parents worked for the government. My dad is a shrink and specializes in PTSD, so I was always around that environment, and the one US store that they would have on base, called the PX, would have a limited amount of magazines and books that would come in, usually just really shitty bestsellers. But they would always have *Rolling Stone* and *SPIN*—and for some reason *MAGNET*, which I always thought was really cool—and on occasion *MOJO* and

NME. That material was always most interesting to me, as opposed to the other reading material that was available, because there wasn't a lot and I didn't speak German. And I just became interested in that type of writing. I liked the idea of removing some of the sort of mythos from the rock gods that I admired through profiles and reviews and criticism. And then in middle school and later high school I got more involved in online communities. Those figures became more accessible, and I became fascinated with that kind of accessibility. There's something about writing about something that could be in your periphery even though I was so isolated in a tiny village in Germany—or what felt really isolating. I'm sure people with a suburban experience feel the same way.

T. Cole Rachel I grew up on a farm in Oklahoma. All of that kind of thing was very foreign to me. But I do think if you really love music and you love seeing bands and are a nerd for the whole culture of music and the history of music—I did grow up reading music magazines religiously and would order records through the mail because there were no records stores where I grew up. I think if you have a really deep love and appreciation for that culture, it kind of seeps into you. I feel like even though I never took journalism classes, when I started to write about music professionally it wasn't such a huge leap because I spent my whole life reading music writing. So those forms and that vernacular were already sort of imprinted in my brain. So I felt like I can speak in this language because I read it for so long and I understand it.

Hua Hsu I'll never forget going to this local bookstore near my house and noticing that off to the side of the magazines were these flat stacks of European tabloids, and in one of the slots was the *New Musical Express*, and I pulled it out and Ice-T was on the cover and inside there were articles about Bob Mould's band Sugar and Sloan, this pop band from Halifax that I had become fascinated with because I had seen their video once on *120 Minutes*, and I just thought, "Wow this thing has Ice-T and Sloan in it. This is mind-blowing." And I bought it and took it home, and from then on every week I would go to that bookstore and buy either the *New Musical Express* or *Melody Maker*, and from there I got into more underground publications and I started reading the *Face* and *Select* and all these British magazines. That was a really huge moment for me, almost more so than the music was seeing these magazines and the discussion about music.

Ben Ratliff My first awareness that there was writing about music came from a book that we had in our house when I was growing up by the writer Nik Cohn called *Awopbopaloobop Alopbamboom: The Golden Age of Rock*. It was published in the late '60s—we had it around the house growing up. It was a speedy and smartly written book of meditations about various musicians in pop music since the '50s, ending around the late '60s. It was on the bookshelf alongside novels and history books and whatever else we had there. But it never had occurred to me before picking it out that one could write about music like that. Partly because descriptive lan-guage was important to [Cohn], he didn't care about picking majority positions, and the book encouraged readers to exercise a little doubt about what was being set in front of them—particularly the later-period Beatles—in a freeing way. It became powerful and useful for me. Later, as an early teenager, I would see *Rolling Stone* and the *Village Voice* and the *Soho News* because I grew up not far from New York City, and my father worked in the city, and he'd bring things home. I read a lot of criticism from those magazines in particular—this is a teenage memory speaking now, but I remember reading people like Greg Tate and Greil Marcus and having a marker in my head for understanding the impulse to be descriptive and discerning and a little bit counterintuitive around music, and that marker was Nik.

Matt Fink I grew up in the '90s. I remember when the internet came around. I was probably about fifteen when we got an internet connec-tion, and I remember just being blown away by all the music writing that was available. I would just spend hours reading the All Music Guide. And around that time was when *Pitchfork* started, and I remem-ber discovering it, which was just mind-blowing. There was this world of music I didn't really know much about. I had read *Rolling Stone* and *SPIN* and *Alternative Press*, and I had some understanding of this indie rock world, but something like *Pitchfork* was my real first exposure to how deep that world was.

Tom Breihan I always wanted to be a rock critic. In high school I would read everything. Nineties-era *SPIN* was amazing. I paid as much attention to the bylines as I did about who they were writing about. It was a big thing for me.

Brittany Spanos I have always known I wanted to be a journalist. As a preteen I was drawn to music history. Whenever I really loved a band, I would need to know what other bands they played with, what other bands they listened to. That kind of got me hooked on music magazines like *Rolling Stone* and *SPIN*, and I just started reading those really voraciously and just started writing.

Ann Powers I've always had a lot of ambition—and probably delusions of grandeur. I wanted to at first write poetry like William Butler Yeats. And then I wanted to write fiction like Joan Didion. I wanted to write books like my favorite literary writers, and music writing just didn't seem like a form that could launch me into immortality, which as a young person felt very important to me. But then I read *Mystery Train*, which really did truly change my life because it made me realize that I could do something beautiful, not just interesting, not just informative, but beautiful and transformative in music writing. After I read *Mystery Train* I actually took my student loan money, bought a plane ticket to New York from San Francisco and then a train pass for the summer, and followed the story of *Mystery Train*. I went to New Orleans and Chicago and Memphis on the train just to learn that stuff that he had written about and to be in the places that he'd written about in the book, going to Graceland and Al Green's church and all that. I realized that music writing could do what I wanted to do. And that's when I committed to it.

Chuck Klosterman In terms of writing about music—it never occurred to me that it could be an actual job. It never did. I always fear I've said things like this in interviews a million times, but it's totally true. In college, I used to read *SPIN* magazine constantly. In 2002, when I got a job at *SPIN*, all my friends from college were like, "Your dream has been realized! That was your dream!" But I am being totally honest when I say that, as a reader of *SPIN* in the '90s, it never occurred to me that working there was a job you could get. I obviously knew that there were people who worked there, and I was a journalism major, so I obviously knew that someone built these magazines. But it was not something I thought I could actually do.

Carl Wilson It's a funny thing—the very first long writing project I ever tried was when I was about twelve. I wrote, in a school notebook, a so-called book about The Beatles. I was writing fiction and poetry throughout high school. That's what I thought I would end up doing.

Matt Fink I think I always liked writing, but I remember I was about fourteen years old and I had my whole record collection and I went through and reviewed all the albums and printed it out and gave it to all my friends. I really don't know why. I just felt some sort of need to weigh in on what I thought was good and bad. And they probably looked at me like I was crazy, but it felt like it was necessary to do, for me to weigh in on what I thought made this music good or bad. And I kind of never stopped since.

Chuck Klosterman In some ways it's weird, because I did do things that would suggest there was always some kind of underlying desire. When I was a kid, sometimes I would make up Q&As with fictional rock bands where I would write the questions and the answers. I found these fake interviews years later, and the hilarious thing is that I had all the fictional musicians saying the most cliché bullshit. It was crazy. I would make up all these bands, and the quote from the fictional guitarist would be, "Our next record is going to be a lot bluesier. It's going to be heavier."

Those are the quotes that I would make up for these guys! It was so odd. Even in my fantasies, everything was boring. But I still thought it was fun.

T. Cole Rachel I wasn't like a lot of other music writers who made zines when they were a kid.

Brandon Stosuy I started writing seriously when I was a teenager, when I started a zine. That was an important moment for me. I grew up in southern New Jersey in the Pine Barrens in a town called Chatsworth that had, and still has, a population of eight hundred people. There was nothing there in the way of punk or underground culture, and a zine connected me to the parts of the outside world that interested me. This was pre-internet, and so I didn't have e-mail or anything like that. I had a friend in another town with a car, but the zine really was the way I corresponded with people, and met people into punk and books and art. We would trade our zines and write each other long letters. I'm still friends with a bunch of people I met that way, when I was fourteen.

Jessica Hopper Through reading fanzines and really feeling part of that community I was immediately thinking of that as a way to participate. The main thing that spurred me was when somebody wrote something sexist—or at least reductive—about Babes in Toyland, and they were my absolute favorite band, and I called the local magazine that printed it and was like "I'd like to write like a rebuttal." And they were like, "Have you ever written before?" And I was like, "For school." I was in ninth grade. I'd never written anything professionally before. But they didn't take me up on my offer, so I was like, "Fuck it. I'm going to start my own thing." So many people I knew did fanzines or self-published comics or whatever. And as I had sort of gotten more immersed in the music scene I wasn't necessarily encountering a ton of other girls my age there. But the music scene in Minneapolis was so small I just knew people, especially hanging out at the record store or eventually working at the record store, and I just started writing. I was writing for Minneapolis' *City Pages* when I was sixteen. That was my first pay-check. By tenth and eleventh grade I had a column in that same local magazine that said "No, we won't let you write." Basically by the time the second issue of my fanzine came out people were hiring me.

Brandon Stosuy My father grew up in East New York, and my mom grew up in Queens. My grandparents were in Brooklyn most of my child-hood, and we would go to the city to visit them quite a bit. So I had ac-cess to this bigger place, but I grew up in a very, very small place. Once I was back in Chatsworth—especially before I could drive—I'd be stuck. I can't overemphasize how small it was. I lived off a dirt road, and the nearest convenience store was a half an hour away. Zines were the best way to communicate with the world. I would go pick up the mail and there'd be tons of them—I'd be trading with people and people would send me stamps and money and cassettes and records, etcetera. That also really was the way I started writing with my own voice, with a bit more confidence than I had when I was struggling to write a paper for school, or whatever. It was how I learned to write like myself. There's this zine called *Jersey Beat*, which still exists. A guy named Jim Testa runs it. Through reading my zine he started asking me to do record re-views for him, and that was my first attempt at writing, outside of some-thing for myself. It was interesting to be edited for the first time. I found it really helpful, and have appreciated working with editors ever since.

Jack Rabid The magazine [*The Big Takeover*] began in 1980 and reflect-ed the nature of the punk rock scene that we joined in New York by coming in from the suburbs for our last few high school years before we graduated and moved into the city that summer of 1980. Every per-son we'd met there in the late '70s by coming to shows pretty much every free day or night we had was a filmmaker or a poet or a sculptor or a writer or just in the rock scene itself, managing a band, playing in a band, taking pictures of a band. It was such a creative scene. It was just breathtaking to a suburban kid—that here was this thing twenty miles away as the crow flies, and these people were just doing crazy, wild things! I was going through the tenth, eleventh, and twelfth grade dealing with really closeted, uninteresting people worried about what their peer approval would be like. And I stopped caring. It was just very liberating. I was seeing all these people doing creative things and getting involved, and following these passions to the nth degree, and I said, "Wow, I want to do that!" I was a drummer, so the natural thing would be to start a band, which I did with my best friend and two other late teens we knew in New York. Around the exact same time as we started that band, Even Worse, my same best friend, the guitarist Dave Stein, and I got the idea to do a fanzine. We wanted to base it on the Bad Brains and The Stimulators and The Mad and some of the other bands playing around town because those bands were not being covered in the *New York Rocker* and the *East Village Eye* and *Trouser Press* and the other underground press we were reading at the time. So we just decided to start our own to write about them and the other punk rock bands we liked coming to town. The first issue was one one-sided typed page, and it really sucked. We just gave it away for free. That's basically how I started. It was just an accident. There was no thought or plan, and no idea we'd ever do another one.

Larry Fitzmaurice One of the first times I remember engaging with music writing was when I would go with my mom to the salon at or nine or ten years old: they'd copies of *Rolling Stone* and *SPIN* lying around. I also worked at my local library when I was younger, and they would let me take the back issues of magazines that were older than twelve months. Obviously you tell your parents when you're a teenager, "I want to be a music writer when I grow up," they're not too thrilled. But I kept at it anyway. I went to NYU and the Gallatin School of Individualized Study because it was basically the only way I was going to study writing and critical thinking while also taking a few business classes to appease my parents. And so while I was in college I didn't have anywhere to write, so what I would do is that I would listen to records, and practicing essentially, I fill up a notebook with reviews. I was just kind of working through it.

Steven Hyden It started when I was fourteen. I wrote for my junior high paper and I reviewed R.E.M.'s *Automatic for the People* and *Dirt* by Alice in
Chains. Those were the first record reviews I ever wrote. And then the
year after, when I was fifteen, I started writing for my local paper. They
had a teen page called the "Get With It" section, and I wrote reviews for
that. My first review for them was *Zooropa* by U2. I did that for three
years, basically throughout high school, getting paid like ten or fifteen
bucks or something a piece. It was very old-timey. I didn't have a computer at that time, so I would write longhand in a notebook paper and
I'd have my mom drive me downtown where the newspaper was and I
would slip my review into the mail slot. I would fold up the notebook
paper and slide it in, and then someone there would have to input it
into the computer. It was funny because there would be misprints in
my reviews because they couldn't read my handwriting.

Jenn Pelly Growing up on Long Island, a lot of my (male) friends were
musicians, and they were forming bands and booking shows and putting out records. They were doing what they wanted, and they weren't
waiting. We didn't know the term "DIY," but the impulse was there.
I knew I wanted to be a writer—it felt like the most immediate form
of expression—so I just did it, and I think my musician friends really
activated that feeling in me. I joined the school newspaper and took
it really seriously. I vividly recall saying goodbye to my skater friends
after school one day and timidly going to my first newspaper meeting
alone.

Liz Pelly Jenn and I both decided we wanted to be journalists when we
were teenagers, growing up in suburbia. We had each other as a support system, and we pushed each other along. We were also lucky to
be attending a public high school with a newspaper club adviser who
gave us a lot of agency. There was one year where we took a field trip to
visit the local alt-weekly newspaper. They had a page where they would
publish writing by local high school students, and the editors would sit
with you and work through drafts. That was formative.

Laura Snapes I knew by age twelve or thirteen that I wanted to write about music and talk to pop stars. I thought the job was called "interviewer" at the time. I had continued to read pop magazines into adolescence, and got into *NME* when I was about fourteen. I never had any doubt that this was what I wanted to do. I started contributing articles to our local newspaper, and when I learned what zines were, I made a few of my own. There was a BBC work placement that was really important, and one at *NME*. I wrote for the latter while I was at university, and eventually quit to take a job there. My progression into the industry was perhaps unusually linear, especially given that I come from one of the most rural parts of the country and had absolutely zero connections to journalism, let alone music journalism. I think I was lucky to catch the last wave of there being entry-level jobs, and to have come up just when Twitter was becoming a thing, so—even though my writing was atrocious—I was able to catch the attention of some editors. I was also lucky to join *NME* at a time when the junior staffers weren't just expected to pump out news stories all day, and you were surrounded by experienced peers who could teach you about magazine craft and publishing.

Ann Powers By the time I hit the age when you start to get into music, it was just the dawn of punk rock and new wave music. And I got really into that in my local scene. This is pregrunge in Seattle. I went to a big Catholic high school and I got involved in our newspaper and I wanted a way to be in the local scene and hang around but I didn't think I really had what it took to be a musician. I kind of dabbled a little bit in singing in bands and stuff, but that wasn't really my path. I loved to write. And being a writer was a great way to give me a purpose, to be a part of the rock 'n' roll scene, especially for a young woman. At that time you're always fighting the assumption that you are a groupie or that you are just a superfan and you're just hanging around because you want to be with the guys. You don't have a function in the scene—which by the way is a total obfuscation of the truth because of the fact women have always basically run these scenes informally, providing support for the guys and places for them to stay and help them with their work. But I wanted to have a reason to be around, and writing and interviewing artists really gave me a reason to be there. And so there was a local music magazine called the *Rocket* that was published once a month and it was this great alternative newspaper in the classic tradition of alternative newspapers like the *Oracle* out of San Francisco and it heavily emphasized art. Somehow one of the managers of one of the local new wave bands I'd interviewed had a friend who worked at this magazine. And he was like, "There's this teenage girl and she's really good at writing about music. You should hire her." So I went up there to their office and was assigned a feature. Soon enough I was writing reviews and other features and interviewing people like Joan Jett and Jane Wiedlin from The Go-Go's. It was a great way to start out running and learn right on the ground in a local publication.

Jim DeRogatis The first things I ever wrote were a couple of record reviews in my high school newspaper. But I started obsessively reading the alternative weeklies in and around New York—the really shitty one in New Jersey—the *Aquarian Weekly*, and the best alternative weekly ever, the *Village Voice*. When I was barely in high school I very much admired Robert Christgau and Lester Bangs, the star of Christgau's music section. That was something else entirely. This passion and this genius. And then I just ferreted out everything I could possibly find that Lester had written. I was a senior in high school, and all the smart kids, all my friends, all took "Masterpieces of Western literature," and the football team and the wrestlers and the burnouts took journalism because it was short sentences and simple words. And I took both. And I was driving my journalism teacher crazy with all these highfalutin questions about what is the new journalism? Tom Wolfe, right? Literary journalism. What is the role of investigative reporting in the wake of Woodward and Bernstein and Silkwood? What is the difference between criticism and journalism? And he said, "Look man you are a pain in my ass. You've already got an A for this class. Just stop coming to class. Go interview a hero in your chosen field. Write it up. All right?

Do me a favor." So I picked Lester Bangs. In his lifetime he published only two books, one that was a quickie fan book of Blondie that had lots of pretty pictures and Lester filled in the text, and the other that he did with Paul Nelson about Rod Stewart. But I'd found the Blondie book and I wrote the publisher asking can I please get an interview with Mr. Bangs? I was an idiot. I wasn't a very good reporter yet. He was listed in the New York phone book. I didn't think about that. And it's getting to be April and school ends at the end of May. And the journalism teacher probably forgot about me and I could have gotten away with not sending anything in but I was worried about this. And so I called Christgau at the *Village Voice* and said, "Can I interview you?" and I went over and I spent the day trailing Christgau through the Village as he picked up his mail and took it home and opened it up—all the promo records. And he was very kind for the self-professed Dean of American Rock Critics to grant a couple of hours to a fat, clueless, nerdy, acne-plagued kid from Jersey City, you know? But he was very stiff and formal. That dean title he gave himself. He was a professor. I had bought Christgau's *Consumer Guide* book and I gave it to him to sign and he signed it in a very tight, small scrawl, "Good luck in your chosen profession—Robert Christgau." I literally came home from Manhattan that day and my mom was all flustered and she said, "Honey. Honey. While you were gone I got this weird telephone call from some guy. Says his name is Lester. He doesn't have a phone that works and his doorbell's broken but if you go to sixth Avenue and 14th Street and stand in front of Gum Joy Chinese restaurant and shout his name up at the fifth floor window he'll throw down the keys and you can interview him and you can spend the day with him next week." So I spent a day with Lester, and he was incredibly kind and generous. He kept asking me what I was reading and who I love listening to and what I thought, and I'm like, "What are you asking me? You're Lester Bangs! I'm fat and clueless from Jersey City." And you know, that day changed my life. Those hours he spent with me changed my life. It's why I'm here today. And when I gave him that copy of Blondie to sign, he opened it up and he signed it, "Now it's your turn. Best, Lester." And the contrast between "Good luck in your profession" and "Now it's your turn," that was everything. And I was literally sitting in my bedroom in the basement of my house transcribing that interview and listening to WNEW—which was as good as rock radio got—and they say Lester Bangs is dead. He died on April thirtieth, and I talked to him on April fourteenth. I had been listening the radio when I heard that John Bonham was dead and that John Lennon was dead. And I thought, "Wow. They're talking about a rock critic who died." Certainly he was very important to me, and I think he was that important to a lot of people.

Ben Ratliff By the time I was done with high school I was aware that there was a healthy and evolved and nonarchaic tradition of writing about popular music. I wrote a little bit for my high school newspaper and a little bit for my college newspaper, but I didn't really think about it seriously until I took a college course at Columbia at the very end of my time there as an undergraduate. It was with Gary Giddins, the jazz critic at the *Village Voice*, a writer I admired. Because I spent so much time at the university radio station, I had learned a lot about jazz and other kinds of music. So I was ready to encounter a person like this and learn from him. It was a workshop class on writing about the arts. What is arts criticism? How do you do it? I got a lot from Gary—feedback and practical encouragement—and it made me pretty certain that I wanted to do that in some way. But of course I didn't quite know how. Some people in this world are real go get 'em, early-starter types. I was not that way. I did not have great connections, or at least that was the story I told myself. I did not yet understand that reaching out to the people who can help you could look like something other than arrogance or grandiosity. I worked in book publishing for six years after college, writing on the side. On evenings and weekends I wrote a lot for jazz magazines like *Coda* and *Downbeat*. I wrote a lot for a magazine called *Option*, and finally for the *Village Voice*. After a while it became evident that I could start writing as a freelancer for the *New York Times*. That was 1996. I was ready to sort of give that my all.

Puja Patel I basically applied for this internship at the *Fader* when I was eighteen. What I came to realize was that the position was half college rep marketing shill and half quick turnaround writing for their blog/newsletter at the time. This was 2004, and they thankfully did not realize how old I was. I think you had to be twenty-one to even have the gig because of all the different brands that they worked with. I did that for a couple of years. It was an amazing time at the *Fader*—it felt really exciting to have this music publication that was as much a culture publication as it was music, and as much about... the world that surrounds an artist instead of just the artist itself.

Marc Hogan It's easy to draw a line looking back. I was always interested in music, but I was never somebody who thought, "Oh here's my number one thing." I took piano lessons but I wasn't like an especially devoted student of it or anything. But I was a writer. It was always something I knew I loved. In high school when I moved to Arizona I remember my yearbook class—the school started a month ahead of my school in Tennessee, and I got there a little late and was kind of thrown into it—but I remember one of the first days I was assigned to write a story. I can't remember if it was my idea or the editor's, but the first story I wrote for them was about bands on campus and it kind of went from there. Then when I was in college whenever I had an option of writing about whatever I wanted it seemed like it would always go back to music. I interviewed the college radio station DJs. When I had to review something for my freshman year journalism class I remember I wrote a review of Beck's *Midnite Vultures*, and the teacher wrote nice words on it. So I was like, "Hey, I should keep doing this."

Ilana Kaplan I attribute my start in music journalism to one instance that legitimately started my career. One day I went to Barnes & Noble and just started scanning the memoirs in the music section and I saw Rob Sheffield's *Love Is a Mix Tape*, and I fell in love with that book. I fell in love with the way he wrote. And I just was like, "This is what I want to do with my life." This was when I was in late high school. I got my first internship when I was nineteen at *SPIN*. I wrote this like ridiculous cover letter where I talked about how much I loved Rob Sheffield's writing and *Love Is a Mix Tape*, and he at the time was a contributing writer at *SPIN*. What was funny was that it was for a fashion marketing internship. It wasn't even for writing. But I interned there for like eight months. It was a great first experience. After my internship, I ran into one of the people who was employed there at *SPIN*'s Vampire Weekend release party. We were talking and he was like, "Oh my friend is looking for interns at *Nylon*" and I was like "Oh my god, *Nylon* is my favorite publication." And I ended up getting an editorial internship there. That's where I got my first byline. And then after that I went to *Interview*, and that's when I really started regularly freelancing. And that's what really started things for me. I feel like a lot of what spiraled from having those beginning assignments has been a lot of me cold e-mailing people with ideas, friends telling me I should talk to a certain editors, and having no shame.

Jack Rabid We [Dave Stein and I] went off to college. For three months there wasn't an issue two. We weren't even thinking like that. I kept giving away the one we'd done because it was only that one page. And people would say, "Well when is issue two?" And I'd say, "Huh? Oh, you want another one?" I was a little surprised. So I created a second issue, this time by myself, as my friend Dave had gone off to Boston University and wasn't around to do it with me anymore. And this time it was two pages folded over, to make four. And I made four more issues like that over the next six months. And people started to really like it and started to ask for it, which was really nice! I'd just fallen into this thing that was really pleasant, and the bands I was writing about appreciated it, too. The same great obsession I have with talking about my favorite music was quite easy to do on a few pages talking about the gigs coming and the ones that I'd seen, and the albums that were coming out. And what a scene to chronicle! That's the thing. I was just reflecting a genuine excitement everyone in that scene felt. It was plain electrifying.

Christian Hoard It started in college. I went to the University of Michigan in the late '90s and was always really interested in writing. I was an English major, and at the same time I was sort of having like my musical awakening. I was sort of a late bloomer when it came to good music. There was no Spotify in the '90s, and I didn't have a cool older brother or influence, and so I didn't get exposed to a lot of punk records or the great hip-hop records until I got to college. I wanted to be a fiction writer, but I wasn't that good at making up stories. And around that time I just became obsessed with music, and I started reading a lot of critics that I still read and have even gotten to work with, people like Rob Christgau and Greil Marcus, Rob Sheffield, a lot of those classic names. And so my interest in their work kind of dovetailed with my obsession over music, which was this great undiscovered world for me. I wanted to write, but I didn't know exactly what I wanted to write other than fiction. I had a friend who wrote for the school paper, the *Michigan Daily*, and I thought I might as well give it a shot. So I started in the fall of '99 writing record and live reviews.

Emily J. Lordi I was very much into performance growing up. I was a performer. As a kid I was always making up little dances and songs. And I studied dance and voice formally through high school and college, so I kind of thought that I was going to try to be a dancer. I understood writing to be a strength of mine, but I was much more on the performance track. So I continued to study dance and sing in different groups and things, but honestly, by the time I was through college, I was physically tired. I also had a pretty clear, realistic sense of my own future prospects as a dancer, which were okay but not great. So I applied to graduate school for English. I applied to Columbia University, because it was in New York and I still wanted to dance. But I also wanted to pursue something else. And so I got there and that first semester of my master's program I took a course about Ralph Ellison's *Invisible Man*. This was a life-changing experience for me. The course was taught by my eventual mentor, professor Robert O'Meally. He was doing this interdisciplinary work that showed me it was possible to bring together my native interest in performance and my passion for reading and writing through the discipline of black studies. He was looking at jazz especially: he was one of the originators of the field of jazz studies. And he was saying we need to understand jazz if we're going to understand American culture, but by "jazz" he meant not only jazz music but also jazz writing: writing about jazz, fiction inspired by jazz, poetry that took off from jazz . . . Ralph Ellison is like the patron saint of this idea. He not only wrote *Invisible Man* but he also wrote a lot about music—about swing especially, and the blues, and these different forms of early twentieth-century African American music. So it was really in that class and through the mentorship of Bob O'Meally that I understood that you could pursue a graduate degree that would allow you to work across arts forms; that would allow me to learn much more about African American history and culture than I had ever been able to learn before; that would allow me to pursue my interest in literary criticism and literary history; and that would allow me also to think about dance and music and different forms of performance—how they all fit together.

Lindsay Zoladz I studied English and actually film production in college. I went to American University in DC. It was there I was kind of trying to figure out what I wanted to do. I think for a while I thought I might be a professor or go to grad school and do the whole PhD thing. I sort of fell out of that idea. I think I wanted to write for a larger audience of people that could understand what I was saying and not have to speak in this really academic jargon. I think I more wanted to use the ideas that I was learning in my classes but phrase them in ways that didn't require a PhD to understand. That just felt more like what I was drawn to. So I graduated in 2009 and I was not sure what I wanted to do with my life. A friend of mine started a music blog. There were a couple people I knew who moved away and we all just wanted a project to keep in touch. So we started this music blog, just writing about songs that we liked. I was definitely the most reliable person. I would get really frustrated when my friends wouldn't meet the fake deadlines that we imposed, and I really took on the role of an editor of the site. I think that was my first indication that I really had a drive to do this.

Rob Sheffield I wrote for a music paper that we had in college, and that was really where I had the first experience of writing about music for an audience. The first time I got a gig-gig, the first time I got paid—twenty bucks—was a fanzine called the *Bob*, which was a big deal fanzine in the '80s. And I was very into fanzines. I was very influenced by fanzines. The '80s was such an amazing time for fanzines like *Conflict* and *Forced Exposure* and *Why Music Sucks*. Fanzines were really where the most interesting writing about music was being done. And the *Bob* asked if I would write something about a band I loved, a great local punk band called Bleached Black. And I wrote about them and was sent a check for twenty bucks. I was like, "I cannot believe that I actually got paid for this." It was the last time for a while, but I got paid for it.

Brittany Spanos I ended up coming to NYU for journalism and did a special, individualized major at the Gallatin School. I wanted to do a lot of music-history-focused work and a lot of various forms of nonfiction writing. And then I started interning at the *Village Voice*, which was what really ended up helping me on this path to becoming a professional music journalist. Being able to write in a space where I was able to contribute weekly to the "Calendar" section, then also to the music blog, was really important for me. I was able to work with Brian McManus. I was working with him pretty much every day and writing for him. I ended up freelancing for *Rookie* and *SPIN* because Jessica Hopper was doing a column at the *Village Voice* at the time that I was there. I just ended up just going from there, making more connections and freelancing a lot, and ended up working at *Rolling Stone*.

Gabriela Tully Claymore I almost went to arts school to study visual arts, but I decided that I didn't really want to close myself off in that way, which is why I ended up going to Gallatin at NYU, because I thought,

"I can do art and I can explore other things that I'm excited about." I started taking a journalism class and decided through some metropolitan studies courses I was also taking that I was more interested in the culture that comes out of a city environment and less in the actual physical development of a city. Growing up in San Francisco, I was obsessed with '70s New York after reading Legs McNeil and Gillian McCain's *Please Kill Me: The Uncensored Oral History of Punk*. I loved the music that game out of that period, and listening to it made me want to learn more about the historical backdrop. In New York in the '70s there was an economic downturn, the city was practically bankrupt, there was all of this political corruption, and heroin was really taking over downtown. The city became an incubator for a new era of art and music that reflected the tumult of the time. That history really interested me and I was drawn to studying the sociocultural landscape that makes an artistic movement possible. In college I decided I wanted to focus on nonfiction writing. My sophomore year I saw Amanda Petrusich and Ben Ratliff do a talk at Gallatin. I went kind of on a whim, and I remember Ben Ratliff read something that he had written for the *Times* about a jazz artist, and he described this song as sounding like "blue glass," and I was like, "Damn, that's really cool." I loved that he used visual language to describe a sound, and I thought, "I'm going to try to do this."

Eric T. Miller I went to Temple University here in Philly. To make a long story short-ish, I had a number of journalism-related internships. I was majoring in journalism, but I had never given a thought to music journalism. I knew it existed from reading magazines, but it wasn't something that I had ever considered doing. I had an internship working for a reporter who covered the federal courthouse in Philly. Basically, if there were multiple cases going on at the same time, he would go to one, I would go to another. I would take notes, and he would write it up. So I did that, and I was really liking it. Then I got fired. The reporter was really nice about it. He said, "You're always talking about music. Have you ever thought about writing about music?"

Carl Wilson At university I started working at the school newspaper at McGill. They were looking for people to do arts writing, and I was enthusiastic about having a place to write. I ended up spending a lot of my college years working on the paper and was at various points the arts editor and the features editor. So when I finished school, I was like, "Oh, I guess this is the only kind of job I'm now qualified to look for."

Chuck Klosterman I went to college and assumed that I was going to major in English and end up becoming an English teacher and a football coach or a basketball coach at the high school level. That's what I assumed would happen. Maybe I'd go to law school, which is what people had always told me to do, for as long as I can remember. But then I found out that the student newspaper actually paid people to write for it. I had always assumed it was something you did for free, like in high school. But here in college you got paid for it. So I'm covering the football team and I'm covering the wrestling team, and then Warrant's *Cherry Pie* came out and I asked the editor of the paper, "Can I review *Cherry Pie* by Warrant?" And he laughed and was like, "I guess." So I wrote a Warrant review as a freshman, and that was the first time I'd ever written about music for real, you know? I ended up majoring in journalism, initially thinking I would be a sportswriter. That felt real natural. Then I went through a period where my ambition was to become a political writer for the Minneapolis *Star Tribune* or the *St. Paul Pioneer Press*. I was in North Dakota, so I thought getting to a daily newspaper in Minneapolis and writing about politics would be an amazing life. But then a whole bunch of weird things happened and I ended up becoming a full-time arts and entertainment writer. And that's just how it began.

Josh Jackson I was a journalism major at the University of Georgia, and at Georgia you could specialize in certain areas. I was actually a magazine major. So I took magazine writing classes and magazine publishing classes and always had in my head that that's what I wanted to do. But then I went and worked for a nonprofit for a while as their director of communications. So I was managing the publications at the nonprofit and doing a lot of the writing and research for them. Then I quit to start *Paste.* I hadn't worked in the music industry, hadn't really worked in the magazine industry beyond what I had done in college. We were pretty green when we started doing this.

Eric T. Miller So still in college, I started freelancing. There was a local magazine I started writing for. I started going in once a week to hang out around the office and do stuff. And then that became twice a week, and then whenever I had free time from school. It was called *Philly Rock Guide.* It was a glossy free monthly that covered Philly music but also started covering more national music. It was a really small operation. And then a handful of us who worked there decided we wanted to do a national magazine.

Mark Redfern *Under the Radar* started almost by mistake, really. We certainly didn't plan on starting a music magazine that would be our sole livelihood and that would be going for eighteen years now. When we originally started, it was kind of just for fun. I went to film school at USC, and Wendy went to photography school in Florida, and we were both graduated and trying to make our way in Los Angeles in the workforce—me in the movie industry, and Wendy in the photography world. And we kind of were kind of a little directionless, I guess.

Josh Jackson We [*Paste*] started out actually as a website back in 1998. We were selling CDs for some friends of ours who were in bands, and it sort of grew from there with people we didn't know but liked and were trying make a living by being in a band. We started the business that way. We were naturally writing about these bands, and I had always wanted to do a magazine. I worked on some little start-up magazines in college and thought it would be a really cool thing to have our own magazine. So we kind of looked at the landscape and saw there were some great magazines out there covering different niches of music—*MAGNET* and *CMJ* doing indie rock, *No Depression* doing alt-country, *Performing Songwriter* doing singer/songwriter stuff. But when you got to the big general magazines like *Rolling Stone* and *Blender*, it just didn't feel like it was aimed at anybody we knew, people who liked the kind of music we liked. We had a broad taste in music and figured that most other people did as well. So we wanted to do something that was broad that covered lots of different kinds of music but was geared in a way toward music lovers. We figured there was a market out there for it. We didn't do any research or anything. We didn't have money to do that kind of stuff, but we had a passion for what we loved and decided to try and launch our own magazine, not really knowing what we needed to know. Right out of the gate it found an audience. We managed to get it into Borders on the first issue, and so all of a sudden it felt like we had this real magazine. Once we could get advertisers coming in, and people finding it at the bookstore and subscribing, it just sort of it grew from there. People were pretty passionate about those early issues and the CD that came with it so they could listen to the music we were writing about. We were writing about a lot of unknown bands, but our readers could discover them pretty easily and quickly just by listening to the sampler that came with the issue. And it was good music, so people responded.

Mark Redfern I was writing for my friend who had a small zine called *Mix Tape Journal* that was printed on really poor-quality paper and was distributed at local shows or whatever. It was all black-and-white newsprint. And I wouldn't say I had a falling out with the person that was putting it together, but we had different visions for it. So I kind of parted ways, and I had some unpublished interviews that were good. At the time I was already setting up all the interviews and all the reviews on my own, and so I had these interviews that had no home. And Wendy wanted to photograph bands, but you can't just say, "Hey I want to photograph you" and do a photo shoot. You have to have some reason for it. So I thought, "Well I have some friends from film school who are really into music and aren't really doing much in the film industry and are willing to write about stuff," and so we just kind of threw together our first issue in 2001.

Josh Jackson Part of why I wanted to started a music magazine and one of the things I had in mind was that by the time we started I was thirty, and it seemed like I was getting all my music knowledge from things like NPR and the *New Yorker* when they would do a great profile of a musician, and I felt like that kind of stuff, those kinds of stories they were telling, I wanted that all in an entertainment magazine. I didn't want to have to rely on a general magazine for music knowledge. And when I say "music knowledge" I mean really in-depth stories. I was still listening to college radio and finding music various ways, but it wasn't like now where you could go online and look at a million blogs and discover music. There just wasn't anything like that.

Eric T. Miller The first issue of *MAGNET* came out in July '93. I was twenty-one. The three other guys involved at the time were all turning thirty. I was still in school. It was sort of like *Animal House* when it started. You hear about the old *Creem* magazine stories and stuff. There was a lot of that kind of stuff going on. It was very relaxed to say the absolute least. As I've gotten older it's gotten to be, not more serious, but at the same time definitely more serious. I mean, when you have no clue what you're doing, there's really not a whole lot of pressure. Then when you start to realize what you need to do, then the pressure starts. It was chaos at first. Then it became more controlled chaos. Then you get better as you go along. I never thought it would go on this long, that's for sure. I never thought there would be a second issue. The only thing harder than doing the first issue of a magazine is the second issue. We were able to twist some arms to buy ads. We were in dire straits, but we didn't let on we were in dire straits. It was like, "Cool, we got this issue. Oh shit. We have another one next month." So we were trying to sell ads to people for the second issue of a magazine where the first issue didn't fully exist yet, which is even harder. It was like, "Well, where's the first issue?" "Oh, it's not done yet."

Jack Rabid If you read interviews with The Beatles, they kept saying they didn't want to make the same song twice. They were constantly trying to do something they hadn't done. And for me it was like, "Well this [*The Big Takeover*] is a nice, little four-page typed fanzine I have here, but I have so much more than that to say." So I just kept making it a little longer, a little bigger, adding things to talk about, more reviews, more concert reviews, more news. And pretty soon people who were rooming with me would say, "Well I could write some reviews." And the next thing you know it's ten pages long and then it's twenty and then it's thirty, and the bigger it gets, the more people seem to like it. And people were clamoring for more and suggesting ways to do it better or asking to help out. I was still doing Xerox copies. Eventually around 1987 we switched to inky offset print instead. After three issues like that, I think in 1989 we got ourselves a glossy cover so that the ink wouldn't get on people's fingers. I kept focusing on the content more than the presentation, but the presentation was bound to get better, too, by doing it. Every time you do something, you get better at it. And in 1991, a friend of mine volunteered to do it on a computer instead of my tape-and-scissors act of the first decade, and the look got immeasurably better immediately, starting with using color inks. And we've really been a magazine instead of a fanzine ever since, switching from newsprint on the inside to glossy pages. And 1994 was our first full-color cover, with Lush and Bob Mould. Hard to believe we've had this format since then, for twenty-five more years.

Eric T. Miller I was so young. It just seemed like something fun to do. It's like you jam with a bunch of friends and then suddenly you have a record out. Then people seem to like it, and they want another record. And then suddenly it's like a career. There was never that much thought put into it. And then to have the business aspects of it kick in, too, like health insurance and those sort of things that none of us were equipped to really deal with. Having to learn that was a big thing for me, learning how to run a business simultaneously. I sort of got into journalism to avoid being in "business." That took up a lot of time, too. A lot of nights were spent learning how to run a business, and that was difficult.

Mark Redfern We probably worked on it [*Under the Radar*] for six months or so, and the first issue came out in December of 2001. It was all black-and-white. I think I wrote all but one of the articles in it. Some other people did reviews, but all the interviews but one were done by me. Granddaddy was on the cover.

Wendy Lynch Redfern I thought, "Here is somebody who wants to do something just as badly as I do." I wanted to photograph bands, and he wanted to write about bands, and we wanted to go to shows, and we wanted to get free music. And he wanted to do it just as much as I did. And so we were like—not having much else to do—"Why don't we just try to do it?" I happened to have an old, old version of Quark, and went and bought a *QuarkXPress for Dummies* book and just was like, "I'm going to try and lay out a page." And we did it. Of course, if you look at it you can see how bad it is. But that's great because you start. That's the point. We had fun going and photographing things for our first cover that we thought made sense. We had fun doing that stuff. We were young and in love and being creative together, and it was really cool.

Mark Redfern We met and started dating in December 2000. And it was probably around six months in that we started working on the magazine, and then another six months by the time the first issue came out. The first one was distributed for free at shows. We really had no idea what we were doing. If you look back at the first issue, I just cringe at all the mistakes. You look at it and it's all over the place. Each review has different formatting. It's just a mess. We didn't even think about the concept of really proofreading. I remember we got some initial proofs from the very small printers that printed it and we found all these mistakes and we wanted to go make all these changes and they were like, "It's too late now."

Wendy Lynch Redfern They sent us the final proof to just go over one last time, and we showed up the next day with hundreds of changes and they're like, "What? No. No. No. That's not happening." It was a big learning curve. But we had other jobs, so it was like we were doing it on the side for a while. Then that changed. Mark and I both more or less got laid off around the same time.

Mark Redfern About two years into it, around issue five, we both got laid off. I was working at a record store at that point, kind of falling out of the film industry, and Wendy was managing a photo studio. We had to decide whether we wanted make it our full-time job and give it a shot or did we wanna try and go get other regular jobs. And we decided to make it our full-time thing and haven't looked back since then. We had zero expectations. Our expectations were to get free albums and not have to go buy albums anymore. We were fresh out of college; we didn't have a lot of money. But we'd love to go to shows and to get free concert tickets, to get on a list for shows and get free CDs, that was enough at the beginning. We're to the point now where I honestly don't know the last time that I've actually paid for a CD or actually paid for a concert. But those were our initial expectations. Then we started to get more ambitious. The second issue we actually got distribution in Tower Records. They used to have what they called a "Zine Stand," which featured smaller magazines, and somehow we convinced them to carry *Under the Radar.* The third issue was the first one that had any kind of national distribution. Then our expectations started to really grow. The first two issues were all black-and-white. The third issue started to have some color pages. I think it wasn't until issue ten or eleven that we went all-color. Eventually our expectations were to be taken seriously as a music magazine, as a source to be distributed nationwide and to land the biggest interviews that we could. But at first we just wanted free concert tickets and free CDs.

Mark Richardson I kind of started late. I work with a lot of people that are in their twenties now, and it seems more common now—or maybe it was then and I just didn't notice—a lot of people come right out of college to try to start their career immediately. But I didn't do that. I graduated from college and through most of my twenties I just did a lot of different things. In the later part of the '90s I moved to San Francisco. By this time the web was in full swing, and I was pretty early in terms of the fact that I was doing HTML on websites. A friend and I had a little web design company, which was also very early. There weren't too many web design companies in 1995.

Joe Levy I came out of college without a particular direction or sense of what I might do with this interest. It was not clear to me that I could be a music critic, but I had a friend I'd grown up with who interned at the *Village Voice* and he became a roommate of mine in Brooklyn and encouraged me to apply for an internship there with the music editor. Which I did, and I was turned down. At that particular point I was earning money moving furniture in Brooklyn. A few months went by, and my roommate asked the *Voice* music editor if he'd found an intern. He hadn't, and he gave me a tryout. That's where things started for me. I'd been an English major in college. There was no undergraduate journalism or media program at my school, but I hadn't even worked for the college paper. I had no real journalism experience, so working at the *Voice* was a crash course in newspaper basics. I knew nothing, including knowing nothing about writing. The music editor, Doug Simmons, gave me an assignment and spent hours editing my fourth or fifth draft until it was in publishable form. The second time it took maybe an hour less and was maybe a third or fourth draft. I learned the basics of both editing and writing from experiences like that. And after a few of them I took my clips and applied for a job as a columnist for a trade magazine called *Cash Box*. It had been at important music-industry trade magazine in the '40s and '50s, but by the time I got there it was holding on by a thread. I worked there for about a year and a half as a reporter and columnist, and I was lucky enough to keep a freelance relationship with the *Voice*. Doug Simmons sent me to cover the New Music Seminar—a massive convention that no longer exists—because I was working at a trade magazine, and I had some knowledge of the music industry.

And my career path began to be blessed by what was not a plan at the start: a mix of different kinds of experience. In this case, it was a mix of business reporting and music criticism, but later on it was a mix of newspaper and glossy magazine experience, and then after that it was a mix of magazines and broadcast. But that mix of music business reporting and rock criticism experience meant I got do this feature piece for the *Voice* on the New Music Seminar. Someone at *SPIN* magazine read it and asked me to lunch. It was my greatest hope that they were going to give me a chance to write something there, and I wrote a long pitch memo. They ended up hiring me as an editor. And so I went from learning on the job how to be a writer and a reporter to learning on the job how to be an editor. And I basically stayed an editor for most of my career.

Rob Sheffield After college I went to Boston to live with my grandfather and I worked as a librarian at the Harvard science library, the Cabot Science Library. I shelved books all day and listened to my Walkman and wrote about music, wrote about poetry, and applied to grad school. I went to grad school in the English department at the University of Virginia. I had decided to make studying literature my life's work and my life's passion, but I always planned to keep writing about music on the side because it was something I was equally passionate about. It was while I was in Boston in that year between college and grad school that I started freelancing in earnest.

Amanda Petrusich Like most writers, I've done all kinds of weird things when writing alone wasn't paying the rent. Part-time jobs and odd jobs. I was fortunate to have a decent amount of writing work early on—not always glamorous writing work, but writing work. I've written for airline magazines; I wrote SparkNotes for a while. I had a great but exhausting job doing the pop music concert previews for the *New York Times* for a few years. That was a steady income, plus it taught me the importance of writing one really good, really sharp descriptive line. I think all the blurbs had to be under eighty words or something. I also had to spend hours looking up dates and ticket prices and where shows were happening.

Marc Hogan My first job in New York—because I needed a job and was a journalist—was reporting about the mutual fund industry, which I was able to figure out what was interesting about that.

Tom Breihan When I finished school I was working just kind of shit jobs. I worked four years for the Maryland State Bar Association pretty much stuffing envelopes. Luckily I was still writing for the *Washington City Paper.* I was doing reviews, and I would do features on local bands, occasionally touring bands when they were coming through, and I did all my work at my desk at the bar association office because I didn't have a computer at home. I had no internet or anything.

Craig Jenkins My first good paying writing gig came in a moment where I was good and set to quit. I had decided, mathematically speaking, that with the amount of attention and time I was putting into it, writing about music was not lucrative. It wasn't making me any money, so I thought, "I'm going to write one more thing," and that was thing that people saw. The piece wound up catching the eye of some people at *Complex* and *Pitchfork.* And I was on a roll from there. In my twenties my job was retail, retail, and then retail again. I worked at a department store for three years when I got out of college. They fired me. I worked at a supermarket up the block from my house for about a year or so. Then I got a job at a Nintendo store in the city, and I worked at those two places at the same time for a while. Then I took a desk for five years, customer service for a company that sold mattresses. All of my stuff for *Pitchfork* was being written on construction paper in the office when it got quiet. I became a very efficient customer service worker so I could spend the afternoon of my workday writing. I would come home with cut-up paper with bits of a review on them. I couldn't bank on my bosses not checking the history of my computer, so I wrote everything by hand so as to not leave a trail. That's how that worked for a long time.

Larry Fitzmaurice Almost to a fault I'm a little bit of a workaholic. I actually remember when I was working at a restaurant I would log into the Wi-Fi on fifteen-minute dinner breaks to listen to a Caribou song I was asked to review at *Pitchfork*. That's kind of how I worked it in. I'd go to the bathroom during a shift and I'd send an e-mail and be like, "Can I review this record?" Every waking moment that I had that wasn't me working I would be pitching or writing. It was unhealthy at the time. I don't think I ever want to go back to living like that, though it was necessary.

Jayson Greene I didn't set out with the belief that this would be my career. I thought it would be something that I did for fun while I figured out a steadier job. But I got a job right out of college working at a trade magazine. It was technically related to music, but it was pretty distant. And it was just a copyediting job. While I was there I started writing album reviews for free because I just wanted to. It was for a site that's gone now—years and years ago—called Stylus. Then I had a series of editing jobs over the years that didn't have anything to do with music. I chanced into a job at eMusic, which at the time was a little bit more of a player as a digital music retailer, where they had an editorial staff that they treated like the way that the editorial staff at Bandcamp treats music now. The approach was "Let's sort through all this and make an interesting magazine." And that was kind of the first place where I had a job in music journalism. They encouraged you to freelance, so from there it just sort of snowballed slowly as I wrote for *Pitchfork* over the next several years. By 2012, I became a contributing editor for *Pitchfork* on the side while working full-time at eMusic editing and assigning stories. I think that by then I kind of realized that I was all the way in.

Jes Skolnik I took a very roundabout way here. Although I have freelanced for a long time, working at Bandcamp is my first staff job, and I didn't get in until I was thirty-seven. I didn't really conceive of music journalism as a career path ever. I ended up quitting grad school. I was in a combined master's and PhD program, and I did only the master's portion of it because the program got defunded and I couldn't afford to go anymore. That was a major turn for me. It was the mid-2000s and I considered nursing school for a while because I had been doing my dissertation on labor and health policy. I had been spending a lot of time in free clinics. I was like, "Maybe I'll go to nursing school." I was sort of adrift in my midtwenties. The career path that I had thought, where I was going into academic research and academic writing, was not happening anymore. A long-term relationship also ended, and my best friend who was living out here in Chicago was like, "If you need a place for a new start or to feel revived again just come sleep on the floor of my office for a minute and if you like it out here you can stay. If not, no harm, no foul." And I loved it and ended up staying and got a job at a labor union doing contract administration and negotiation. I had helped organize my grad student union, and with a background in labor history I went into organizing, and that's where I was when I started freelancing again. I was pretty miserable at my actual job. I love the labor movement forever and I will always be an organizer and I will always stand up for that kind of stuff, but the place that I was at was a heavily bureaucratic union that was very mismanaged and did not do right by its workers and did not do right by the staff. There were a lot of sexual harassers and a couple of rapists that were kept on staff because HR was unresponsive. It was very frustrating and bad and finally I actually got laid off. So I was applying for tons of jobs, and while I was doing that I went to work at a record store, going back to my job from when I was fifteen. I was like, "Oh cool, I'm thirty-five and I'm doing the same job that I was when I was fifteen." But I was freelancing on the side. And then I got recruited out to do Bandcamp. It's very wild. I feel like this is my third act. It's weird because just from playing in bands and writing zines and doing criticism that way I had just built up this network of people—it wasn't conscious at all—who are just involved in the same world that I am. It was always the thing I did outside of work, and then it became work.

Rob Sheffield Christgau was writing at the *Voice*, and Greil Marcus was writing at the *Voice*. John Leland was writing for *SPIN*, and Greg Tate, he was writing everywhere, and there was all this amazing stuff and these writers who were taking new approaches to music. And music was changing so drastically in the '80s that it was a time where the writers were kind of pointing the way for new ways to talk about all this music that was suddenly in the air. It was a time where it was really immensely inspiring to read about music. I wanted to write for the *Voice*, and Doug Simmons was the editor of the music section at the time. He was great. I called him and he said, "Yeah, okay yeah. Fine. You can call me and pitch ideas if you like, but this is how it works. Nine out of ten times, you call, I'm busy because my phone's ringing all the time. So I'm going to answer the phone and say, 'Yeah I can't talk right now,' and just hang up on you. If that's going to bother you, don't call." So I said, "Okay." And he then said, "Now because you don't live in New York, nine times out of ten, I'm going to say 'no' to your idea before you even tell me what your idea is. If you're going to have a problem with that, just don't call." And I'm like, "Okay. I'm cool with that too." And he said, "Because we're a New York paper we usually run things the week the artist is coming to town, and things are very focused on the show in New York, and I'm almost going to say 'no' to everything you recommend. And then I'm going to hang up." Because he'd laid down the rules so clearly, I was fine with all of that. So frequently I would call. I learned not to call on Mondays because if I called on Mondays, Doug Simmons would answer the phone and say, "Yeah, it's Monday, my dick is on fire. I gotta go," and hang up. And I did not take it personally. It was cool. And true to his word, I would pitch him ideas and before the words were even out of my mouth he'd say, "Nah," and hang up. Finally I came up with an idea he liked. I wanted to write about a new album by The Frogs. The Frogs were on Homestead records and had their first really major album, *It's Only Right and Natural*. And I was really excited about The Frogs. So he was like, "Okay, you can try that." And so I wrote and I put my heart and soul in this review. I was really proud of it and I sent it, and Doug Simmons was like, "Yeah, I think I can use this." And he said, "Accepted," in this really formal way, which was really kind of funny because it was like a performance for my benefit because he knew I was this young rookie writer he knew would get a real thrill out of hearing the words, "Accepted." He said, "The band will come to town in two weeks so I'll run it then." And I was like, "Oh my god that's amazing." And so like many inexperienced, rookie writers before me and after me, I made the mistake of telling literally everybody I knew, "Hey my review is going to be coming out in the *Village Voice* next week." And the *Voice* came out that week. It came out on Wednesdays in New York, and in Boston we got it on Fridays. I saw my Frogs review was not in it. And I thought, "Well it must have been pushed back a week." So that's what I told all my friends to whom I had bragged too soon about this review coming out. "Yeah I think it just got pushed back a week." Well, the following week the *Village Voice* came out and it wasn't in it either. And then a couple weeks went by and it just did not run. And I slowly got the message in my head that I bet this review just got canned. And I thought, "Well, I could call Doug Simmons and ask, but you know what? I'm going to show off what a grown-up I can be. I'm going to take this opportunity to show off. I'll be cool and collected and let a couple months go by and then I'll call about something else and not even mention it and it'll be like it never happened. I'll be showing off my maturity and poise and sophistication." So I didn't call to bug about it or ask about it or anything like that. And then a couple months go by and at this point I've moved to Virginia for grad school, and one day I get a check in the mail, a check actually paying me for this review that didn't run. It wasn't even a kill fee. It was the full $250, which was two months' rent for me at the time. I was so blown away. So I called him to thank him. I didn't even sign a contract, so they didn't even really have to send me even a kill fee. But I called Doug to say "Thank you for this," and as soon as he heard my voice he's like, "Sorry about the review. At least I didn't fuck you over on the money part of it." He said, "It's good that you learn this way when you're young. The most important three words a young writer can learn: 'editors always lie.'" And he's right. Ever since then I've always assumed something's not coming out until it's actually in print in my hands.

Stephen Deusner When people ask me how I got into this as a profession, I always feel like I have the worst answer because it was totally accidental. It was nothing where I sat down and said, "I'm going to do this!" Having come from a small town very much off the grid as far as the music industry goes, it always felt like a closed circuit to me. It seemed impossible that I could write for a place like *Rolling Stone* or something like that. When I was living in Memphis, I started writing book reviews for the local newspaper and working at a publishing company that specialized in chamber of commerce materials. It wasn't great, but the guy in the cubicle next to me would always bring in these great CDs to listen to as he was working. And we got to talking and struck up a friendship. It just so happened that he eventually left the company to become the music editor at the local alt-weekly, so he was like, "Hey you do you want to write some reviews for me?" and I was like, "Okay, sure." And that was it. I feel like I've just been tripping upward every step of the way.

Andy Greene My senior project in high school I worked at the Rock and Roll Hall of Fame, which was just downtown. It was a month working for free for part of my senior year, but I made good connections there, and they hired me that summer for a job. And then during my college breaks I was always working there and I got really close with the staff. It was fun. I mean, I started in human resources. I was an office assistant when I was an intern, but it was nice to work with the curators and help do small things to help on the exhibits and whatnot. And Jim Henke then was a chief curator, and he was an editor at *Rolling Stone* for a very long time, from the '70s to the early '90s. He did a lot of great cover stories and he got me an internship at the magazine when college ended. At the same time I got offered an internship here [*Rolling Stone*], which was unpaid. I got offered a paid job at VH1 as a production assistant. It was it was a tough choice because at the time I didn't see myself as a writer. But I figured *Rolling Stone* was more up my alley than getting coffee on the set of dumb VH1 shows. So I came in here. I interned for about five or six months. But after even just six weeks they started to give me small assignments, and I sort of taught myself. I had no experience as a writer. I'd never written an article in my life, but I just sort of saw it at my graduate school. I watched the magazine process happen. I watched how they did interviews. I was right in the middle. I sat by Austin Scaggs and just sort of observed everything and then slowly started to do it myself.

Michael Azerrad I knew I wanted to work in music, somehow—if I didn't make it as a musician. So a couple of years out of college I started working at a place called Rockamerica, which sent music videos to nightclubs. Music videos were huge then, in the mideighties, and even though I had a lowly job, it gave me a priceless introduction to the music biz, and I got a good look at a lot of different facets of the industry. Sheerly for promotion, Rockamerica published a little magazine— glossy paper and everything—that went out to all sectors of the music business. They always needed writers, and the editor, a very sharp lady named Lyn Healy, figured that since Michael (a) had gone to college, and (b) played in bands, he could write about music. The thing was, I hated writing. *Hated* it. Always had. In college, I would rather have gotten a tooth pulled than write a paper. Many was the time that I was tempted to throw the typewriter out the window. But after much cajoling from Lyn, I was persuaded to try writing about music. And it came out pretty well! I was surprised at how much I actually enjoyed it. So I kept doing that, and one thing led to another; within a couple of years, I was writing for *Rolling Stone.*

Andy Greene I was a complete amateur, but I was learning from these professionals and seeing my pieces just get torn apart and watched how they get reconstructed. I would sit down with somebody and they would show me things I did wrong and I would just absorb all of it. I was working like twelve-hour days. I was just always in the process. I would transcribe stuff as an intern. I would watch everything. It was just osmosis after a while. And then I eventually developed a voice. It took time. I think after writing a lot of bad articles I started to write good ones. And they hired me April of 2015 as an editorial assistant. Now I'm a senior writer.

Mark Richardson I had always obviously read a lot of music press. I read *Rolling Stone* and *SPIN*, and I read books about music and I collected records and I bought a lot of music. And I was very into writing. I had written fiction and a lot of writing of different kinds, but I hadn't really written for money. But my friend and I, we got very into the Bay Area hip-hop scene. This was '96, '97, and it was a pretty exciting time there. DJ Shadow was a thing and we were very into the scratch DJ scene. It was kind of ground zero for it. If you look at scratch DJing or turntablism in late '90s in San Francisco, it was really at its peak, and we were there for that. We were going and seeing shows all the time and buying mixtapes and we thought, "Let's start our own online magazine." So we did that. We had an online webzine where we covered shows and covered releases. I interviewed some DJs. I don't know why. It was just like, "Let's do this." And it was a very, very small thing, but from there I kind of realized I enjoyed writing about music. And in 1997, somewhere along the line as I had been working different kinds of jobs, I saw *Pitchfork*. A lot of people don't know it's been around that long. This was before Google and it was very hard to find online. But I somehow found the site and they had a listing that said they were looking for writers. So I applied to write for them using some of the writing I'd done on my own website. And Ryan Schreiber hired me as a reviewer. I started reviewing records for them in 1998.

Nitsuh Abebe I'd always been nerdy about music and liked to talk about it, hanging around record stores. I worked at a record store for a while. I basically got into writing about it through message boards and online forums like that. There was one in particular that I think a lot of my age cohort of critics spent time on. It was actually a lot of really smart people just talking about music and typing long things back and forth, talking about whatever. I think that just sort of got me into the habit a little bit and introduced me to some people who were also involved in it. Ryan Schreiber, who started *Pitchfork*, was in Chicago. I know he looked at and occasionally posted to some of the same sort of internet areas that I was looking at, the same message boards. At some point we got in touch and asked if I would like to write some things. In addition to the indie rock that was *Pitchfork*'s main beat, I was really into a type of music that *Pitchfork* didn't have a lot of people covering or paying attention to—which around 2001 was trashy electro music from New York and pop. This was when *Pitchfork* was run out of Ryan's apartment. It was a corner of his living room basically. There were huge piles of CDs, and as a writer you could drop by and he'd tell you to take some home and listen to them. So I just started doing that occasionally. I don't think I was ever that heavy of a contributor. There were people who were reviewing four or five things a week. These were the people who were the mainstays of the site, whereas I would do one a month or every other month or something like that. I kept doing that for years, writing occasionally. I moved to New York and worked on lots of other things, had regular jobs, but I'd contribute reviews and features when I could, and had a blog on the side. Eventually I started a column. It was called "Why We Fight." It was this idea of, "What's the sort of weird thing that people are arguing and getting upset about in music this month and what does it tell us more deeply about how we think about music?" Somehow in the process of doing the column, just sticking my face into the sphere of writing about music, someone from *New York* magazine gave me a call and basically asked if I'd be interested in coming in and having some conversations about becoming their music critic. I was actually very unsure about it, but I at the same time I was like, "Why would you not just try? If it goes badly, it goes badly, but you've got to give that a shot."

Tom Breihan In 2005 I moved to New York. My wife, my girlfriend at the time, was going to NYU for social work for grad school, and so we just decided to move up there. It worked out really nicely because I got a job at the *Village Voice*. And for about three years I wrote a blog on the *Village Voice* website. It was completely different. The mid-2000s nobody really knew what writing on the internet was going to be. I would write a little bit for the *Voice* print edition but not very much. But my whole job there was I just wrote one music post a day and that was it. I would pick a subject. I would do an interview or I would write about a live show or I'd write about a song or whatever. I'd like come up with some random half-assed list and then do it. And I built up an audience over time. I did that for a long time, and people still talk to me about that column.

Puja Patel My first true start as a writer was when I pitched the *Village Voice*. They had put up a listing for a nightlife reporter. It was in their music section, which was helmed by Rob Harvilla and was made up of Rob, Camille Dodero, Zach Baron, and [regular writers] Chris Weingarten and Tom Breihan, and then I became their nightlife reporter. I was so freaking arrogant. I sent this e-mail to Rob—I still have it and look at it sometimes—and I said, "I don't have a ton of writing samples. What I do know is that I know music, and I know emerging trends and I follow lots of different communities. This section is called 'The Sound of the City' and here is all of the city that you're missing." Bless his heart for humoring me and being like, "Sure." He gave me a couple of assignments, with my constant badgering. I truly have to thank him deeply, because he really quickly just let me write about whatever I wanted, to the point where I had a nightlife column and was writing for the *Voice* three to four times a week. At the time I didn't realize how significant that was, but in retrospect I fully recognize how significant it was, and how the spirit of an alt-weekly really informs the way that I learned to approach journalism, in that they're really focused on reporting and really focused on human interest stories. There's this spirit of being fearless, honest, and directly engaging with the world that you live in.

Lindsay Zoladz I ended up submitting some of my blog pieces to websites while I was looking for service industry jobs. One of them was called Coke Machine Glow. They were the first ones to really give me my first break. They put me on as a staff writer. It wasn't a paid position. No one there got paid. It was just this passion project, but it was my first experience being on staff somewhere and it was really exciting. I eventually got a job at a bakery and would write my stuff on nights and weekends. That led me into the flow of doing music writing and doing album reviews and learning about the structure and how to work with editors and stuff like that. From there I just kept pitching things to the *Washington City Paper*—the alt-weekly there in DC—and started getting little blog assignments for them. Those were the first paid things I did. And then I started getting bigger and bigger stories from them. The more I did, it kind of snowballed, and I started freelancing for other places. This was all while I had other desk jobs. I was doing other work that didn't really fulfill me, but I think that made me work harder on the stuff I actually cared about in my spare time. Eventually I got enough freelance stuff under my belt to quit my desk job and basically try and succeed somehow at making a career as a freelance writer, and that was around the time that *Pitchfork* got in contact with me.

Carvell Wallace In college I was absolutely obsessive about music. I would read artists' biographies over and over again, including this one Jimi Hendrix biography over and over again, and the way the author wrote about music I just started imitating it whenever I had a chance to write about music. So in college I took some writing class and ended up writing this really ridiculous essay about Jimi's performance of "Machine Gun" at the Fillmore East on New Year's Eve 1970, which was still to this day my favorite recording. So I practiced writing about music but I never had a gig doing it. Then around 2014 I wrote a little bit about Mike Brown and the Ferguson situation for a very small blog called *The Manifest-Station*. And even though it didn't have a lot of readers, for whatever reason a lot of its readers are celebrities. So that piece that I wrote ended up getting retweeting by Cindy Crawford or someone—I'm not exactly sure who it was. But then it just suddenly turned this whole thing on Twitter and then I guess Jessica Hopper found it and asked if I had ever written about music. And I was like, "Yes." I knew that I could, because I had spent so many years obsessing over music, talking about it with people, living with people who obsessed over music, and I played music for all these years, and I had a really good year for composition and arrangement. And I just kind of knew that I could probably pull something off. And then I think Jessica was really looking to shake up the way that music writing went. She was on the lookout for different kinds of voices that she thought could explore facets of criticism that had been explored before. And so I wrote two pieces for her that did really well, and then the third piece I wrote was sort of a turning point because it was the review of *To Pimp a Butterfly* for *Pitchfork*. And she asked me if I would be willing to write about it. And I can say this now, but I had pretty much never listened to Kendrick Lamar. I knew who he was and I knew that he existed but I had never listened to him. But I have a habit of saying "yes" to things and then quickly learning how to do them. And so what I did with the Kendrick Lamar piece was while I was waiting for him to drop the record—because, if you recall, that album drop came as a surprise in that there was a date that was floating about but it wasn't clear if it was actually going to drop on that date or not—while I was waiting I was just reading all the reviews anyone had ever written of Kendrick and in the process just learning kind of what the linguistics of music reviews were. And I just started noticing some patterns in the way the people wrote about rap and about Kendrick and about black music in general. And I sort of have this theory that when you're learning how to do something you should look at everyone else who's ever done it and figure out what you like and figure out what you don't like. And so I found there was a lot of stuff in the way that people wrote about rap that just seemed to me to be problematic. And so when the record finally came out, because we really wanted to be the first one out with the review, I really only had a chance to listen to it once. I think I was even listening to the last half of the album as I was writing. That's how quickly I turned that review around. And so I didn't even really have time to dig into the music. It's a different kind of review than I may have written if I had a few days with it. But I felt like it was an opportunity to review the way people review Kendrick and the way that people review rap. And so I ended up doing that not knowing if that was right or wrong, but it just felt like the right thing to do. And I guess people were thirsty for that because Jessica said that piece had more numbers on the site than anything she ever edited. And after that it was kind of over. That's when I started getting a lot of DMs from editors and so forth asking if I would be willing to write for them and that's sort of launched everything.

Rob Sheffield In late '97 Joe Levy went to *Rolling Stone* and I came on board with him. And the first thing I wrote for *Rolling Stone* was about Bob Dylan, which was intimidating enough. It was funny because it was the end of 1997 and I was writing for the year-end issue. And so I was writing about things that had happened in music all year and I was writing about Bob Dylan putting out one of his all-time best albums, *Time Out of Mind.* And I remember thinking it's weird writing in an editorial infrastructure that I haven't written for before, and it was weird writing for a magazine I hadn't written for before. And it's *Rolling Stone* and I'm writing about Bob Dylan. It was like I was writing for the Vatican newspaper and I'm writing about the transubstantiation or something. And I was like, "Well are they going to let me be myself? Are they going to let me be bitchy and irreverent?" And I was like, "Well I may as well find out now. If they're not going to let me be myself, I might as well piss them off writing about Bob Dylan and we can end the suspense here." As it turns out it was a perfect match.

Steven Hyden Pretty much anything I wrote in my twenties, it's like in a black hole. A lot of what I wrote is pretty terrible, but it's sort of like being a band that just played clubs for like a really long time before they kind of got a national audience. Like The Beatles had to go to Hamburg for three years to hone their craft. And I really believe that that's good for writers to do in obscurity for a while, to hone your craft and to fuck up in the darkness. Because there are some writers now who are so young and they're writing for national sites and they write shitty stories, and they just embarrass themselves because they don't have that benefit of obscurity like I got. I got to write like two hundred shitty columns in obscurity that no one's ever going to read. It wasn't until I could write a halfway decent column that people could actually read my stuff. You can kind of arrive more fully formed in a way if you have that benefit.

Nitsuh Abebe I used to get really nice e-mails from people who were like, "Yeah I'm just finishing college and I'd love to just go get coffee with you and talk to you about how you wound up being the music critic for *New York*." And I would often do that, and they would do all these sort of strategic questions about how all this happened. And honestly my answer was, "It's not that I made job decisions to make this happen. I literally had a different job during which I wasted a lot of time sitting on the internet arguing with people about music." It seemed to me that the way to grow as a writer wasn't necessarily to angle yourself through some series of jobs that would tell you what to write, or make you churn out content every day—it was to have space to write stuff you really wanted to, stuff you believed in, about things you cared about and were genuinely involved in. If you're writing things that are good, there's a better chance that someone says, "Hey you're good at doing that."

Steven Hyden I was obsessed with kind of taking the next step in my career and I just couldn't do it. I failed so many times. I would send out probably at least ten portfolios a month to various newspapers. And not only did I not get hired anywhere, I didn't even get an interview. The greatest moment of my career will always be the moment that The A.V. Club gave me an interview. Not even the moment that they hired me, but the moment that they gave me an interview because I waited six years just to get an interview from somebody. That was such a big deal.

J. Edward Keyes For people who are just starting out, as many publications as there are and as many opportunities as there are, I still think it's hard to break in. And I think for people who don't come from the background—if because of where you were born, you're not connected to the right people, or you didn't get to go to school for this profession— that sucks. And I think that's still a wall.

T. Cole Rachel Everything that has ever happened for me professionally has sort of been an accident, but has also been because of relationships. If you want to be a part of this world and write about it, a part of that is just going to shows and becoming friends with other people that are in that world. It's not trying to aggressively insinuate yourself with people or force your clips on an editor that doesn't know you. Sometimes that can actually do you a huge disservice. People can sense that a mile off and they don't want anything to do with it. So there's a delicate balance still, like how you present yourself to people. But I always tell them you can't engineer or force organic relationships to happen. But you can sort of put yourself in a position where those things can happen. So much of what happened to me just happened because I would know someone and then that would lead to something.

Chuck Klosterman There are many factors involved: your ability, your work ethic, your ability to think critically. But the biggest factor is luck. It really is. I mean, I graduated from college in 1994. By chance, the newspaper in Fargo, North Dakota, at that time, in that highly specific summer of 1994—their fear was the idea of Gen X readers. "Who are these people wearing hats backward and listening to Soundgarden and carrying skateboards? They're confusing and apathetic!" Now, what a smart publication would have done is look at that demographic and say, "Well we need to update the entire paper. We need to consider stories that young people are interested in." But that wasn't their philosophy. Their philosophy was, "Every Thursday let's put a sixteen-page insert into the paper called *Rage*, and this sixteen-page tabloid insert will deal with all issues involving people in their twenties." And a ton of people applied for this job because—and I think it might even be illegal—the ad said you had to be under thirty to apply. So of course every young reporter in the upper Midwest applied. I ended up getting this job partially because the guy who was doing the hiring had gone to Michigan State and was a huge basketball fan, and I think I was the only applicant who knew anything about Big Ten basketball. So we had a great dinner together and I got the job. This is why I say random chance is such a huge factor: If I had graduated in 1993, I would've gone to graduate school or moved away or done something else, you know? If I had graduated in '95—well, then somebody who graduated the year before me would have gotten the job. But I happened to graduate when the job was open, and that really accelerated my career.

CHAPTER THREE

Interviews

Music, like any other art form, comes with context. A song, an album, is always framed by the artist that made it. Influence. Intent. Process. These are just a few of the gaps that interviews fill, confronting an artist in relation to his or her art. "If you like a piece of art you want to know about the artist, and that's kind of compounded with music," says Chuck Klosterman. "Because the content is more opaque. Understanding who the person is kind of necessitates a discussion."

Said discussions, of course, are not something that occur naturally in everyday life. Interviews are a conversational cheat of sorts, where relative strangers are given license to largely avoid inert small talk and fast-forward to more meaningful conversations on identity, love, happiness, success, failure, fear, anxiety, and so many other emotional points of life's little intricacies. There's an implied understanding that your whole purpose is to pry, to expose the kind of personal truths and emotions that are normally reserved for the closed doors of a therapy or counseling session, and then to use those answers to develop a narrative that will inevitably be consumed by a large audience of readers. It's a jarring kind of intimacy.

And while the average person will likely never view the stakes of a musical artist interview as being tantamount to those conducted with political figures or world leaders, for music journalists and music lovers, these interviews and these stories are important. They are an opportunity to peek behind the curtain, to demystify, to humanize, and yet somehow make the art of songwriting all the more otherworldly and in-explicable.

Josh Jackson I've always been fascinated by the people who make the things I love, and whether it's a TV show or a book, the idea that there's real people behind things who are following their creative passions, you want to know more about those people and their stories and how they became the kind of person that would be able to create this kind of thing that you love. But more than that, what is particular about these stories that I'm drawn to is that outside of the fact that it's about an author or a musician, there is a story. The stories themselves are interesting. When you have a writer who can tell a great story—and that was one of the hardest things when we were starting, working with writers—who could not just go through the motions and ask the questions and give you the typical music profile. The writers that I really love and am excited to find are ones who can go and connect with a person on a deeper level, to really tell their story, to give us some new and fresh perspective that makes you see the world in a different way. I'd much rather read a really interesting and engaging story about some person that I'm not familiar with or am not a fan of their work than I would a boring story about somebody that I care about deeply.

Michael Azerrad Not many music journalists are reporters in the sense of someone who researches and conveys a news story. Mostly, music journalists write profiles, which involves establishing a rapport with the subject, rather than digging up facts and describing a situation. So to be a music journalist, as opposed to a newspaper reporter, you have to have a knack for drawing out the subject to get the great quotations and revealing scenarios, and one can get there many different ways. A newspaper reporter does a lot of legwork, and isn't so much of a thera-pist; they just need to get facts, not feelings.

Chuck Klosterman Reporting and interviewing are art forms that seem to be disappearing. Up until the advent of the internet, the assumption was that almost no young journalist would ever be allowed to do criticism or to write columns or work in an essayistic style until they'd proven that they could succeed as a traditional reporter. And now that relationship has reversed. Now you can become a national writer at the age of twenty-three without having interviewed anybody in your entire life. And the problem is that this kind of person—a talented person who achieves major notoriety at a very young age—will slowly mature, and he or she will want to pursue pieces that demand that they interview people who aren't already their friends. And they are not able to do it, because those skills are part of a larger craft. It's like blacksmithing. You can only get good at it by doing it constantly. That's the only way. There's no other way to learn. You cannot be naturally great at interviewing. It's impossible. It would be like looking at your two-year-old kid and thinking, "Oh, he's just naturally great at talking. He could have his own podcast tomorrow." It doesn't work that way.

Christopher R. Weingarten What's most exciting for me is telling the story. When I say telling the story, the underline is on "the." I like having *the* story. Whether it's a famous group or a not-famous group, or someone I respect or someone who's music I don't even like that much, I'm excited to tell a story and fit it into the culture at large. You know, there's a lot of people whose music I'm not incredibly psyched about but they have great stories and people are into them. That is more important to me than just letting everyone know how psyched I am about a particular artist.

Gabriela Tully Claymore I like talking to people. I do a lot of interviews. I think that profiling is really fun. Obviously you're trying to create a narrative and you're following more than a couple threads. You're following the story of the album, you're following the story of how this person got to where they are, and then you're also trying to follow your interaction with that person and how it goes and calculate a way of describing that because you're hoping that the reader feels like they're along for the ride.

Jes Skolnik As a trans person, as an intersex person, as somebody who has always been on the outside in a lot of ways, I'm very interested in letting people tell their stories in their own voices and try to raise that up.

Ilana Kaplan It's to facilitate the storytelling, to help someone's voice shine through in a different way and to get them seen through a different light than what's in their music.

Jayson Greene I've always loved asking strangers about themselves. Personally it's one of my favorite things to do. Having an excuse to do it in a professional context is awesome.

T. Cole Rachel I was not always so interested in the musical lineage of bands as I was interested in sort of the cultural lineage of bands, if that make sense. And I think that's still kind of true. I'm much more interested in talking to people about what they do than I am interested in writing criticism or anything. If I never wrote another record review, that would be totally fine with me. But I love interviewing people. I love talking with people about where they're from and how they started and why they make what they make. And that part of it was always really interesting to me. Seeing those bands and coming from where I was coming from, I was just sort of like, "What makes someone make this? Where does this even come from?" And that was always really interesting.

Gabriela Tully Claymore I think what draws people to musicians is just the fact that so much of it soundtracks really important moments in other people's lives. And I think that a lot of people want to know what made this kind of thing possible.

Michael Azerrad One of my favorite quotations is from *Noise: The Political Economy of Music* by the French cultural theorist Jacques Attali: "Music is a herald, for change is inscribed in noise faster than it transforms society." Musicians tend to be mostly unconscious cultural visionaries, and it's a good idea to pay attention to what they're thinking and feeling and doing, and how the business of music functions, because they tend to anticipate larger movements in society. Also, music is incorporeal and abstract, so hearing people try to describe their own music is inherently interesting.

Ilana Kaplan I feel like the humanity behind the music is really what fuels the music and the tangible product that you're listening to, that you connect to. I've often been seen less as a critic and more as an interviewer. I think that bothered me for a while, and sometimes it still does. But I just really like talking with people and connecting with them, especially when their music has such a connection with fans. I want to know what prompted them to create what they do best. I think people are really complex and really layered, and I honestly just love talking to creative people and getting to know them.

Bonnie Stiernberg I love when a great feature will not only give you a sense of the music and the band or artist but a sense of them as people and what makes them tick and why they're doing what they're doing and who they really are. That for me is always the most rewarding and fascinating part of music journalism and just journalism in general. Just telling people's stories. Giving people a sense of who someone is. I think it's really easy to get sucked into the formula of "Oh, so-and-so has an album coming out this month." And people think that that is a pitch. "Oh, I'll just talk to them about the album." And it's really easy to fall into that. But for me the stories I really love and are the ones I try to write are the ones that can kind of go beyond that and get to the heart of the artist and why they are the way they are.

T. Cole Rachel For me it's just a general curiosity with all the kinds of interviews I do. Where did you come from? Why did you do this? Why did you start doing this? And it's always interesting to see how people's personalities weigh on the kind of art that they make. I like that. That's the most interesting thing to me.

Laura Snapes They are their work. An actor is taking on roles, an author is translating their experiences into fiction, an artist's work is a lot more ineffable. A musician is right in the middle of what they make and generally a key part of the overall effect. I am a very prosaic, unartistic person. I might be very cynical about a lot of music, but most of it outside the nakedly commercial realm still works on me like a magic trick: what moves that person to want to do something that is so alien to me, and how do they do it? If I'm interviewing a musician that I really like, the subtext of all my questions is basically *How do you* do *that?*

Clover Hope When you're sitting down with an artist it's like you're sitting down with all of their fans. You have this emotional attachment that connects thousands or millions of people to this one person. This one person represents millions of people. It's strange and scary, but often rewarding to be a conduit for the artist's narrative.

Christian Hoard They make people feel something. They've captured a grand audience, so there's going to be a grand audience that wants to learn about them. They tend to be unusual people. The people who do it well are eccentric or weird or just different in a way that kind of fascinates us. And it's fascinating to try to understand how they do the things they do. I also think that if you're going to love the music, it's just natural to want to understand who the person behind it is. I've always found that learning more about the person who made it makes me appreciate the thing more. It's always been a piece of my fandom. One of my favorite things to do is read a biography and listen along with it, to dive deep into the music. There is a symbiotic relationship between the music and learning about the person that made it. That's fandom to me.

Ryan Dombal With reviews, it's more like you're teaching other people. But when I'm interviewing people for a feature, I often feel like I'm enriching myself. With a reported feature story, you don't have to know everything about a person or subject before you start to write it. That's kind of the point—learning.

Clover Hope A lot of times interviews exist as an artifact for music writing or the music industry. You can look back on stories, say, for example, about Mariah Carey, and see the context of her life and where her career was at that moment in time. It's like a time capsule for entertainment, and my role is to kind of contribute to that time capsule.

Matt Fink There's that quote about how every photographer who does portraits is basically taking a self-portrait with every picture that they take, and I suppose with writing we're kind of telling our own stories as much as we're telling the artist's story. Because we gravitate toward certain ideas and certain themes that are uniquely us. I think it is a form of self-expression.

J. Edward Keyes I mean I think it comes down to the fact that music can speak to you and it can speak to your life experience and you can really connect with something and it can move you. And I think when something has that kind of emotional impact on you, you want to know more about the person who made it and you want to know what their life is like and what experiences they brought to the record. And I think that's where a lot of that comes from. It's like just wanting to have more of a connection with these people who make music that moves you. I think that's that part of the reason why people are so interested, I guess.

Amanda Petrusich Interviewing is so weird. Everything about it is weird. There's no way around how weird it is. And there are so many things you're pretending. It's a performance on both sides of the table. You're pretending that everything the other person says isn't going to end up in a national magazine. You're pretending that you know each other a lot better than you actually do. You're demanding really personal confessions from someone when it's arguably not in their best interests to disclose them. It's nothing like a regular conversation, but you do your best to pretend it is. When else would you do something like that?

Larry Fitzmaurice I hated doing interviews at first because I had a lot of anxiety about it, but then I realized it's really just talking to somebody about who they are and how they feel. And once you realize that they are just another person, it's so easy to get to know them, and you form a connection. I guess some people would say you exploit the connection a little bit, but it's in the service of telling a story and helping an audience understand who somebody is, and I've found to some extent it helps the artists understand who they are on a deeper level.

David Marchese The advantage of talking to a stranger is that you know you're never going to have to see them again. So you can ask things or bring up things that maybe you wouldn't ask if you had to see that person the next day. That's coupled with the advantage you have of being able to learn about the other person and get ideas about them ahead of time. It's sort of like having a conversation with somebody while you're both looking at the same piece of art in a museum, but you have the opportunity beforehand to learn about the specific artwork and the other person you're with, who's also looking at the same piece of art. You just have so much more conversationally to draw from.

Ryan Dombal Asking people about their personal lives in interviews can be weird. I mean, I have causal friends that I don't talk to about personal things like that. It's funny, being a journalist gives you this license to ask.

Michael Azerrad Anyone you interview is a grown adult who knows what interviews are for and about, and is doing this of their own volition. So they know the drill: someone they may never have met before is going to ask them intimate questions. It's just part of the deal.

Andy Greene It's an advantage we have over TV, because when you have makeup, there's lights in your face, and a boom over your head, you're very aware that it's an interview. When you're in your own house or a restaurant, or you're talking to somebody on the phone, there are fewer barriers that are obstructing the conversation, so it can go well.

Maria Sherman I understand why there are therapist/patient comparisons to be made about interviewing. And as a kid of a shrink, I really enjoy the analogy. There's something about the practice of sitting down with somebody or a group of somebodies with the mutual understanding that they have to reveal some part of themselves to you, and learning how to do that tactfully and in a way that is meaningful for some nebulous third party who at some point is going to interact with it and digest it. It's really fascinating. It's a strange practice.

Andy Greene It's a very interesting dynamic, because you're sitting there with somebody and you're talking to them and they're just talking to you, yet you're taping it and they're also talking to the whole world. And they know that you can take their sentences and they have to trust you to be in context. They're right to be concerned. It's a scary thing to be on the record, especially in this day and age when one sentence on Twitter can be posted as a tweet out of context and it can destroy you. There are people whose lives are destroyed by a single sentence they say on the record.

T. Cole Rachel I think sometimes people take for granted what a really profound kind of emotional experience it can be to do an interview with someone, both for you and for them. And often it really goes to a place that's really surprising. I mean it's always weird to interview people that you sort of worshiped when you were young, and that is its own surreal thing, but often it can be really surprising.

J. Edward Keyes I think if you're a writer and you're being assigned a story on somebody, your first responsibility should be reading as much as you can of what other people have said about them. And then I think you just have to kind of immerse yourself in it to find out if you have something distinctive, really, to say. I think for me I would almost describe it like unscrewing the face of a clock or something, looking at the gears and seeing how everything's moving and what's setting what off and trying to get into that aspect of it.

David Marchese The actual doing of the interview takes a much smaller amount of time than the preparation and the writing of it.

Craig Jenkins Fifty percent of interview prep is freaking out and then getting myself to stop doing that. I never know fully what I'm going to ask until a couple of hours before. I'll have stuff lined up, but usually it will all come to me in a freak-out hours before. I'm always thinking long-term about what I want to talk to a person about, but it's meltdown city until then.

Amanda Petrusich For me, I'll do an aggressive amount of research. I'll try not to ask or report on anything that's already been asked or reported on. I'll write out a bunch of questions, but then I tend to keep all that stuff in my backpack and just start talking. I try to remember to listen.

Jayson Greene My goal when I go into a conversation that I'm going to write about is to prepare as much as possible beforehand and then be as loose as possible when I'm actually there. I want to prepare so that I can completely turn off all those guards and just *go*. I have a list of questions, I prepare them, but the act of preparing is more important than anything I wrote down. It is that sense of preparedness that I take with me into the interview. I may ask three of the ten questions that I wrote down, but I always know where I could go next and so that gives me confidence to continue that conversation in a good direction. If you don't do that prep, you will stall, you'll stutter.

David Marchese I just want to be as familiar with the subject's body of work as I can be, so that if they reference things I can know what they're talking about and also follow up on it. I'm sure everyone's experienced this: when you're in an interview and somebody mentions something they've done that you don't really know about, but you sort of fake like you do know about it. On the few times that's happened, I've both found it extremely uncomfortable and been frustrated that I couldn't ask something interesting in response—because I didn't know the work. So the preparation is about familiarizing myself as much as possible with the subject and their work. I also find too that when the subjects recognize that you know their work and respect their work in a serious way, it helps them open up to you, because it suggests a level of respect and seriousness.

Jayson Greene I find for what it's worth that whenever I do bring my questions, it's good I've forgotten that I have them.

T. Cole Rachel I kind of had this moment of epiphany. I interviewed Stephin Merritt when *69 Love Songs* came out. And I was terrified. I heard all the stories about what it was like to interview him. And I went in there with this list of questions and then all of the sudden I was like, "You know, I've absorbed this material through research. I'm just going to talk to him." It got to be less of having a list of questions that I'd like to ask and more just like, doing as much research as possible, and then just talking to them and seeing where the conversation goes. Which is hard because I'm actually a really introverted person socially.

Ryan Leas I was more introverted when I was younger, and I guess this job really forced me to not be. In hindsight I'm kind of surprised I haven't been more awkward in some of these situations.

Andy Greene I had a mild stutter, so it was sort of nerve-wracking to get on the phone with people and do interviews. At first I'd be kind of terrified. I just had to get over that.

T. Cole Rachel I think back at some of the first big interviews I got to do, how nervous I was. When I listen to them now, it's so cringey. I'm so awkward. I'm reading questions off a piece of paper, looking at my notes.

Andy Greene There's so many things that can go wrong. Time is a prob-lem. There are interviews where you know that you have twenty min-utes. There's been times I've been cut off and been furious. There are times where you ask one question and the person talks for eight min-utes straight and you're like, "Oh fuck! I've twenty questions. I have twelve minutes left and I got one of them." I've had my recorder die on me. I've gotten lost on the way to people's houses and [was] almost late. There's been so many things.

Stephen Deusner This is why—no kidding—I use at least three recorders when I do an interview.

Gabriela Tully Claymore I feel really nervous all the time, period. But also when I do interviews. It's weird because I'll get anxious when I'm doing literally the chillest thing, something that is so quote unquote "easy."

Matt Fink I still get nervous before I talk to somebody who I really, really admire. That's kind of the thrill to me. And to be able to form some story out of what they've told me—that's kind of thrilling too. I guess it feels like you're interacting with that musician. You're part of their story in some way. I interviewed Yoko Ono years ago, and still, to this day, in my head I'm thinking *she's had conversations with John Lennon*—and now I'm talking to her. It feels cool that even though that's not a big deal—she talks to people every day—I'm some part of that story, even if it's a very minuscule part that no one cares about. It's kind of cool to even be in that narrative somewhere.

Bonnie Stiernberg I mean, I've done who knows how many interviews over the years that I've been doing this and I still get that little rush of adren-aline before an interview, regardless, even if it's a small band that I'm not necessarily nervous to be talking to. It's almost like an involuntary method to get psyched for it. I start fidgeting ten or fifteen minutes before the interview. I guess it's nervous energy, but I'm not nervous I'm going to have a bad interview. It's almost like when you play a sport or something and you're getting yourself ready for the game. That's such a dorky comparison, but whatever. I just know that no matter who I'm talking to, ten minutes before it's time to talk to them, I'm gonna be pacing around or picking at my cuticles or maybe feeling a little weird in the pit of my stomach. It's something that takes a while to ease into. Almost every interview that I do, I will ask my first questions and think, "Is this going to be a good one?" And then after I get that first question out and get a feel for how the interview is going to go, I sort of flip back to normal and relax.

Matt Fink I grew up reading about these artists who hated the press, like Lou Reed, who would just be really combative in interviews. I didn't really know what to expect before I interviewed an artist, but that was sort of what I was thinking could happen, that it would be very adversarial. Then right away when I started interviewing artists I was really surprised by how normal they seemed and how often it did just feel like a conversation. I had this idea in my head that these were artists. These are people who exist on a different plane than the rest of us do. But talking to them I very rarely get that impression.

T. Cole Rachel I really feel like so much of it is just some kind of psychology about body language and how you approach people, and I really feel like most of the time what you give off to people is what you get back from them. If you come into it with a good vibe, that's usually what you get back. It's a weird skill. You do have to be able to read the room and make people feel at ease and not be a fucking weirdo with people. That's harder to do when you're first starting because you're nervous.

Amanda Petrusich When I was younger I was so intimidated and nervous when I would go to interview someone. I'd be terrified. I'd be shaking. The power dynamic of an interview is so strange as a social interaction or just as a human interaction. It took me a long time to get comfortable with it, and to recognize my power and my agency in the transaction. I think previously it was like, these are heroes of mine or they were famous musicians or they were not-so-famous musicians, and I felt like, "What am I doing here?" Now I head into those things feeling a little more in control. I'm the one that gets to go home and write the story. They can say whatever they want and do whatever they want, but I've really got all the power. Not that I would encourage anyone to think of it that way. That's sort of a terrible way to think about it, but when you're feeling nervous or intimidated it's good to be reminded, "Look, I'm in control at the end of the day. I've got the platform. I've got the megaphone." And I think when you stop being so afraid, at least for me, I could act more like a normal person in those situations instead of freaking out.

David Marchese I guess insofar as I feel like there's any dispositional aspect of myself that is useful in these interviews, it's that they just don't feel weird to me. The celebrity aspect doesn't play into it for me at all. Fundamentally I like talking to people, and when I'm in the conversation, I'm just talking to a *person*, you know? It doesn't matter to me that they're famous, and therefore I'm not worried about asking a question or bringing up a subject that is going to make the famous person like me less or anything like that. I don't have that worry. I talk to strangers. When I'm sitting at an airport by myself, I'll talk to someone. If I see somebody on the subway who's reading a book that I've read or reading a book I want to read, I'll ask them about it. I like talking to cab drivers. It's that kind of thing. And the emotional tenor of those conversations to me doesn't feel different, whether it's the waiter at the restaurant I'm talking to if I'm eating alone or it's an artist and I'm interviewing them for two hours. It's all just talking to people.

Amanda Petrusich I'll try to have just a conversation with somebody that maybe isn't about the thing they made or isn't about the work that they do, but is just sort of about being alive. I try to come at it that way and learn something about them that way. Sometimes it's just a question of hanging around long enough. Sometimes if you're just there, and you're there long enough, you get to see some interesting things happen, or you get to notice more interesting things. It's just a question of per- sistence at a certain point. You're taking this very contrived transaction and trying to make it a little less weird. It's kind of like being on a date, just trying to be comfortable and find a thing that you both can happily talk about. Sometimes it goes better than others. I don't know. There's chemistry in an interview too that, just like dating, you just can't pre- dict who you're going to get along with. It's weird, right? Some people you sit down with and you're both just talking at once and it's great and amazing, and other times it's like pulling teeth.

Chuck Klosterman The first thing you need to do is size the person up when you meet them. You need to get a sense of how interested are they in do- ing this at all. Because that's a big part of it. When I interviewed Bono, it was clear that he views journalists as psychiatrists. He wants to ex- plain who he is. He wants to talk. And in those situations, you just sort of gently move them toward the areas you want to examine and sort of let them do the work of getting there. You just kind of guide them where you want to go because they're already into doing it. Marilyn Manson is the same way. He's not like Bono, but he loves being interviewed. He views himself as somebody who could have been a journalist, so he has a real understanding of how an interesting feature about a rock star is supposed to unspool. You can ask him a very straightforward question and he will sense what you're really asking and will just immediately jump there. But more often than not, the person either doesn't want to do the interview at all, or they want to do it but they really just want to get it over with. And in those cases what I do—and I used to do this nonverbally, but now I do it directly—is say to the person, "Look, we're not going to become friends. This is the only time we're ever going to speak. I'm only here because I'm a journalist. You're only here because you're promoting something. That's the only reason this event is hap- pening at all. It's totally constructed. But there are things about your life that I find authentically interesting, and I want to ask you these questions, and it would be cool if you responded." And very often the person will be like, "Yes. Thank God this is how you're doing it."

Jillian Mapes The rookie mistake is that you don't actually listen to what they're saying. You're just too nervous thinking about what you want to ask. You're not listening closely and you're not actually following up and paying attention. Everything has to be a conversation. Don't make it into a doctor's appointment. I've actually found that if I know a lot about an artist or I'm familiar with their music but maybe don't know much about them personally I find it a little more interesting to—I don't want to say not prepare—but I think it's really interesting to not have an agenda. I feel like some of my biggest mistakes in interviews have been asking overly complicated questions, so what I try to do is try to be a human first. That's kind of my philosophy. Be a human first. Give people the benefit of the doubt, listen to them, make eye contact. Be a human first. Just try to have a good conversation. Be genuinely interested, and just go from there. I also think interviewing people it kind of behooves you to get along with the person. Some writers are like, "Cool. I want to provoke you and have a hostile environment and I'll get things out of you." But that's not my style. That's not what I do. Being a human oftentimes works in your favor because then they recognize you're being genuine and they start to trust you and they open up and you can get more out of them in the long game.

Lindsay Zoladz I think the challenge of any interview is to make that person feel comfortable and feel like an actual human being and not just someone you're there to sap information out of. Interviewing is a really weird, transactional process. Everybody gets something out of it, but on another level it's just two people sitting down to have a conversation. You're never going to get away completely from that transactional thing, but those moments of humanity and sort of going off script I think are what I'm always striving to get out of an interview. And sometimes they don't happen. You'll get someone who's really wooden and only wants to paraphrase a quote about their new album or artist bio or something. That's the biggest frustration is when you don't penetrate that wall. I've tried to get a little bit better and work on that over the years because that can be really intimidating when you're just starting out.

Ilana Kaplan I used to be very clinical about interviewing people. I would kind of stick to my questions more. I think that's a natural thing to do when you're starting out. And I realized over the years that sometimes people go off topic and that's fine. That's what makes your story better and that's where you can ask them more questions and have it be more conversational and get something that maybe somebody else won't.

T. Cole Rachel I always tell people when you do interviews, everybody is different. Other people have very different approaches to how they do it, but for me you just talk to people like you're talking to a person, someone that you know. It's always a little weird because there is this false sense of familiarity with someone while you're interviewing them. To sit down with a stranger and start telling them things about your life is weird, but I just approach people in the same way I would approach anybody else, and people tend to respond to that. It's never been my style where I would be really antagonistic with people or try to provoke people or push them in a way to get them to say something crazy. People have often said things to me that were crazy, but usually we get to that point in a really different kind of way. There's a kind of intimacy sometimes where it's surprising what people reveal to you. People always want to know who was a jerk or who was not nice or who was the worst, and I can only say that has hardly ever, ever happened to me. And when it has happened, it usually wasn't that they were a jerk. It was usually that they just got off a plane and had been awake for twenty-four hours, or sometimes people are just really shy and it's not like they're trying to be a jerk to you, it's just they're not comfortable talking to a stranger. I could probably count on one hand the number of times I felt like someone was just being a dick.

Matt Fink There's definitely been some people I've really, really enjoyed talking to, people that in your head you think, "If this person was in my life, we'd be good friends," which is probably just something I tell myself to feel better about how awkward I am in an interview.

Craig Jenkins Honestly, the hard part is staying a journalist. In order to get a really good snapshot of someone you have to really be invested and there's a level of careful distance you have to keep. And that's the tough part. It's hard to bounce between getting to know the person and being able to maintain that distance and maintaining that critical eye. It's weird.

Ryan Dombal It's cool when artists offer themselves to be profiled in a real way because it shows that they're confident enough in who they are and what they're doing to allow somebody to really get inside.

Amanda Petrusich Good profiles are simultaneously doing two things. They're either very zoomed in on something, that fly-on-the-wall perspective of "This is what's happening, this is what she's drinking or she's eating this sandwich like this," hyperattention to detail. And then it's this very zoomed-out thing of like, "What does this mean? What is she doing in these songs, the way she's talking about these things, the way that she's writing? What is that? What is this thing that she's doing and what does it mean?" You're a thousand miles away looking at Earth from the moon at that point. For me where the writing tends to get a little tedious is when it occupies the middle ground, that middle distance. I feel like you want to be so close or you want to be really far back.

Ryan Leas I tend to want to talk to most people about bigger picture things, how they're thinking or operating in the current landscape. One thing I try to veer away from is when people get too granular about recording techniques and stuff like that. While I enjoy those details, putting that into a feature is often really dull. I think the layman reader who is consuming this stuff mostly doesn't care about that. Musicians obviously do. They're not always thinking about their art in the same way we are. And they're not supposed to, you know? That's what journalists do. It's understandable that musicians, especially early on in their promotion cycle, might not really be thinking about why their album represents X or Y about American music culture in 2014 or 2016 or 2018.

Lizzy Goodman My ex-boyfriend Marc Spitz, who was my mentor and taught me a lot about how to do this, basically told me that your job is to make your reader feel like they were in the room with this person. And I know that's very basic, but it's really true. You learn to be attuned to these things that are going to help you flesh out the way it feels in a sensory way to sit in some shitty hotel room with someone that everyone wants to get close to. Those are the things that make me stoked, being able to peer behind the curtain. That is just a very natural instinct that I have and one that I've been taught to develop through this work.

Jayson Greene It's nice to be wrapped up in the details of someone else's life. It's enjoyable. I think that good profile journalism is very much about—without exhaustively noting a bunch of trivial details—putting someone into a scene where they feel like they're there, too. I can remember really great profiles that I've read and felt very much along for the ride. I think that's the key phrase. It's somewhere between a short story and an interview. A lot of them are very nonsensical and full of empty calories and things that aren't meaningful because you don't really get to know someone in those contexts. Sometimes you can read meaning into almost anything and the worst examples are the really high-up celebrity ones where it's basically a journalist sitting down with an incredibly famous actor or actress in a restaurant in a hotel somewhere for like twenty minutes and then you have to read about the salad they ate and there's nothing there any of real interest. But I think when you're given a glimpse into something a little bit more interesting, it just speaks to our inherent interest in other human beings and how they go about their day. It's like watching a short film starring that person.

Andy Greene You really want color. I'll be like, "Hey do you mind if I take pictures on my phone? I won't publish it. They're for my reference." So then you can take a picture of a bookshelf that you walked past, then you can go back later and can see all the books. And then you can describe them. You take a picture of one room then describe the fireplace in real detail. It's a really good way to not have to take notes and still be engaged. I sort of walk around with a camera in my hand and with permission just kind of snap like one hundred pictures. Then I go back later and you can take one picture and turn it into a whole little scene.

Michael Azerrad I'm paying attention to everything: you have to be very highly alert and yet also relaxed. But the main thing with interviewing someone is simply to *pay attention to what they're saying.* Which sounds obvious but actually is rarer and more difficult to do and vastly more important than it seems. If you're just firing off a list of questions as if it were a pop quiz, you're probably not going to get much good stuff. You have to listen closely to the other person, think of follow-ups based on what they just said, and be aware when the story is taking an unforeseen turn, and have the humility to give up your preconceived notions and follow that turn.

Andy Greene I will have the tape recorder in my pocket and when I leave the car, before I even ring the doorbell, I'm taping. Unless they tell you they want something off the record, you want everything. Because you never know when something will be said that's interesting. Never stop taping.

Ilana Kaplan One thing that I was also taught in my writing classes was how the inclination is to talk more. Interviewers want to talk more. And I love talking. I will talk forever. But the thing is you should also really try to not interrupt them. Let them speak. Let them have their stream of consciousness because a lot of times it'll be a more comfortable conversation and they might open up more.

Matt Fink I try to use silence to my advantage. That's something I really had to work at, to not want to fill every silent moment with me talking. Perhaps to even let an awkward silence kind of linger. I feel like someone's gonna fill it, and often it will be the artist who will fill it, and they might end up saying the most interesting thing that they say in the whole interview. When they've felt like they've said everything but you're not saying anything so they have to say something else, that might knock them off their talking points a little bit and they'll say something they hadn't planned on.

David Marchese I don't think people have a problem with being asked, "What do you mean by that?" or "Can you tell me more about that?" I've had a few people, students and journalists, say to me, "How are you comfortable being combative or pushing people?" and that makes me thinks my interviews can come across on the page as more combative or tense than the conversations really were. It's extremely rare that I ever have a tense or combative moment with someone I'm interviewing. I'm conscious of those moments and I try to make sure there aren't too many of those moments because they're not useful. At least not to me.

Lizzy Goodman The other thing Marc always said was that you reach a point where you hear the quotes coming out of a person's mouth and you can see them on the page. It really is weird. Someone will say something and you'll be like, "Oh, that's going to be my lead."

Jayson Greene It's a bit more of a contact sport socially. You're very much in the moment. Sometimes someone will say something and there will be a little bit of a voice in the back of my head saying, "Oh this will be excellent context for …" and there'll be a little subthread running in the back of my head about how I could use what they're saying. But I can't indulge that for too long because they're still talking to me and I might miss something.

Andy Greene There are some people that are hard to interrupt but you have to be willing to cut off anybody, even Mick Jagger if you have to.

No matter how famous they are or how rich they are, it is still your interview and your questions and you are in control.

Amanda Petrusich The part of the reporting where you have a formal interview with someone, where you ask, "What's this new record about?" That usually gets the most stilted responses. So for me I either try to get that stuff really quickly as soon as I get there, or right at the end. Or sometimes I won't do it at all while I'm actually reporting the piece and will try to make sure I have access for a phone call later where I can sort of ask the—I shouldn't say boring questions—but the rote questions that every reporter's gonna ask them. The who, what, where, when, why of the new album or whatever it is that they're promoting.

David Marchese Having that second phone call is helpful. Sometimes I find I forget to ask very basic questions, almost like housekeeping questions, because I'm more engaged in deeper questions. So it's good to be able to go back and get the basics.

Lizzy Goodman Honestly, this is so cheesy that I'm saying this—Philip Seymour Hoffman as Lester Bangs got it right in *Almost Famous*, which I maintain is the best and most accurate depiction of music journalism ever. It's really pretty good. He says, "You have to make your reputation on being honest and unmerciful." You have to tell the truth. You don't serve your subject. You are there to respect them, and you are there to tell the honest truth about them.

Ryan Leas Some say there's way too much of people in their own articles. It's a tricky balance. I've mostly done it in situations where it was called for, or sort of inextricable from the experience. I don't know. I don't think any of that should be black and white anymore. When people talk about that being some kind of cardinal sin, I don't see it that way. There's going to be twenty pieces during an album cycle, and if you have a unique experience with somebody or an interesting way to do it, then you should.

Matt Fink I think there are times when the way that the artist reacts to you as a person is perhaps the most revealing thing in the whole interview. I know there have been times where I've had to allow that to be there, even though it makes me uncomfortable. There are a number of artists who are very, very personable and you learn more about that artist through seeing how they relate to other people, and that's what I like as a reader too. I like to read pieces where you see the writer reacting to the artist as a human being. I think you can learn a lot about that artist as a person just through seeing that, where if they're just discussing their album, you lose that. Then you're just in a press agent role where it could just be anyone who worked on the album talking about it.

Laura Snapes Listening is the most important part. And watching their body language and facial expressions. And trying to keep track of subconscious themes to what they're saying that accumulate into a bigger issue that you might not have thought to ask about, or they might not even be aware of. I prepare a lot of questions, or as many as seems appropriate given the allotted time, but I prefer to barely look at them and to just follow the conversation where it needs to go. The most fulfilling aspect is if they come to understand something about themselves that they hadn't realized before, or if the conversation illuminates things about them that you didn't know going in.

Gabriela Tully Claymore One of the things I tell my interns when they're anxious about doing an interview is that it's okay to ask the tough questions. Just ask them at the end.

Clover Hope It's like a live experiment, getting someone to open up.

T. Cole Rachel There are going to be times where you know you're more than likely going to get to a topic that's uncomfortable or there's something you're going to have to address. But you can't open with that. You have to establish some kind of trust and rapport with people before it's like, "So tell me about getting arrested," or whatever it is.

David Marchese I think people in conversation are likely to mirror each other in some fashion. So if I'm showing vulnerability or honesty or a certain nakedness about the question I'm asking, I think it's just human nature that the interview subject is inclined to respond in kind. Trying to be explicitly provocative or hard-hitting—that works for some people. I don't feel like I know how to make it work for me.

Andy Greene If I'm doing a half page in a studio on somebody's new album, I'm not going to bring out their scandal or whatever. If I'm doing a profile of somebody and I have to fill six pages and there's an obvious question that the reader will have, like what happened with their arrest or whatever, you have to bring it up in a tasteful way and let them respond to it. Don't make it the lead of the article and don't dwell on it, but if something's happening in their life that's really interesting, even if it's something they don't want to talk about, you sort of have to go there. You don't want your article to just be about their personal life because that's not going to be interesting, but you need a balance. When you're profiling somebody, it's their work, it's their life, it's everything.

David Marchese I'm conscious of asking questions in ways that are not going to get somebody else's back up. And that's in terms of specific language that I use, vocal tone, and body language. Sometimes I'll say to people, "I know this is a difficult question, and if you don't want to talk about it that's okay, but," and then I'll ask the question. And it's very rare that somebody then says, "I don't want to talk about that." They might not give the insightful answer that I'm hoping for, but it's rare that somebody will totally shut off the line of questioning after I've acknowledged that a question may be difficult.

Michael Azerrad The *Almost Famous* syndrome is one of the most difficult aspects of the gig. It can also be one of the most fun, of course—getting to have an in-depth conversation with your favorite musicians is a real kick. But you also have to be prepared to make some unflattering observations about musicians you admire—and suffer the consequences.

The funny thing is, you can't always predict what will or will not set someone off. They might not mind something you thought for sure they'd object to, and they might go ballistic about something you thought was insignificant.

Jayson Greene Personal questions are really, really good. Questions that aren't about music at all, questions that actually aren't about what they're being asked about, that are about their lives, are incredible ways to open people up. They've already talked about whatever it is they're supposed to talk to you about. If you're being interviewed, you get on the phone with a list of talking points that you want to get out. You want people to hear you say five or six things, and that person on the phone with you is a medium for you to say those five or six things to them. And so whatever questions are being asked you are preparing in your mind to find a way to direct the conversation to those five or six things. So if someone asks you what your favorite movie was when you were ten, you are completely thrown off momentarily, and often you are more engaged because you actually begin talking to the person on the phone for the first time, and it often reawakens the conversation. I've often asked people what their first song they ever wrote was. How old were they? What were the words? Could you perform a little bit for me? That always disarms people because it's funny, it's usually embarrassing, and it makes them think about something they probably haven't thought about in a while, and they certainly aren't prepared to talk to you about it.

Gabriela Tully Claymore There's always asking, "Why?" It sounds really basic but it's because people are always asked what something is but they're not always asked why that was the choice.

Josh Jackson I love hearing about people's childhood. If they're a musician, what was it like growing up? Were they surrounded by music? Did they have an interest in music? Were they playing instruments? Was dad playing Dylan records in the home? Was this something that you latched onto early or was it something that came later? I like going to the start. I like origin stories. When R.E.M. was breaking up, I got to interview Mike Mills and Michael Stipe, and I used that opportunity to really talk about the very beginning and frame the story around the beginning and end of R.E.M., going back and forth between these kids getting to know each other to all these years later hanging everything up. I love the origin story.

David Marchese There's a couple questions I often ask, but I feel like those questions usually yield answers that end up getting cut out of the final piece. They're more about developing some comfort level early in the interview. If somebody has a new project, which is usually the reason why they've agreed to do an interview, I often ask, "What about this thing represents growth for you or shows a new side to what you can do?" I think people usually have something to say about that because I think in their minds nobody likes to think they're just repeating themselves in their work. So in what I hope is a nonobsequious way, it's a flattering question that doesn't always result in something riveting to read, but it is good to ask early on. I also often ask what's something the subject has made that they're most proud of. Sometimes the popular thing somebody has made might not be what they think is the best thing they did. So that answer can be kind of revealing. The other thing, which is lightweight but I'm always curious about, is asking people what books they are reading, what TV shows they are watching, what music they're listening to. It's kind of a fun glimpse into their lives that's not necessarily related to the work that they're doing.

Stephen Deusner One question I picked up and started thinking about a while back that altered the way I think about music is asking artists how their songs change for them over time. I guess I'm trying to figure out what it's like to live with a song. Jessica Lea Mayfield wrote a fantastic album about surviving a very abusive relationship. It's very frank and very brave. When I interviewed her, I was trying to get her to talk about these very emotional and raw songs. What does it mean to get up and sing them night after night? What does it mean to know that you're go-ing to have to get up there whether you feel like it or not? That's an extreme example, but I mean any kind of confessional songwriting can be very raw. That's what draws people to it. But then the artist is stuck living with these songs night after night. Do they have to dissociate themselves? Do they become actors, or do they relive that moment over and over and over? I find that that opens up a lot.

Bonnie Stiernberg People always make fun of stereotypically bad ques-tions like "Who are your influences?," but there are so many factors that can determine whether an interview's gonna go badly or not. Did they just finish a set? Are the two of you at dinner in person somewhere, or are you their twelfth phoner of the day? One of my worst interviews from years ago that I still cringe about to this day was Elvis Costello. He had been doing press all day, and after I got my first question out, he just paused and said that the answer had been pretty well documented at that point. And he was right! It totally had. But what I couldn't say is "Well, yeah, I know, but I just need to get a quote from you about it." But it taught me a really valuable lesson about not asking questions you already know the answers to and taking extra care to phrase things in a way where you're hopefully not gonna get an answer like that.

Gabriela Tully Claymore I think process is really interesting, and I don't think everyone feels that way. Some people are going to want to know fun, crazy, weird stories or get a good sound bite, but I feel like some-thing I always want to ask is where something was created, what were the circumstances that made it possible. And for some artists the an-swer is boring. They might be like, "I went to Philadelphia and I record-ed the album in my friend's basement and I slept on their couch for a week and that's how we made it." But the reverse is true, too. For exam-ple, an artist like Grouper, every album she makes has an attachment to a certain place and time, and there's definitely a story there and the environment influences the music.

Jes Skolnik For a long time I've always asked everybody that I interview, "If you have any closing thoughts, what are the things that nobody has ever asked you about that you wish that you could say?" And that always gets really interesting answers. I like leaving things open-ended for people to create their own narratives because the media is so good at placing very distinct narratives onto people about their lives, particularly marginalized people.

Matt Fink What I often like to end an interview with is asking the artist what they hope their listener will take from their work. I ask that one a lot, and I get the impression they aren't asked that question very often, and it often doesn't get a very good answer. But sometimes that can get a very interesting response, because I'm very interested in wanting to know what this artist wants out of our experience as listeners. When someone hears their work, what do they want that person to hear? What do they want that person to experience? Often they just say, "Oh I just want them to experience what they want to experience." But I kind of think that's a cop-out answer. I think they have an idea. I think they have a desired outcome. I don't think they want the listener to pick it up and say like, "This album infuriates me and I hate it, but for some reason I'm going to keep listening to it." I think they have an idea in their mind of what they would like the listener to do with their work, but they maybe haven't thought about it or don't feel comfortable imposing that on a listener.

Michael Azerrad I don't think I have any standard questions for musicians. I try to tailor each one to the particular person. To do otherwise would be to impose my preconceptions on them, and the whole point of the article is to illuminate *their* way of thinking about their music, not mine. But if I had to state a general theme for what I'm interested in, it's the pragmatics of being a musician—by that, I don't mean what effects boxes you use, but demystifying the process of making music and, in so doing, perhaps revealing its true magic.

David Marchese I would hope at some level I'm surprised by every answer I get. I don't want my subjects to be giving answers that I'm expecting they'll give, and I definitely don't want to ask questions that I already know their answers to. I remember—and I'm so appreciative that he answered honestly—when I interviewed Dave Matthews and I asked a question about drinking and he said that by some standards he probably drinks too much. I was surprised at the level of candor in that moment. And I would almost say the surprise didn't really register most fully until the conversation was over and I was reading the transcript. Sometimes you don't know what you've got until after the interview is over.

Jayson Greene Transcription is very dull, but I find listening to your interviews really, really helpful as a way of reexperiencing them. This is especially true for in-person interviews, because you remember everything about the encounter as you relisten to it. You remember where you were walking, or where you were sitting, or something else that happened. The story tells itself to you if you are open.

Amanda Petrusich These days getting meaningful access to an artist can be really hard. I turn those assignments down now, but when I was freelancing full-time and needed the cash, you end up taking jobs where you're going to get fifteen minutes on the phone with someone and then you've got to write a 1,300-word story and you're just pulling things out of your butt. There's just nothing there, and it's so hard. I really admire writers who can do that well, though I don't know if there are actually writers who can do that really well. It's an impossible situation. That's really hard and I think it's getting worse because artists are very protective of their privacy, and perhaps rightfully so, but this is the format that exists, and we can't keep going on in this way if we're not going to get the access we need to write a story. That's really hard, feeling like you come home with nothing or you come home with a few quotes that they've said to fifty other journalists before you, and then you have to find some new and interesting thing to say about them.

Ryan Leas You hear these stories from the '70s that are fucking insane. I once met a woman who is an older British music journalist. She had written for *Rolling Stone, Creem,* all the old guard. And her stories were unreal. She was on tour on a plane with The Clash for a feature, shit that wouldn't happen now for so many reasons. Nobody would let you do that now. That kind of unfettered access would be fucking crazy.

Andy Greene The challenge is some of the biggest artists in the world, they don't want to submit themselves to that kind of profile. Beyoncé or Kanye West or Jay-Z or Rihanna—these are people that we would love to have on the cover but they're unwilling to sort of submit themselves to a profile because they know they can go right to their fans without having the filter.

Ryan Leas Everybody's a little different now. Everybody is so aware that everything they say or do could be online in minutes. I think they behave differently. You don't really have bands throwing TVs out of windows. They're forced to be fairly savvy as business people, not just as musicians. I think we kind of lament that there aren't as many characters these days, but if people behaved the way that those people did back in the day, we wouldn't really like them. It's weird. I think the whole thing is a little more tame and matter-of-fact than the past. Part of that's reality, part of that's perception. I also think that there's also a little bit of a shared experience that there might not have been back in the day. Obviously there were smaller bands that didn't have money back then, too, that may be bigger now in our cultural memory, but I don't know what it would have been like to be in that position in the '70s or '80s. These people were, I think, elevated to a different position in a lot of cases and were sort of godlike and had these insane lives that were so radically different. I still interview people who have lives that are insanely different from mine, but a lot of the indie-level bands I talk to, they aren't getting crazy rich off of this. Their lives look a bit more like ours.

Jillian Mapes Artists don't need us. They have Twitter and Instagram. And I feel like so much of the news that we report on in music or entertainment culture, it's not announced through traditional means. It's not a press release. It's somebody said something on Twitter or Instagram. They don't need us to get the message out. If you're somebody like Frank Ocean—if you're on that level—you can just release a film and say whatever you want. You can dictate the context and the narrative of a piece of work.

Andy Greene The person you're talking to is usually trying to sell something. And there's always a gap between what you want to talk about and what they want to talk about, and the broader that gap is, the more difficult that the article becomes or that interview becomes.

Matt Fink Sometimes when I'm interviewing an artist, when it comes time to write the actual article I feel almost like that artist's publicist in way. I feel like there's been a certain set of talking points delivered to me through the interview and I feel like I'm just kind of repeating the story that was in the press release. You really have to work hard to get off that—those talking points—to find something new. And I feel like if you have an especially focused artist that knows exactly what those talking points are it can be really difficult to even get them away from them. I think our goal as writers should be to tell those interesting stories that might be beyond what the publicity team thinks is important, but I do think that is getting more difficult.

Andy Greene It can be really sticky. There's some people who are really tough personalities, really brittle people who often are really wealthy and are surrounded by yes men and are used to getting their own way.

Ryan Leas It's always surprising to me who's reticent to give you more time and who's open to it. Those moments are the cool ones, where somebody's really down to talk and you get to know them to some extent. Then there are some people who just don't like doing press. The

PR apparatus is a lot different than it used to be. There are the times where you get an hour. And I've done it plenty of times where you have to get a feature out of that.

Andy Greene It's a dying art. Even cover stories for some big magazines now it's like a forty-minute lunch with somebody. And we never do that. We insist on days and days of access to produce a real quality feature about somebody.

Lindsay Zoladz It's getting kind of bad with access and getting to spend time with artists and do that reporting. Even at a respected magazine we often don't get the access that we want. I know the big example that everyone has been citing was that Beyoncé was on the cover of *Vogue* and she didn't even give an interview to the journalist. And I think people are becoming terrified that that's becoming the trend, especially with big pop musicians who are really good at cultivating their image on social media. In a way they can do that promotion themselves and don't need the help of journalists they once needed before. I don't actually think that's true. I think as a fan you lose a lot from that if you're just getting the artist's point of view. And obviously I'm biased because I'm a journalist, but I think there's a slightly alarming trend away from the sort of access we used to get and it's hard, especially with print stuff for magazines. There's a lot of scheduling at work and the timing has to be right. And when we get access to this person there are certain exclusivity rules where certain competitors of ours can't be running a rival story. Stuff will get killed for that reason. There's a lot of behind-the-scenes challenges with it. I'm lucky that in my job as a critic I don't really need access to anybody to do my work.

Andy Greene I've had people tell me they'll talk to me if they get copy approval and I'll be like, "What are you talking about? That's not happening." There are some outlets that say yes to that shit. Or some people will say, "I'll talk, but you can't talk about about X, Y, and Z." and I say, "No I'm not doing the interview." It's ultimately rare. But I think as this industry struggles, for some people there are some outlets that are willing to do those things to get the story. But we have our standards. We will never agree to question limitations. Copy approval is ridiculous. I mean, no outlet would do that, that's respectable. We'd rather not have a story than have a compromised story.

Amanda Petrusich We're in this Taylor Swift–era where everything, including basic human emotions and reactions, are so aggressively engineered. Nothing slips through the cracks. You're just trying to see someone do something human or real instead of this weird performance of humanity. And so much depends on the publication you're writing for. I feel like if you're writing for a smaller place it's virtually impossible to get real access. It's a nightmare. For me at least I've started to say no to those assignments, which is a luxury I have because I also teach full-time. I wrote a cover story for *Paper* magazine a few years back. It was about Miley Cyrus, and it was a phoner. It was all they could give us. And granted, it was a long phone call. We were on the phone for maybe to two and half, maybe three hours—a long time—but that sucks. It's really so hard. And she's a great interview. She's very colorful. She's very smart and honest. She says whatever she's thinking. She's pretty unfiltered. I did a *Brooklyn* magazine cover story not too long ago about St. Vincent. And I think she's great and amazing. I think we chatted awkwardly while she was getting her hair and makeup done for the cover shoot. You can't really talk to someone while all these people are around, listening. And then we had maybe a thirty-minute phoner after that. And I had interviewed her before for another publication, and she's a notoriously difficult interview in that she's very savvy and she's very careful, as she should be. I don't fault her for these things, but I remember having to go home, and I had like a few quotes from the photo shoot and this sort of stilted, not-great thirty-minute phone interview, and it was just like, "What do I do with this? This is boring. She's not saying anything." And maybe I didn't ask the right questions. I'm certainly not absolving myself from the situation—and I had a great editor, and the story turned out fine—but it was just like, "How is this beneficial to either of us?" No one's going to remember this story because neither of us is saying anything. Why bother? I don't know, maybe that's a fatalistic way to think about it.

Jayson Greene Most major superstars don't even grant interviews anymore. And if they do, the fact that they did is its own story. "We actually sat down with Rihanna" is more than enough of a headline already. It doesn't even matter what the article itself contains. Readers don't need to know what she said to get them in the door. The fact that she showed up at all is tremendous news in celebrity world. Beyoncé doesn't do interviews at all anymore. She's the subject of writing. Even Madonna at her height was leaping into the fray and grabbing microphones and talking to every available person and giving quotes. That was part of her oxygen. That was part of the ecosystem she was in. Now, that's not necessary. And in some ways it doesn't even benefit them. With someone like Drake or Kanye, it's like interviewing a dictator from a small country where they say, "You're coming here on my terms. I'm going to handpick my reporter," and I think that's what it is right now. So it's almost like we're just interpreting the actions of the gods from underneath. That's how all the writing strikes me. "Beyoncé blessed us with this…"

Puja Patel Just the way that the album rollout has changed is so significant. Where music was once pretty accessed-based in terms of doing anything that involves reporting, it's nearly impossible to do that for some of the most iconic musical acts because they've become so protective about their narratives and are really insular on that front. And yet—and this is just my personal perspective with regard to helming a music publication—I think what that does to benefit journalists is that we are given the distance that we need to do actual reporting. Nineties-era *SPIN* to me was the ideal mix of criticism and reporting within a feature story. You could be with an artist for a very long time and be extremely honest about what your time with them was like.

Chuck Klosterman Prince was ahead of the curve on this. Prince's thing was, if you interviewed him, you could not use a recording device. You could not take notes. Everyone thought, "Oh, he's crazy. He's afraid people are going to misquote him." But that wasn't it. He was afraid they were going to quote him correctly, but use it in a context that didn't reflect what he really meant. But if you just had to sit with the guy and listen to him, and you couldn't transcribe or record anything he said, all you could really write about was your general impression of what he was like, and he was confident that would be positive.

Matt Fink I'm so envious of these writers who live in New York City and Los Angeles where every interview they do is in person. That's such a luxury to have that. You can look the artist in the eye and you can catch their reactions to your questions and you can talk about how they interact with their environment and the people around them. That's so revealing about a person. Whenever you're doing anything over the phone you really have to kind of guess that. I've done some Skype interviews that can give you a little bit more of that content, but it's still not perfect.

Amanda Petrusich There are rare cases where I'll prefer a phone interview. Usually it's a secondary interview when I actually need information, as opposed to a profile where you're just trying to get a sense of somebody. Writing anything more than a Q&A with just a phoner is really tough. I feel like readers don't always know how hard that is. You're like running in place. It's really tough to write scenes or to write color or write anything at all about this person when you've got, like, a Wikipedia page and some lame quotes. At least in person you can kind of see how a person moves, see their face. You can pick up on more subtle things.

David Marchese I find that older subjects are better for the kind of pieces that I do. They just have more life to talk about. That's not to say you couldn't have a fascinating conversation with an eighteen-year-old, but in my experience there are going to be more interesting conversational avenues to go down with a sixty-five-year-old. They've had more ebbs and flows in their life. They can talk about when they've been on top of the world and when they fell back down. They've also had the time to develop greater perspective on those experiences. And people like Quincy Jones whom I've talked to, you can tell they've reached a point in their lives where they don't care as much as maybe they once did about what other people might think of what they're saying. Having a more unfiltered conversation is always going to be good for me.

Chuck Klosterman The best time to interview anybody is at the very beginning of their career or at the very end. Old musicians are great because they don't give a fuck. They'll say anything. Interviewing someone like Robert Plant is awesome, because it just means nothing to him. And interviewing somebody on their very first record is also good, because they're being themselves and still trying to figure out who they are. The absolute worst person to interview is the person who got famous with their first record and is now releasing the second record, because they have just been fried down to nothing. I did a profile on The Strokes when their second album was coming out. I've used this example many times, but it's just kind of mind-blowing when you think about it—by the time The Strokes were releasing that second album, Albert Hammond Jr. had probably done more interviews than George Harrison did with The Beatles just because of the proliferation of media. If The Beatles went to perform a show in Cincinnati, maybe somebody from the local newspaper interviewed them, maybe not. If they did do an interview, the reporter wanted to talk to John or Paul, and the whole thing lasted twenty minutes backstage. But when The Strokes put that second record out, that's all they were doing for two months. They were being interviewed constantly. Sometimes eight, nine times a day. And I could just tell from talking to those guys that they were asking themselves whether it was worth it. Did we make the right choice?

Josh Jackson I love a really good profile, and still maybe my favorite one I ever wrote was on Josh Ritter. And it was because I got to spend so much time with him, I really felt like I was writing something defini-tive, that nobody else had taken the time to do. And it's not like he's the hugest person in the world, but I was able to tell his story in a way that I knew had never really been told before. I had been following his career from the beginning and had encountered him on several occasions and then for that piece I actually took two trips, one to Chicago, where he was recording—we went to a Cubs game—and then I went out to Idaho and saw where he lived and had dinner with his parents. I got to write about a musician in a way that I wish I could read more of. You know, when we started *Paste* I would read those kinds of pieces in the *New Yorker* when they'd occasionally profile a musician. It was that kind of access, that kind of comprehensive story. You were getting the whole history of someone and you were getting a fuller understanding of a person who made something that you love. And I love doing that as a writer.

Andy Greene I love the opportunity to talk to artists that I really admire, people like Bruce Springsteen or Peter Gabriel or Elton John, and just have carte blanche to just ask anything I've always wondered about their lives and really burrowing deep into the process. I love Elton John, and to just be able to spend an hour on the phone with him and just get really in-depth on something I've always wanted to know and I ask a bunch of follow-ups, it's very it's very gratifying.

Ryan Dombal I interviewed Daft Punk around their last album, which was memorable. They were one of the first electronic acts I really fell in love with as a teenager, largely from watching all of their wild videos at the time. I interviewed them during Coachella; they had rented a mansion in the desert and were just hanging out by the pool with their friends. It was a surreal. A couple of my friends asked me after the interview, "Did they wear the masks during the interview?" And I was like, "No that would be bizarre." But just the fact that that question was a fairly legitimate thing to ask made the whole thing strange.

T. Cole Rachel I went to Atlanta to do a story on Deerhunter for the *Fader,* like when the band was first kind of really blowing up, and I had a really crazy but also kind of amazing and very moving experience with frontman Bradford Cox. It was not what I expected it to be at all. It became something totally different. I remember I spent a day with Courtney Love, which was crazy but also really kind of touching. She was really very sweet and very nice to me and very candid in a way that almost made me uncomfortable. It was like where people say things in your presence and you're like, "I can't really—I should not print that or it will be a problem."

Stephen Deusner I interviewed Robert Plant for an *American Songwriter* cover story a few years ago and had the best time talking with him. It was one of those things where I had made my script of questions, and he mentioned something and we just took that and ran with it. We ended up having this really casual, loose, yet very informative conversation that never felt like it was an interview. I don't know what it was like on his end, but as somebody who does a lot of interviews, it was nice just to have a conversation. I also loved talking with Mavis Staples. I didn't even ask a full question. I think I got about half the thought out of my mouth and she just started talking. She was just so funny and smart and gracious and enthusiastic and everything you want Mavis Staples to be. She's literally my musical hero. If I ever met her face-to-face, I would be a blubbering mess.

Andy Greene The best was Roger Waters. With Roger Waters I was doing a big Q&A with him about *The Wall* movie that was coming out, and I always like this to start with small talk, so they just get used to talking. And like literally two seconds before the phone rang there's breaking news on the TV that Joe Biden was not going to run for the presidency [in 2016]. It was this breaking news story. So then the phone rings and I go, "Hey Roger, did you see the news about Joe Biden?" And he was like, "What?" I said, "Did you see the news about Joe Biden? He's not going to run for president." And he goes, "What did you say?" And I said, "Joe Biden is not going to run for the presidency." And he's like, "Aaannnnnd?" And I go, "And I'm surprised." And he goes very sarcastically, "Oh, thanks for sharing your opinion. How Fascinating." And then my whole heart sank into my toes. I thought, "Oh god. That did not go very well." So then I had to just switch gears instantly, and I said, "Okay. *The Wall*. How do you see *The Wall* now, like, differently and then you saw it before? Does it mean anything different to you now than when you wrote it? And he goes, "[Sigh] Do you know how many times I get asked that question?" And I was like, "Oh god!" But what you have to do is not show your fear. I plowed forward, and it got good. I mean, he really yelled at me once. Later on I had asked about a Pink Floyd reunion, and he starts screaming at me. And he's like, "You know how many fucking times..." and he starts screaming, like really loud. But he yelled on the record, which is good. So the Q&A was great. I put in parentheses "[screaming now]" and people loved it. So if they want to yell at me, that's great. Just do it on the record. I mean, at the time I'm horrified, but when you read it, I get very happy. I love Roger Waters. I love him. He's great. He was honest with me. He didn't care that it was an interview. He just spoke his mind. That's awesome. I wish more people were like Roger Waters.

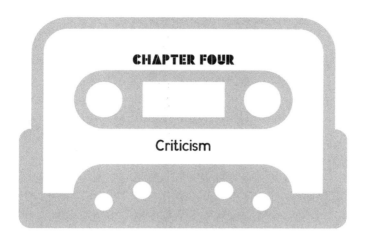

CHAPTER FOUR

Criticism

I f interviews, profiles, and features are at one end of the music journal-ism spectrum, criticism is at the other. There's no scheduling of phone calls or designated rendezvouses with a subject, no recording or tran-scribing conversations. Any personal interaction with an artist or band is unwarranted, if not outright discouraged. It's just you putting words to a page, making a point about the importance (or lack thereof) of a particu-lar song, album, or performance. "I tend to love musicians as people," says Rob Sheffield. "I love hearing them talk about what they do and what their ideas are. I love that. But at a certain point as a writer that stopped as my main interest. I'm not interested in their story about what they were try-ing to do. I'm interested more in what the music actually does. What they were hoping that the music would do is often hugely different from what the music does do and where the music goes. So for me my favorite per-spective from which to write is as a listener. To me the weirdness of the stories in the music is so much weirder than the musicians themselves. It's just letting the music tell the story. It's not even that the artist is using music to tell the artist's story. It's almost like the artist is making the music and the music decides what the story is."

Just as a good interview places an artist in context of the resulting mu-sic, a good piece of criticism puts the music in the context of everything else. It's not trying to argue, but to analyze, dissect, and interpret. This is perhaps why in the hierarchy of music journalists, the critic is regarded with more prestige and respect than the profiler or reporter. It's why even today we know the names of Lester Bangs, Greil Marcus, Robert Christgau, Ellen Willis, and the progenitors of the form. Critics then and now aren't just taking a snapshot of a particular artist or event in time but are contributing to a conversation about what that artist or event means in the cultural landscape's past, present, and potential future.

It's easy for a cynic to argue that all a music critic's job is is to tell a listener whether an album or a song is worth listening to. But that argument—from a paradigm of gatekeeping, consumerism through recommendation, and the teenage-addled question, "What am I going to spend my hard-earned money on?"—doesn't hold up anymore. With the advent of the universal jukebox through the internet, progressing from Napster's online file sharing, Apple's iTunes store, and the rising dominance of streaming services such as Spotify, the idea of reading about a piece of music before actually listening to the track or record for yourself is archaically quaint. Factor in the trend of artists suddenly surprising everyone—critics included—by dropping a new album or song and making it available to everyone at the same time, music critics have had to abandon their long-standing role as a sound-describing go-between.

The consequences have been a blessing in disguise for critical music writing. No longer arbitrarily compelled to conjure unnecessary adjectives for the way a guitar part sounds or convoluted metaphors about sonic textures, critics are provided the opportunity and challenge to discuss what a particular piece of music is reflecting back on us, confronting larger topics such as race, gender, diversity, social class, politics, power, relationships, mortality, and other grand themes. Critical music writing is thriving in its modern form because it's no longer just about the music but also what it is playing parallel to in the wider world.

Carl Wilson One of the things I sort of figured out when I was in my twenties doing various kinds of journalism is that I'm not really a reporter. My social skills are such that I don't really like talking to strangers. I get pretty shy if I go to someplace to interview people. It's hard for me to walk up to people and ask them questions. Criticism is really where my more natural voice is and where it clicks with how my mind works.

Nitsuh Abebe It's weird where you have to wake up in the morning and your job is having an entertaining opinion about something.

Carl Wilson Taste is this engine of how artwork gets treated in the world. And there's an implicit kind of scale of cool that operates in different cultural spheres that people are always either consciously or subconsciously creating hierarchies. Hopefully part of what criticism does is subvert and complicate that and make us think about how those processes work.

Josh Jackson It helps you understand and better appreciate a piece of art. Not just appreciate, but it helps you better experience a piece of art. Criticism can help clarify things that a piece of art was doing for you and to you in a way that makes it more enjoyable but also where you're getting more out of it. It becomes more effective on you. And also it can teach you what is going on in a greater context. Criticism can lead you down a rabbit hole.

Ben Ratliff I think that critics contextualize and make connections from the subject they're writing about to areas of knowledge outside of it. They describe. For me, description is a central and basically ritual activity that complements or mirrors the ritual of the making of the art. By doing so I'm contributing to the discourse around some art. That's it, and that's all, and that's good enough. Whether my judgments will be heard widely or live on through the years—I couldn't care less. Art isn't made for the void. It's made within a context of people communicating back at it or around it. I'm one of those people.

Emily J. Lordi I think that it can give us a different understanding of the art. Because it's not always the artist's job to say everything about their own work, you know? They have their own perspective on it, which of course is valuable, and you take that into consideration, but I do think that often what a critic says about a work is more interesting than what the artist might say. Because they place it in a context—that is their job, to find a proper, and properly illuminating, context. This is especially useful when it comes to the work of artists who aren't as interested in saying very much, in providing that much commentary on their own work. They might say, "The work expresses how I felt." Well, okay. So the question for the critic is, "But what does it *mean?* What does it mean to us, as very different sorts of listeners? What does it mean at this particular time, in light of this present or historical context?" I think that that's really a critic's job, to be able to distill this broader significance and therefore help people appreciate the work even more.

Hua Hsu I think as, like, a literary historian I have this weird highfalutin sense of what critics have been able to do over the past two hundred, three hundred years. I think back to this quote I read from the British literary critic Terry Eagleton about how the early critics were a bulwark against totalitarianism. And I think it's true that one thing that a critic does—and this is probably why people hate them—is hold a mirror up to society and question why things exist or why things are popular. There is a way in which you are a level of friction against business as usual, the business of culture, with popularity, populism, and things like that. I don't necessarily think it has to be that, but I think that's always been my interest, what it means to inhabit this moment, what it means to be alive today, how we see ourselves, how we imagine ourselves, how we understand the limitations put on us, if any. I think those are questions I'm interested in as a critic.

Ben Ratliff What good is the critic when there are interviews to read with the artist? That's an important thing for critics to think about. I believe that critics shouldn't just take dictation from the artist about what the intent of the artwork is. Critics should be coming up with their own ideas, interpreting the work for themselves, after having immersed themselves in it and its context—as wide a context as possible, even wider than the artist built for it. This is different from misrepresenting an artist—I have no interest in doing that. Find a balance. Listen to the artist, but don't think too much about exactly how they want their work to be understood. D. H. Lawrence wrote a book called *Classic Studies in American Literature,* in which he wrote, "Never trust the artist. Trust the tale. The proper function of a critic is to save the tale from the artist who created it." I think that this, within reason, is good advice. I am not saying that artists are deceitful, misguided, trying to put one over on us—nothing like that. I'm just saying that the aim of the artist is the aim of the artist. And the aim of the critic is not the aim of the artist. Critics are allowed to believe that the artwork tells its own story.

Craig Jenkins The challenge is synthesizing what the thing means and how I feel about it. I think it's cutting through the noise. I think what I try to do when I write about a subject is present what the dialogue is, present what the conversation is, present what the art means and what it does, and then whether or not it does that well. The challenge for myself is always being evenhanded, and I don't know if that's necessarily the job of a critic, but I feel like my favorite stuff is always something that's been deeply considered. I don't want to get too far into my own opinion and think that I'm correct, that if there's this thing that I don't like it's bad because I don't like it. I try to see the value in things that don't necessarily interest me.

Joe Levy Opinions are easy to come by and not necessarily the center of the work. Opinions come down to "I liked it. I didn't like it." And they can be more interestingly explained than that. But the relationship between the audience and the performer deserves some understanding even as you work to explain why something is successful or why its success deserves something other than celebration. And that's something that I learned to take seriously early on.

Larry Fitzmaurice I was terrible at math. And I still am. But you know how mathematicians work backward to finish the equation. That to me, when I write something critical, positive or negative, it's usually, okay, I have an idea that "This artist is fill in the blank." So how do I get there? What are the steps I have to take and draw it out?

Amanda Petrusich I think sometimes criticism can get dismissed as this kind of succubus writing that's thriving on the creative work of other people and is in fact not a creative work in and of itself—that we're all failed musicians and blah-blah-blah, making garbage writing. I don't really buy any of that. When art gets released into the world, I think this idea that there's a person that sort of shepherds it from one side of the river to the other—I think that's lovely and useful. I think there's a real utility to criticism. I think it helps people find their way to art or to music that could be powerful or transformative to them. I think it helps people avoid things that maybe wouldn't work for them—even beyond the consumer guide aspect of it. I think the interpretive work of criticism is important to the artist. I think the fact that there's somebody listening and trying to figure out what's the narrative of this thing, and how does it exist in the world, I think artists need that almost more than people who read criticism. I think it's tremendously important, actually, that there be a studied response to that stuff. It's hard to imagine what the landscape would look like if critics just disappeared entirely. People would still be having conversations about music, and people would be seeking out others to talk to or read on music.

Ben Ratliff What I enjoy most about writing about music is getting to a place where I feel that I understand a piece of music as well as I'm going to, and that I can use my own writing voice and sensibility to describe it and take it apart. I can get my writing around it. I can have my writing interact with this thing.

Jim DeRogatis When I was seventeen Lester Bangs said to me when I asked him why he was a rock critic, "I've always had fanatical opinions to inflict on people. I'm a fanatical listener. I'm a fanatical record collector. I'm fanatical about playing music, and fanatical about writing about it." I mean, I think it all comes from the same place. Teaching it, talking about it on the radio, writing about it, playing drums in my stupid punk rock band, having a million records, it's all the same impulse, you know? Which I think is living. That was my fanzine: *Reasons for Living.*

Mark Richardson If you've been doing music criticism for a while, I think it's really hard to not listen to music and think at the same time. Every time you hear music you're thinking about all the things around it. There's a tiny element of that that's kind of annoying, probably just because you might be missing out on some kind of pure experience. But I think there's a part of your brain that switches on as a critic, where you're listening and maybe enjoying and loving it, but there's this small part of you that's always interrogating what it means and trying to understand what it is. You're not just enjoying what you're hearing but trying to understand why, or if you don't like it, trying to understand why. I think that part of your brain becomes hard to turn off with music once you've been doing it for a while.

Chuck Klosterman My perspective was always that music criticism is for people who like music so much that they enjoy thinking about it, even when they're not actively listening to it. I mean, that's how I always was. I wasn't just into *listening* to KISS. I wasn't just into *listening* to The Beatles. I liked to think about KISS. I liked to think about The Beatles. So when I read someone writing about those artists, it was always great, because I knew that the next time I played that music I was going to inject what I had learned—what the other person's opinion was or their perspective on what makes something good or bad—back into the music. That's really the only role I saw. It was just like, "I want to write something that people enjoy reading." The fact that it was about music was almost secondary.

Steven Hyden I would say that a critic is someone who is maybe more articulate than the average casual fan, someone who is probably more self-conscious in a way about the listening experience. I think a lot of people say, "I either like something or I don't." But a critic says, "Well if

I like it, why do I like it?" There's this sort of self-interrogation process that happens, and that's how you sort of end up intellectualizing the listening experience. I mean, it's hard for me to say what casual listeners are like. I'm not a casual listener. I haven't been for a long time.

Puja Patel I think we're also being way more aware of how the current cultural, political, and social narratives affect the way that we write about music. I think people who are glib and don't take context into account when tied to music are now being forced to—it's the norm now. Where before trumpeting your opinion was the strongest cultural norm, being thoughtful is the cultural norm, which is astonishing.

Carvell Wallace For me music criticism is just a branch of culture criticism. When a song comes out, when a piece of music appears and people want to know what to think about it, to me the question that's most relevant is, What does this work of art and what does this artist mean at this moment? What does the existence of this mean in response to our collective cultural moment, where we are headed, what we are fighting against, what we are fighting for, where do they fit into that? If you exist and you're making stuff on a public stage, you're in it. You might not have meant to be in it, but that in and of itself is a thing. Nothing is apolitical. If you exist and the politics of culture exists, then what you create exists within the context of the politics of culture. Just because you didn't mean it to doesn't mean that you're not. If you go and stand somewhere, you take up space even if you didn't mean to take up space. You still take up space. That's just a fact. So I think if you release a work, then your work is situated somewhere in the cultural context whether you intended it to or not.

Emily J. Lordi It's a political act. To be a critic of black music especially is a political act in a couple of ways. Number one because black musicians haven't always been thought of as artists, as craftspeople, period—they have historically been framed as just naturally talented entertainers who just stand up and sing because they're just good at it, or play an instrument because they just have some kind of innate gift for rhythm. And these primitive stereotypes are still with us in a lot of music criticism, especially when it comes to the work of black women. And it might be subtler, but I still see black women portrayed as people who just kind of naturally do things, as if they don't think very strategically about how they're going to present themselves, who they're going to collaborate with, and so on. Someone like Beyoncé, to give the most obvious and polarizing example, has an incredible amount of control over who she's going to collaborate with, how she's going to represent herself, what she's going to wear, how she's going to dance, every part of these massive productions. And I just think that there's so much more work that we need to do as critics to respect and evaluate those sort of choices *as* choices, to think about artists as agents who are also intellectuals and are visionaries and have ideas about what they want to do. So our job is to take that seriously and then to work to translate the meaning of what they're doing.

Jim DeRogatis I thought I had coined this phrase, but I hadn't: investigative criticism. It turns out there's a Pulitzer Prize–winning architecture critic at the *Philadelphia Inquirer* named Inga Saffron, and apparently when you win a Pulitzer you've got to write an essay for the book at the dinner. And she wrote about being an investigative critic, of how she had been a reporter in New Jersey covering development and crooked politicians' land grabs and how that reporting is part and parcel of all the criticism that she went on to do about the city of Philadelphia and its architecture. And that's what led to the Pulitzer. I think we should all do this. Everyone's a critic. You, me, the fifteen-year-old Taylor Swift fan, and the seventy-five-year-old Rolling Stones fan who doesn't think anything's good that has been made since their beloved Rolling Stones. Everybody's a critic, so long as they back up their opinions, and there's three ways to back up your opinion. I teach my classes context, evidence, and insight. The pizza in this place sucks. That's mere opinion. It becomes a review when you say the pizza at this place is awful because the crust is soggy, there isn't enough cheese, the sauce is sickly sweet, it's overpriced, etcetera, etcetera. That's evidence. Insight. You know, you and I are two different people. We stand in front of Edward Hopper's *Nighthawks* at the Art Institute of Chicago and we see two different paintings. We see the world differently. What criticism is, is the conversation between people who care passionately about the art. And when you tell me what you saw, and I tell you what I saw, we perhaps not only come to a deeper understanding of that art—not to change your mind or you to change mine—but what did you see that I might have missed? And also you tell me about yourself. Oscar Wilde said, "Criticism is the only civilized form of autobiography." When you talk about what you're seeing or hearing or tasting, you're telling me about you. And so insight and evidence in a context—Where did this art come from?—I think we need to investigate that to some degree. Every one of us, when we're listening to something or watching something, I don't think we have to be obsessive about it. I don't think we can apply a moral litmus test. I think 99.9 percent of the time we can separate the art from the artist. On the rare occasions we can't, we should be aware of the context of that art. Where does it fit in this genre? Who were these artists? How was this made? I think it enhances our appreciation of the art. And so, yeah, I think we've all got to investigate and criticize. Sometimes it's a little more dramatic than others. Who is Courtney Barnett, and why is this second album brilliant? I think understanding the context is going to make you have a deeper appreciation of that.

Joe Levy It's about intention and effect. I would like to be able to write about a song or an album from as deep an understanding of intention and effect as I can. And that could be musical intention or process, narrative or lyrical intention or process. The effect is obviously subjective and is almost always individually based—although not exclusively so. Ideally you get to write about songs or albums from a deeper understanding of them, and you don't always get to do that.

Amanda Petrusich One tough thing about being a critic is having to point out where someone else has faltered or fallen short. It's not fun.

I don't trust any critic who is relishing that that. But then it's this sort of ideal we have of, "Well, who is qualified to make those judgments?" Aren't all of us, as listeners and fans mindful, thoughtful consumers of this stuff? Doesn't that qualify us to have an opinion about it? Do I need to be able to annotate this music on a staff? Do I need to be able to identify all the different technical bits that are happening? Do I need to hear everything else this band has made before? Do I need to hear every recording in the history of time? At a certain point I don't know if that person, that ideal critic, exists. And again, in terms of having a real, honest, human communion with your reader, I feel like that person probably isn't your reader, either. Your reader is probably just like you—a person who likes this band and maybe heard a little bit of their stuff before or maybe heard other bands that sound like them or are operating in the same genre or mode. That's the person you really want to serve. But it is hard. Certainly it requires a lot of hubris and a lot of self-confidence in a way that I don't think comes naturally to most writers. I doubt myself all the time. I certainly don't know more than anyone else does. But you do hope your opinion is at least worth sharing, that maybe someone somewhere will glean something from it.

Jessica Hopper I think as I've become older, I'm much more interested in the other perspectives that haven't really had as much of a platform, lost histories, people who have sort of been erased. I'm like an activist judge. That's more where I feel like I want to be. I want to be someone who helps usher in critical conversation. I'm not interested in just talking about the aesthetics of something removed from a box. I really love context. I was never a passive consumer of music, but I realized most people are. You can love music and still be a really passive consumer. I worked with a guy briefly who was like, "You know how you listen to a song a thousand times and you never thought about the lyrics?" And I was like, "No. I'm literally not the person to have that kind of conversation. I've literally never done that." I'm the person who listens to "Little Red Corvette" and was like, "Wait, she had used condoms in her pocket or the condom wrapper?" There's a big difference. I'm not that person. I've never been that person.

Steven Hyden If you're a music critic and you have followers or readers who know who you are and they really like your thing, you become a person that they'd want to take a road trip with where you just talk about music and listen to records. Maybe they don't have a friend like that anymore that they can just talk about records with, but they have you. That's what I feel like music writing is like now. If you can be that for a reader then you have value. It's really about you, what your voice is, what your perspective is, and if you can provide something that is unique for people.

Lindsay Zoladz A lot of times when a piece of art makes you feel some sort of way, a lot of times you can't really articulate it. It's complicated. Very seldom do we listen to a record and it's the extreme of "This is the worst thing I've ever heard and I never want to hear it again" or "Oh my god, this is the best thing that I've ever heard in my life." Most experiences with art are somewhere in that vast spectrum between those two things. Especially nowadays with the internet, where everything has to be the best or the worst—or the loudest—to get attention, those complicated feelings in the middle, which are most of the ways we respond to music, those can be really hard to articulate. I think that's the job of a critic, putting into words the stuff maybe you don't have time to sit down and really think through or that you couldn't put into words yourself. The reviews I most like to read kind of pick up something that was somewhere in my brain but was like a preverbal idea that I couldn't quite articulate. Like, "Yes! That's was exactly how I felt all along. I just couldn't say it like that." That's always the highest compliment I can get when people say that to me. Not that I want people to agree with me all the time.

Amanda Petrusich I will say—I've thought about this so much—writing about music is so fucking hard. In my experience, it's so much harder than writing about anything else. When I started writing about film, I found it so much easier. I just remember feeling like I had been run-ning with cinder blocks tied to my legs, and suddenly someone had cut them off. It was just like, "Oh, narrative, and character, and a scene I can describe, a story I can recount!" Writing about something as abstract and nonnarrative and complicated as music is extraordinarily diffi-cult. When I was really grinding it out as a young critic for *Pitchfork* I was writing two reviews a week, which maybe doesn't sound like a lot, but man, you really learn how to describe things that are not easy to describe. And I feel like that skill I picked up early on by virtue of having that job—even now, it serves me well in my writing. Learning to be a music critic is really good bootcamp for any other kind of writing you want to do because you're describing things that are not easily de-scribed, and you have to really work to do it well.

Steven Hyden I feel like songs never sound exactly the same way to every-body. It's always a little bit different depending on what your perspec-tive is. So if you're a music writer there's a lot of imagination that has to be infused into it because you are writing about something that you can't see or touch.

Maria Sherman With music writing we've dedicated ourselves to creat-ing ideas out of something that is so hard to define and describe. And the language for it changes so much as music continues to change and genres become more hybrid.

Jillian Mapes So much of critical language too is so adjective-based. We have this joke at work, this dream of writing a record review with no adjectives. Can that exist and can someone actually do it?

Lindsay Zoladz I've talked to so many music writers who are just like, "I'm out of adjectives about how ethereal something sounds."

Craig Jenkins I spent a year or two writing for this experimental music blog and they were tossing me stuff I had never heard before and stuff that didn't have words or lyrics. Sometimes the music could be this long ambient drone. And so talking about the sound of a piece is the easiest thing to do for me. That's fun. That's dancing.

Ben Ratliff There was a time, I am told, when nongraded reviews of albums were widely read and widely discussed, and seemed to generate some kind of excitement or discourse. It has been decided—at least with the publication where I primarily worked—that this is no longer the case. Who decided that? It's not a who but a what—it was media analytics. Well, it's a what interpreted by whos.

Maura Johnston It's easier to position a record in somebody's head as a cultural product instead of an aesthetic product.

Mark Richardson Many people who I'm very close to in my life enjoy music, but they don't really enjoy thinking about it at all or it doesn't really occur to them to do so. My dad, for instance, will like something and I'll ask all excited, "Well what do you like about it?" And he'll be like, "I dunno. It's good." And that'll be the whole thing. You gotta have to respect that for some people. It doesn't need to go any further than that.

Steven Hyden Music writing is not essential in the same way that it was when I was growing up, where I would often read reviews of records that I'd never heard. That was sort of the norm. You'd read *Rolling Stone* or *SPIN* and they're talking about *In Utero* and talking about how it's so abrasive and unlistenable and so different from *Nevermind*. And you, having never heard *In Utero*, you're like, "What the fuck is this record going to sound like?" And you're just sort of imagining what it's going to sound like. And you're sort of letting the critic guide your imagination.

Lindsay Zoladz I think the role of the music critic has changed. In previous generations, when stuff was just out there on vinyl and the radio, the role of the critic was often to really describe how it sounded, because these were songs you hadn't heard. I'm a big fan of Ellen Willis, who was the *New Yorker* critic in the late '60s and early '70s, and if you read a lot of her reviews now, a lot of it is describing what this Creedance Clearwater Revival album sounds like and whether or not you should buy it. There was a consumer choice at stake of "Is this good enough for me to spend money on it?" I think a lot of the best writing from that time honestly brought up larger questions too, but they were describing this experience for the listener before they had it. I think the biggest difference right now is that we're hearing this stuff at the same time the listener is. If a new Kanye song came out today and tweeted out the link on his SoundCloud, I'm hearing it the same time everybody else hears it. My job is no longer to describe what it sounds like because you've heard it already. I think there's some people who still get hung up on the old form and don't want to let go. I think some people who are more pessimistic than I am could say that means the critic is not as important now, but I just think it's a shifting of the roles. The responsibility of the critic is no longer to describe whether you should buy something or not. With streaming you don't even have to buy it. It becomes more about the ideas and the larger trends behind the songs and what this is saying about the artist rather than try and get in the nitty gritty of communicating what it sounds like.

Ryan Dombal There was a tipping point—I forget exactly when but I want to say in the late 2000s—when streaming music became more available. We made this deal with this service called LaLa, which was eventually bought by Apple, which was one of the first streaming sites where you could basically embed an album into any website. So, for the first time, people could read our review and then just click a button right next to it and stream the album. Now it seems quaint, but at that time, it was like, "Holy shit." It was such a moment. Since people have that access now, I think it's changed the writing for the better. People don't feel like they have to describe how things sound as much, which is oftentimes the most boring part of reading about music. Now you can just assume the reader can listen to what you're writing about, and it allows you to go into other aspects of the music, whether that's the lyrics or how the music or the artist is positioned in the culture—it frees you up to engage in these other things as opposed to trying to describe the guitar sound.

Steven Hyden What music criticism has become now is about creating this parallel experience where the person who has sought your review has made the decision that they love music so much that they want to experience it from someone else's perspective. In the same way that people love sports so much that they want to experience it through the perspective of their favorite columnist who's going to analyze it, it's the same thing with music. It's like "I've already heard the record, but I want to relive this, and my own perspective is kind of limited, so if I can hear it through this person's ears in a way it's like hearing it again for the first time."

Jessica Hopper Criticism now is I think engaged with some pretty different principles, and expectations on artists. I think because artists are much less accessible to journalists, and often much more filtered and media trained—there is sometimes less to entertain, consider, and engage with in terms of the ideas or execution of a thing—song/album/aesthetic. We are more on the outside trying to analyze sometimes assumed intent. There is I think a greater expectation on artists to make stands, and still I think a lot of art is less engaged politically and personally for that reason. Also, plenty of pop music is written by six people crowded around a laptop, and so what is political and personal when it comes via committee?

Ryan Leas The circumstance of the digital era is it's like everybody can have all this in their pockets at any moment. Not only all the new stuff, but they can have the whole history of popular music. It used to be that somebody maybe needed to tell you about this British band called New Order. And you had to decide based on that advice whether it was good enough to spend fifteen dollars, or whatever, on a record or CD. That doesn't exist anymore because you can stream whatever you want and find it for yourself. I think the liberating element is that we don't really have to play like consumer guides anymore.

Jayson Greene There's a huge inflection point happening. I think in some ways there's always going to be a need for critical writing, but there is also—I am trying to think of the way to put this—there's more music being produced than ever before in human history. There's more recorded music than ever before. And that changes the rules of engagement for everyone trying to write about it. It is really, really, really, really different from any other era of culture writing. The idea that we have a tidy and clearly defined separation between pop stars and underground rock, that's a relic of an earlier era where there was just less of everyone doing everything. Now there are so many artists working in so many genres that it's like dipping a ladle into the ocean. Who knows what you are coming up with, and what's in there could be a lifetime's worth of study. One person could devote the rest of their career to studying the various protozoa floating around in that one ladle. The word that everyone uses in the culture industry is "discovery"—I tend to shy away from it because it's so overused. But at its heart the idea is that you need to be guided through this landscape, and someone will do that for you. And so that naturally raises the question: If you are guiding me through a vast ocean of possibilities, why would you point out the shit that's not worthwhile? Why would you waste my time saying that something is not worth my attention when there is already an endless amount of stuff happening, and I'll only ever even hear a tiny fraction of it to begin with? In that way, music journalism's whole goal shifts. It's not making sense of an arena we can all see. It's guiding you through the infinite. I think that changes everyone's mission statements on some level. The work of a site like *Pitchfork* becomes ever harder when the idea is that we are trying to give you a snapshot. Because again it's like trying to take in the ocean. What are you really capturing? Those are intense trends to reckon with. It has profound implications for what the future of the field focuses on, how many directions it splits off into, and whether or not there will even be another major publication that is the publication of record for music.

Hua Hsu I think the main problem is that for the industry as a whole there's a surplus of opinion but very little interest in other people's opinions. It's that old adage of everyone being a critic. It's true to some extent in that everyone has an opinion, but I think because everyone has an opinion there's less of an appetite to seek out opinions that stray from yours or come out of different contexts or opinions that are "professional."

Ryan Dombal I was doing college radio at Northwestern University around the time AllMusic got big and the internet became this ultimate encyclopedia. There was this one guy who was a DJ there too, and he was on the snobbier side. He clearly liked knowing more than other people about music and would hold that over them, which is not a belief system I subscribe to. And one day he was looking something up on AllMusic and he was like, "I can't believe how easy it is to know about stuff. It's almost too easy. It's almost unfair." But I don't see any downside to the idea of people having that access to information. If someone's personal brand is being a snob, I guess that might be a problem, but I think that democratization of information has something to do with the fact that indie snobism has waned over the last fifteen years or so.

Carl Wilson There's really more value in the critic's ability to help you think about things that you've already encountered. A lot of criticism has shifted in that direction. Now in a lot of ways there's much more conversation about pop, and unfortunately less conversation about lesser-known artists. Part of that is driven by editorial priorities of online sites, but another part of it is driven by what's functional. Of course there are places like Bandcamp that now have people writing articles to try to help guide you to content, and a lot of the streaming services also have people writing recommendations. That's a part of the field that's opened up in a different way. But a lot of us have gone to saying, "Okay, here are the things that are already out there in the culture circulating widely and making a big impact. The interesting thing to do is discuss and debate what that impact is, try and pull that apart a little bit, and deepen the conversation."

Jes Skolnik I think that there is a lot to be said for the fact that now you can go and listen to at least a sound sample of something as a means of discovery. As you're looking for stuff to buy you can listen to at least part of a track if not a whole album before you buy it. And that has really changed how we do criticism. Before, so much of it was describing. So much of it was, "Okay, you can't listen to this right now, so I'm going to get into that," as opposed to building out the context around it and explaining what makes it special.

Mark Richardson It's interesting. Say fifteen years ago, you still might be looking at reviews purely to say, "Well what should I buy at the record store?" That would have been a normal thing to be doing. File sharing was happening, but CDs were still selling well and physical music was still the dominant mode before Apple's iTunes store. So back then it would be like, "I'm going to look at some reviews. I'm going to find an album that I want to spend money on and buy." In those days—and certainly going all the way back forever in pop music criticism—the idea of the record review as a buyer's guide was very prominent. Sometime in the last decade the idea that you're reading about things that you want to buy, that fell away a little bit. I think there's still a small part that's true in that you're still guiding people toward things to pay attention to. So even if you're not spending money now, you are still spending time to seek things out and listen to them. But I think the more salient part of it is that—and this was always inherent in record reviews—is that we're now reading about records in order to enrich our understanding of them, broaden our appreciation, and just make for a richer experience. Just by virtue of reading about things you can say to yourself "Oh I didn't think of that" or "Here's a way that someone else hears it. Now I'm hearing it the way they hear it or hadn't thought of." I feel like that kind of thing is much more prominent than it used to be. I also think that the people that really read record reviews primarily as a consumer guide probably don't read very many record reviews anymore, and that the people that are left want to read them because it enriches their understanding of music.

Ben Ratliff　I think what critics are struggling with now is, how can we create a piece of writing about music that can contend with simply streaming it for free? What the hell use is criticism when you can just listen to the fucking song? Why do you need a critic in that equation? In the old days you'd have to get off your ass and go to a store and buy the thing with money, and it was the critic who was sort of there to put it in context and, possibly, if they wanted to, give you a sense whether it was worth spending money on. The word "value" has become debased, but I'll use it anyway: now the critic really has to create some extra value. And I think it always comes down to the fact that while you're writing about the record or the musician, you'd better also be writing about something else, a question larger than the record or the musician currently under the microscope.

Carl Wilson　That's what's enjoyable about the game, right? I know a lot of critics try to avoid having their opinions contaminated by other people's opinions about the same thing, but I actually enjoy it best weighing in on something when I can go and read twenty-five or thirty things that people have already said about it and think, "Where do I fall in that spectrum of different opinions, and what do I think this conversation is about from the things that people have been saying about it?" The discourse around art is always just as interesting to me as the art itself. I don't really come at it as a pure fan or even an appreciator or connoisseur. I am interested in the debate and in the ideas. One of the benefits of the internet has been that it's much easier to be in contact with all of these other voices and have a more direct exchange, whereas when I was younger all these things that I was reading in magazines were very far away—especially as a Canadian, who wasn't in New York or LA, where there is a concentration of writers. In the past twenty years I've been able to bridge all of that much more easily, and now I really feel like I'm a part of that community, and that's really a pleasurable thing about it to me.

Nitsuh Abebe The idea of "Oh, I'm going to break down to you what this sounds like" becomes sort of pointless. If we're all listening to the song, conversation shifts to what other ideas you might have about it—people bring in ideas about, say, race in America, or perceptions of different archetypes of women. So that stuff becomes more interesting and popular to talk about than what genre the drums seem to be influenced by.

Stephen Deusner When you've got so much stuff on Spotify or iTunes or YouTube or however people listen to music, basically everything is accessible, so how do you even proceed? What kind of roadmap do you need? Maybe my job is that of a cartographer, where I'm drawing out the landscape for people to move through in a way that is rewarding for them or at least doesn't waste their time. But you're talking about these things, so that there's a record of them. I love to go back and read older music criticism to see what people thought about classic albums when they first came out. I'm always shocked to see people dismissing Led Zeppelin or Leonard Cohen. "Alienated Young Man Creates Some Sad Music." That's the headline to Cohen's first review in the *New York Times*, and it's very dismissive. I like that. I like the idea that none of it set in stone. That first impression is maybe not the one that lasts, but it's still an important impression.

Mark Richardson There have been a lot of other shifts in cultural writing that happened at the same time that shed more light on why people still read about records. The one that comes to mind most is how much writing there is now about television. There's so much great writing about TV, and say if you watched the new episode of *Mad Men*, the next day you read something about it online. You weren't reading it to see if you should spend time watching it or to see if it's any good or for any other reason. You saw something interesting and you wanted to hear what a writer says and kind of commune with their experience of the thing you just saw. So I feel like record reviews in some ways have become similar to that for a lot of people in certain situations.

Ben Ratliff I think that my work includes a lot more uncertainty now, and I'm fine with that. When I'm confronted with a piece of new music, writing about a piece of new music, in the old days I would try to determine whether or not the piece of music was *any good*. These days I don't really have to do that so much anymore. What's more in my mind is an extremely simple question on the order of "What is music for in the first place?"

Chuck Klosterman I reviewed records the same way all newspaper critics reviewed records. Every critic has, at some point in their life, reviewed a record having listened to it only once or twice or three times. There was no way around that. And at the time, when I did this in the '90s and the very early 2000s, the key was explaining that experience to people who hadn't heard the music *at all*. What is the expository nature of this listening experience? But that's gone now, because now we have to assume the reader has probably listened to the music before they read the review, or that maybe they're listening and reading at the exact same time. I just try to take the experience that I'm having mentally and make it tangible, to explain that experience in a way that makes somebody feel as though my experience is temporarily their experience. There are a lot of people who get into this business because they have a real craving to be a tastemaker. It's very important to them, the idea that they somehow can shape what people choose to listen to, or that they can promote the music that they think is significant and erode the music that they think is bad. I've never felt that way. I have no interest in persuading people to think the same way I think, and it's odd that so many other people want to do that. When I'm writing anything, all I think about is "What's the most effective way to do this?" I want to be clear, I want to be interesting, and I want to be entertaining. That's as far as it goes. Whatever it takes to get to that point is what I do. Sometimes that's just listing things. Sometimes it's writing about something that's totally unrelated to the music. Sometimes it's writing about something you remember about the artist before they made this record and how that memory is now changed. That's just sort of the way I do it. My style is no style.

Amanda Petrusich With reviews—and this is going to sound dumb—the challenge is just having an idea. Sometimes you put a record on and you're like, "Oh this is fun," or "Oh, this is good," but that's not an idea. And sometimes for me, no matter how many times I listen to something, I'll just be like, "I don't know. It's fine." You can't write eight hundred words about how it's "fine." At some point something has to click for you. Something has to open up into a bigger idea about what's going on here or what it means or how it relates to a particular moment. And sometimes those things appear and sometimes they don't. It's like rubbing the bottle and hoping the genie comes out. You just never know. That's the hard part for me with the review, having a real idea about a record.

Jim DeRogatis Number one is don't be boring. The problem is 90 percent of everything is mediocre, in any art form. Five percent is so truly awful and sometimes so offensive that you can get really worked up about how much it sucks. And then the other 5 percent, if we're being generous, is brilliant and genius. So the biggest challenge as a critic who is writing about it is assessing it in a "professional capacity." Is this something that we can get worked up about and passionate about, either because it's so bad or because it's so great?

Jenn Pelly I think it's important to remain an open and curious listener while also knowing yourself and knowing what you care about, because music is so endless. If you know what you care about and what you want to do with your work, you can resist getting distracted by the endlessness and you can form your own perspective. It might sound simple, but I try to do the type of music writing that I want to read. I think it's healthy to know when you should detach from the echo-chamber consensus of other critics in order to figure out how you actually feel about something. I think Twitter is an inadequate place for that, most of the time.

Mark Richardson I think developing your own ideas is a huge challenge, probably because you're inundated with the ideas of others now. Albums now are kind of collectively digested and they become part of a collective public perception and experience. So being able to meditate and develop your own ideas is hard. It's not a place that everybody can get to. Fighting against a kind of groupthink and really trying to get to what you think about a particular record on an individual level is one of the hardest things right now.

Hannah Giorgis I think there's a fundamental difference between—and this sounds superbasic—"Do I like this piece of work" and "Is this a successful piece of work?"—not in the commercial sense but, "Did this artist do what they set out to do?" And I think there are plenty of things that I can recognize as being good or being great that aren't going to be my favorite thing. It feels like my job is to say, "Well here are all the little pieces motivating and behind and around this piece of art, and I'm going to present them to you in such a way that makes evaluating this art for yourself—as a reader—either easier or more rewarding." That to me feels more important than necessarily evaluating on a rubric.

Laura Snapes If I'm trying to assess a piece of music, or a show, I suppose I either want to illuminate its cohesiveness, if it's a good, well-thought-out piece of work, or its contradictions if it's flawed. I'd like people to read my criticism and come away having understood something about a record that they might not have thought of before. I also always want to give marginalized artists the serious consideration that their straight, white, male peers automatically command from a large number of critics with large platforms. The biggest challenge: it's easier to point out all the reasons why something is bad than why it's good. I think that's something that most people find. If you think a piece of work is great, it's pressing buttons within you that you might not even understand, whereas I think most people are acutely aware of their bugbears. My view of criticism has changed insofar as I used to think an album was a puzzle that needed solving, that I needed to connect all its loose threads into a coherent thesis. But years ago I read a great Rebecca Solnit essay on criticism and understood that a good critic lets the work breathe, and doesn't try to pin it down to a single meaning.

Jes Skolnik That's the thing that I always tell people who are writing reviews for me. Just pull out what makes this special. Pull out, whether it's contextual, historical, its approach, instrumentation, just pull out what you think are the constellation of things that make this record stand out to you.

Emily J. Lordi I think my strength as a music writer is much more about the detail. I'm never going to be the person who knows all the things. My husband is more like that. He's a completist. He wants all the obscure outtakes and sessions, and I think jazz in particular has inspired that kind of drive to acquire and listen to everything. And that's just not me. I don't know everything, and I'm fairly comfortable—especially the older I get—with not knowing everything. But I think my particular strength is to kind of zero in on a moment. Even small things. Like why did this singer breathe in this particular place? Or what does it mean to intone a line or a phrase in this way? And that approach is as much informed by the poet Nathaniel Mackey as it is by any of the music writers that I've read. Mackey is a poet who writes a lot about jazz, and he also has works of criticism where he will read into, for example, the gravel of Louis Armstrong's voice—and he'll do a lot as a poet with that and generate a great deal of meaning from that. What does that gravely sound tell us about the possibility of black expression? What does that tell us about black life, or Armstrong's very particular life, as expressed through his art? That ability to move from the very, very particular out to the massively significant was something that I was really struck by in his work, and that was the kind of thing that I wanted to do.

Ben Ratliff It all starts with listening in real time. If I feel that if I understand too much from the start about any record based on its words or its concept, I feel uneasy. I want it to get back to the music as much as possible. I trust that the music is going to be telling the truth about what it is, even more so than the words, and definitely more so than what the artist is saying in interviews.

Carvell Wallace Learning how to observe is a lifelong art. It's not just seeing. It's seeing and seeing again and seeing underneath and then asking questions and then seeing more. And so given who I am and where I'm situated in society, if I am good at observing, then I'm going to see things that are important and that have to do with race and class and power and systemic oppression. And if I do the reporting part well, which is putting those observations into words, then I'm going to communicate those things in a way that people hear and feel. And so if I do my job, it's inevitable that I will bring forth a narrative that is maybe somewhat different from the dominant narrative. Because the dominant narrative still has a long way to go before it's completely inclusive. I don't think of it from the outside, "Oh I have to bring something that isn't there." I think that if I do the tasks of being a writer and critic, then I will inevitably bring something that isn't there.

Jayson Greene Note taking is what makes writing writing. It's the only way to really work. As I collect notes, I see what they say. Usually everything I do starts a little mass of notes and then it becomes clear to me what I'm trying to build.

Jes Skolnik The dominant mode of music criticism for so long was this very flowery bullshit. And I think that a lot of us learned to write to that and it's not necessary. If I never see the word "ethereal" again I will be so happy. Or "glimmering." You don't need as much purpleness as you think you do. Sometimes the thing that you're the most self-satisfied about where you're like, "Yeah, that phrase is good!," cut that shit out. There is a balance you can strike between beautiful writing and effective writing. Finding that balance is a lifelong challenge, and I've gotten a lot better at it, and I look forward to getting even better in future.

Mark Richardson I taught a college course for a semester in Chicago a couple of years ago. And you really get a sense of when people sit down to write a record review if they're doing it for the first time. They often think that a record review is about expressing your opinion. While there is certainly opinion in there and you need to have a take on the music, the fact of having an opinion and telling somebody about it, that in itself is not at all interesting. Everybody's got an opinion. Who cares? Is the opinion the most important thing or is it everything else around it? It takes a little while for younger writers to understand, to click into that. Talking about what the music is and how it works and how it delivers what it's trying to deliver, the relationship between the music and other things that are going on in music, that's where the really interesting stuff is. And accessing that kind of stuff takes a lot of work and practice.

Hua Hsu I think as a writer I've had these moments where I've kind of tried on other people's voices or other people's personas—maybe not in ways that are superobvious—but I think when I started off I was definitely more polemical, being a skeptic or even maybe a cynic about certain things. It's not that I thought everyone should be listening to what I'm listening to, because that sort of robs you of whatever you think is unique about yourself. Now, I think I always try to leave space in a piece for the reader, and even if I sound really authoritative I'm really just trying to perform an authority over my own reaction to something. I tell this to my students sometimes: it's different to be an authority over your own experiences versus an authority over an argument or a premise or body of knowledge. I'm always trying to give the reader some sense of why I am reacting a certain way, but I don't necessarily assume anyone else will feel that way or has to feel that way. That's how

I approach it. I don't necessarily feel like it's my job to tell you whether something's good or bad. I'm more interested in—and this is a weird way of putting it—I'm just more interested in why it exists and what forces caused it to appear now.

Puja Patel I think that we can still speak from a point of authority while acknowledging the subtleties and the nuance of something.

Amanda Petrusich Because you're not necessarily reporting when you're writing criticism. I feel like the writing can end up being really static because it's all sort of born from the recesses of your mind, so I will sometimes encourage my students to include action of some sort—somebody doing something, a description of someone doing something, and to write that scene. Or you can watch performance footage, or watch an interview and find a way to describe how someone does something. Just to try and get some action in there, so it's not just all editorializing.

Carl Wilson I don't know if there's a general template. A lot of it depends on whether I'm already familiar with the artist, how conversant I am with the genre they work in. There's a form of listening that's just "What is this?" And then when you have a stronger sense, you then go, "How does this relate to and change and develop from what's gone before?" And then you just sort of wait for things to jump out at you. A couple of listens in, you start going, "Oh, okay. I see this thread that's swimming through here," or that there's a musical technique or sound or timbre or texture that is being introduced. So it's different every time. I try to listen as much as possible without making judgments the first time, which is a struggle because your mind naturally does that. You've got to go "Nope, shut up and just listen."

Jes Skolnik I come from a background where my undergrad and graduate studies are in American studies—and in particular labor history of the Americas. So my background is as a historian. That's something that is important to me personally, and it's been something that has always jumped out in the criticism that I really enjoy, providing that sort of contextual understanding. It's something that can give you multiple perspectives on a piece of art in a shorthand sort of way. It grounds it in the histories of certain movements, the histories of certain artists. You can get at the personal aspect of things, you can get at the cultural aspect of things. There's no truth in criticism, but building out the history gives the reader more of an informed background, and you can get at some very complicated stuff in a very simple-to-read and -digest way, which I think is really important.

Lizzy Goodman I studied classics in college, among other things. And when I was a classics student, obviously I studied all this mythology. And early on I really felt strongly that pop stars were the sort of gods and goddesses of our contemporary society. The pop stars are the top of the food chain of celebrity. If you're at a miscellaneous entertainment industry party, the actor is always kissing up to the rock star. It's really weird. Not-even-that-awesome rock stars will have more power in a room than really famous actors. It's so strange. But that's the kind of hierarchy. Britney Spears was really interesting to me not because I necessarily loved Britney Spears's music or thought she was some powerful artist—although I might also make that argument in a separate case—but I was obsessed with her and interested in her and wanting to write about her because of the phenomenon of her. What does it say about us? What does it say about that moment in our culture that we're worshipping her? What are the things about her that we're worshipping? It's a mirror. Who you choose to worship as a society is a reflection of how you see yourself and what you value. For me that was kind of the way in. Pop stars are Demeter and Hera and Zeus and Apollo. That's who they were to me. These are these outsized caricatures of our sense of self. And that's what I want to write about.

Hanif Abdurraqib I think so much of my interest in criticism is less about getting people to like a band or musician or whatever and more about seeing if I can challenge them to go on an emotional journey. I could talk about the technical aspect of music all the time, but I'm more interested in the emotional aspect and trying to build a bridge to someone who otherwise might not listen to something. For me at least, with music there's always a feeling first. I'm often trying to translate that and what it means. I've always viewed music as emotional first and then cerebral.

Carl Wilson There's a middle stage where you do start having theories and making judgments. The last stage is to question those theories and judgments as well and see if you might be going the wrong direction. Ultimately it's about what the things are that call to me most strongly, and if they don't, then why not?

Ben Ratliff I like the critical procedure of intermittently zooming backward into an absurdly long view: pretending that you're coming from another planet and looking at the subject—the music—looking at it, listening to it as if you're not intimately familiar with it and everything around it. Pretending to have some kind of objectivity. I call it "squinting," in that you're able to sort of fuzz up your vision of it. You can just sort of make out the outlines of it. You're listening to the outlines of it and the general suggestion of it. You're thinking, "What does this remind me of? What other thing does this suggest?" This is a way of making criticism not become a bunch of inside baseball, cliché, or received sales pitches. If you can connect a new record by a musician that you know really well to other tendencies in the world beyond it, other thoughts, other energies, even other shapes, that's great. It lets air into the thing. It confirms that this record, by Jlin or Neil Young or Horace Silver or Mitski or Györgi Kurtág or Rihanna or whomever, has a place in the world outside of a small group of music obsessives, or a place in the world outside the mediated understanding of the work that the marketing team has designed for it. And then, of course, after the squinting and imagining and connecting, you have to zoom back in, because if you've done your work, you actually do know a lot about the work and its context, and you're nobody's fool.

Carl Wilson I like to filter my thoughts through an outside object. There's that initial sense of looking at something and doing the research and putting it in context, and then the interesting part is to think, "Well then, what do I want to say about this, and why is that important? Why does it matter to me?"

Chuck Klosterman With criticism it's almost the purity of its subjectivity. In so many other kinds of writing there is inevitably some kind of objective anchor. If you write about sports, certain teams win and certain teams lose. There are statistics. If you're writing about film or novels or plays, it's hard to write about those things without spending some time on the plot and the characters and the mechanics of how a television show works or how a film works. Music is not like that. You can be a music critic and never talk about lyrics. You could also be a music critic who only thinks about lyrics. You can be a music critic who usually just ends up analyzing the kind of person who listens to that kind of music. You see this with people who write about the Insane Clown Posse or the Grateful Dead, or any group where there tends to be a greater emphasis on the ancillary culture than the content of what the band is producing. What you're really doing when you're reviewing a record or reviewing a song is you are literally trying to translate an emotional experience into letters and sentences. That's literally what you're doing. You're intellectualizing an experience that is consciously meant by the artist to be emotive. It quite rare that you find a musician who would say, "My only real interest here is that someone will intellectually respond to this." So with music, it's almost like the writer invents the meaning. Now, there's a certain kind of critic who would hear me say that and they would be outraged. They would be like, "That's not true." They would say, "There is a quantitative difference between the Talking Heads and Kansas, and it doesn't matter how you personally feel about Kansas. The Talking Heads did something more important, more meaningful, and more artful." And I totally get that. I make those same distinctions myself, all the time. But the fact of the matter is that if the writer is entertaining and talented, he or she could convincingly argue that Kansas is better than the Talking Heads. That absolutely could be done.

Carl Wilson Taste is a tool that you use. It's not extraneous. You need to be able to be sensitive to your own reactions and your own value judgments and all of these things. What I came to in the course of working on my book [*Let's Talk About Love: Why Other People Have Such Bad Taste*]—and the book was an outgrowth of having thought about that subject while doing criticism for several years—is that taste isn't the end goal. It's easy to mistake that for the end goal of criticism. Being able to *examine* your tastes, being aware that other people have different tastes, and thinking about what the relationship between those things means—that is a vehicle to get you to a conversation that's more interesting than ranking things or just proclaiming the superiority of one thing over another.

Jillian Mapes When I review a record, I'm less interested in the really technical. I'm more interested in how music works for the people who are listening to it, the function it serves in culture, those kinds of more macro ideas. I know you can't review every record like that. It typically has to be a record that does play a role in culture and work in that way versus a very small band. But for me, I love criticism.

Carl Wilson I think for most critics when they're young there's pleasure in writing the slam review where you think you're being very clever. You're either unleashing a stream of insults or making some argument for why this music is the reason the world is a bad place. I try not to do either of those things anymore. If I am going to say what I find messed up about something, it'll be couched within a counterargument with myself. It's like, "Okay, something seems wrong or off about this or perhaps something's wrong about the way that it's being received," and I'm trying to figure out what the sand in that itch is. "What's the issue at play here?" So it therefore becomes not so much about whether this artist is bad or in bad faith, and more about what's at play in this reaction, whether it's my reaction or a reaction that we're seeing at large. Radiohead is a good example. I've never understood the acclaim. People whose tastes are fairly similar to mine are huge fans, and I was always a little mystified by it. And so when Radiohead's *A Moon Shaped Pool* came out, I intended to write about this lifelong indifference and antipathy to Radiohead. But it turned out that with that record, for some reason, I felt like there were no stakes left in that argument for me. The thing that annoyed me when they were in their prime has gone away. So what went away? That became what the article was about—whether they had changed or whether the context of the music had changed.

Ben Ratliff As a critic, I'm not writing for the artists. By that I mean I'm not writing so as to give them advice about how they could do it better or differently next time. I'm writing for other people—everybody else in the world except the artist. I think artists value their fans and have sophisticated ways to access them—manage them and sort of organize them. Critics almost by definition are beyond their easy control. They can't be managed by the artist, or oughtn't be. I would imagine that annoys certain artists greatly, but I don't think about it much.

Brittany Spanos There's a constant dread of a surprise album.

Tom Breihan With the speed of the internet you do feel a great deal of pressure to sort of have that thing in your back pocket and to say something about that thing that just came out. It's kind of fun though. It's like a race to figure out your take on it. I always try to couch it in like, "Yup, I'm just hearing this too, so this is just my initial impression." It's exciting when everybody's thinking about something, everybody is trying to come up with ideas about it, and everybody is trying to write something good but also write quickly. I feel like most publications try to put their good writers on those crucial releases. There's something about, "Okay, I'm the go-to guy when this album comes out, and I can get to see what Jon Carimanica says about it or Lindsay Zoladz says about it," all these writers who I love and respect. And I'll get to read their things and be like "Oh fuck. I wish I had thought of that" or "Oh, I think I handled this idea better." It's like in *Ghostbusters* when the alarm goes off and we're all running to throw on our proton packs. That's the exciting conflict. That's when the adrenaline really gets going.

Carl Wilson It's the biggest shift in how this work gets done in recent years. There is a way that it's superfun for fans, and a part of me tries to engage in that spirit: "There's this new record. It didn't exist yesterday and it exists today." At its best there can be a feeling of being in a festival of discussion and debate. But it really squeezes out the space to be more reflective. You're much more likely to be wrong—just flat-out wrong about things, because you've stayed up all night listening to this thing and formed what impressions you can. Even three days later you can be like, "Yeah, no. That wasn't really it." And that's a frustrating thing. It's also frustrating to be asked to stay up all night, in terms of the working conditions of the job.

Hua Hsu Something comes out, by noon the next day everyone will have their review up. All these people just stay up all night writing. I have very dark memories of doing this and being filled with self-loathing and regret. But I feel like now what happens is there are those first responders, so to speak, but there's also now this pattern that we recognize where there's the first response and then there's the response that comes right after that, where people say, "Well, was the initial take the right take?" And then maybe the next week there's the even more metaresponse about what this back-and-forth says about this moment. And I don't think that's bad. I think that all of these kinds of conversations are necessary.

Carl Wilson Culture is available with a click, and while that means you might be able to jump around and sample it yourself, there's still a value in having somebody out there who's dedicated more time and maybe has more context than you to recommend things that are worth checking out.

Jes Skolnik I think that right now we're in a space where people really respond to critics in a very different way than they ever have, and have access to us in a way that they never particularly did before. Twitter's a fucking wild and terrifying place, and I hate that you have to maintain a Twitter presence in order to be a freelancer in this world.

Brittany Spanos I think a lot of writers fear, like, major fandoms coming after them, these fans who just disagree with your take on something. I know that a lot of writers have gotten death threats from fans and things like that. I feel like Twitter has made things more volatile.

Andy Greene You get thick skin with the comments because so many are just telling you to go fuck yourself or something like that.

Mark Richardson People have a very visceral emotional response to it. It's hard for a lot of people if they really love something to see somebody say this is really bad, or vice versa. I think in some ways it's human nature for people to take that personally and think "Is there something wrong with my opinion because I'm seeing this drastically different one?" It makes them question themselves. It creates this kind of cognitive dissonance for a lot of people where they want to get defensive. There's just a lot of feeling wrapped up in it.

Jessica Hopper Sometimes that's the bigger compliment. Rather than people saying, "Oh your writing influenced me" or "I agree with you," it's those who take your work seriously enough to fucking fight you over it, be pissed off, or run a counterargument.

Mark Richardson On social media an artist and critic are presented on an even plane. The idea that an artist and a critic are aware of each other, and they're both speaking in a space, and fans of the artist might also be aware of the critic, it kind of creates an unusual situation. There's a closeness to it that really wasn't there much before. For a younger writer particularly there's a certain amount of fear there, because if you write something about an artist that is maybe not totally glowing they may say something about it and their fans are going after you. It can be pretty unpleasant, you know? I mean if you're twenty-two and you're not totally confident in what you're doing, it can be a pretty harrowing experience, I think. Just as an example, there was that time Ryan Adams covered Taylor Swift's *1989* and I wrote a *Pitchfork* review. I didn't think it was very good and I said so. And Ryan Adams, of course, is an artist who's on social media and he also speaks his mind and has got a reputation as being somebody who will call someone out. So he said something about my review and something about me personally. I can't recall. But for many days on Twitter I was besieged by Ryan Adams fans saying I was an asshole or an idiot. It's definitely not a big deal, but that was one of my glimpses into the world where I thought, "Boy if you were a certain kind of person and maybe you were younger and early in your career and this was happening, this could be pretty harsh and frightening and make you feel bad, and probably the next time an opportunity came around to write something maybe you wouldn't because you're like, 'Oh God I don't want the grief.'" Which is fair. If you're going to do criticism and talk honestly about what you think of records, including things you don't think work, you've definitely got to be ready for people to say that about your work.

Jim DeRogatis I teach "Reviewing the Arts" as one of my classes. It's people who are passionate about video game design and film and music production. Columbia College is an arts school, so I have all these different majors who have to take a writing class and they write about the art that they love. And if they write about it well and have that conversation that I define as criticism, their lives are better for it. They appreciate the art that they love more. And even if they never write another review in the future, I think it's helped them come to terms with assessing the art that they love and the art that they dislike in whatever their field is.

Ben Ratliff At a certain point it gets beyond a job. It gets beyond cranking out a piece of copy. At a certain point it feels very physical. Listening to music is a physical experience. It's immersive. You get inside it. You feel it through your body. Then of course the writing itself becomes very physical. You're using your body and your mind. And so at a certain point it all kind of comes together. What good is the writing to the reader? I hope that they enjoy reading it; I hope that they don't feel pain when they read it, and that they are given an idea by it, or even a feeling. I hope that readers get some sense of the ritual aspect that I'm perceiving in any music. Occasionally a reader tells me, "I felt like I could hear the music that you were writing about when I read what you wrote"— even if they have not heard the music at all—and I'm usually happy to hear that. I don't take it to mean that I am involved in the musician's enterprise, or working in tandem with the musician. I take it to mean that my writing embodied something about the music in order to help clarify it from an outside position.

Steven Hyden If you can offer something that's unique and distinctive and can be insightful and smart but also funny and engaging and entertaining, that's the kind of music writing that justifies its existence.

Ben Ratliff I don't tell anybody that music criticism is a growth industry, but I do think that criticism has grown—both proliferated in volume and broadened in scope. The great promise of criticism is that it's is as flexible as, say, fiction. It's as flexible as any form of writing. It's constantly changing and constantly pointing to the future. And you can do anything with it.

Amanda Petrusich People turn to criticism and will continue to turn to criticism as a way—it's almost like finding your people, your tribe. What do other people think of this record? Are other people feeling the same things I'm feeling? Is this normal?

Ben Ratliff I do believe that music criticism is its own art, or at least that it's a literary endeavor. It reflects music, or is reflective about music, but doesn't need to have a parasitical relationship to music, because criticism is not only there for an evaluative function, to award a grade or a thumbs up or thumbs down. It has its own virtues and values beyond telling somebody whether or not they should spend money or time on a piece of art. That's consumer advice, which is at most a small part of criticism, if it should be there at all.

Mark Richardson I still love writing record reviews, and I think what really excites me is the idea of sharing ideas. The simplest way to put it, sometimes I'll hear a new record, I'll be listening to it, and my mind starts going. I start thinking about things. I start thinking about how this record makes you feel and what I'm experiencing. I'll start thinking about how it fits into what's going on in music now. I'll start thinking about the progression for this particular artist. All these ideas will just be rattling in my head. And then I just get excited about the idea of trying to put those thoughts in a coherent essay and share it with people. Maybe it's partly because I trained myself. I've written hundreds and hundreds record reviews at this point, but sometimes I'll just hear music and my mind will just start turning and I'll start thinking about it. Just the excitement of sharing those ideas is still there with me.

Jim DeRogatis It's a conversation between people who care passionately about the art. No critic worth her salt is trying to change your mind or convince you what to think about this art. They're trying to write about the world and themselves through the prism of this art. I don't think the vast majority of people think that deeply or passionately about music or film or food or poetry or visual art or photography, but those who do are living life to the fullest. And I think that being intellectually engaged and passionate about this art—and really what is more important? Politics? Sex? Religion? All of that's in the art. All of that and more. Every experience you care to name in life is in this art. Right? So this is just the forum for our conversations, for engaging with the world.

CHAPTER FIVE

Print versus Digital

The phrase "rock is dead" has been used numerous times in every decade rock 'n' roll has ever existed, and yet every time the supposed corpse of rock seems well and buried and the attendants of its memorial service disperse back home, it somehow manages to zombie its way out of the ground to shamble on in some redefined form. Parallel to rock's seemingly eternal demise has been journalism's own fatalist mantra: "print is dead." While it is certainly shortsighted to say that print as a form is completely kaput, it is has become undeniably diminished within the past few decades, particularly for music-based publications. "The internet has changed everything in countless ways," says Andy Greene.

The state of print periodicals varies from publication to publication, from those that have completely shuttered their print production and ceased altogether to those that have cut their ties with their former physical product for a new digital existence to those that somehow manage to make a survivalist stand, often with the monetary assistance of crowdfunding loyal readers, creative ad revenue, and sheer will.

Print has essentially become the publishing equivalent of vinyl, where a select but devoted group of traditionalists keep the medium alive. There are many music publications that now cater to these inveterate supporters of hardcopy by offering what amounts to a high-end, concept-driven supplement to their established digital enterprise, a collector's item in print worthy of a bookshelf's limited real estate.

The truth is, our readings habits have changed in a substantially short amount of time. For consumers, the majority of any newspaper or magazine article read today is filtered through some piece of technological hardware, whether through a computer screen or on the go with a mobile device. With this digital accessibility comes an unprecedented immediacy, even in music-related coverage. The pace and presentation of think-piece essays, reviews, and exclusive interviews all leave the print-cycle approach to writing to diminishing windows of timeliness and short attention spans. While desperate times may very well lead to a boon in go-for-broke moments of creativity in music journalism's remaining outlets of print, the pull of the web will undoubtedly dominate the writing form's foreseeable future, with all the good and ill that comes with it.

Tom Breihan What is crazy to me is that the job I had at the *Voice* where I wrote one blog post a day—and that was all I had to do—I felt no pressure because the bosses were barely aware of what I was doing and they were happy with it. Shortly after I started at the *Village Voice* the New Times Company bought the paper and started running it into the ground and making a series of terrible decisions, but they left me alone. They laid off all my friends. They laid off goddamn Robert Christgau. They laid off Chuck Eddy. Legends. But I kept my job and part of the reason was because I was writing on the internet, and they were trying to get some shit going on the internet, and people were reading my stuff to an extent and people were not reading anything else they were doing. All their terrible ideas were nonstarters and my terrible ideas were doing okay, and they left me alone. Nobody will ever have that job again. That's gone. That is a lost era.

Nitsuh Abebe I happened to be in these online conversations talking about music when that was not a thing that people were paying attention to. It was sort of expanding. A lot of the people who were there doing it at that moment in the early aughts were all in conversation with each other, learning from each other, and were poised to do really well with it. And then that space was sort of occupied. You have a bunch of nerds who talked about what was happening and then the established magazines would eventually cover it.

Mark Richardson During the early part of the last decade was really the rise of online file sharing with Napster and Audiogalaxy and some of the things that came after. *Pitchfork*'s rise in some ways correlated with the idea that a lot of online music fandom, discussion, listening, and consumption was now happening in a web space. Before that, to be a music fan was not to be in front of a computer. It was to be on a magazine rack or a record store or venue. In the early 2000s the idea of what it was to be a music fan definitely migrated to being in a computer space, and *Pitchfork* just happened to be well situated for that since it was a native digital magazine as opposed to a print magazine that had a website.

Steven Hyden I think it's easy for people to forget how insurgent *Pitchfork* was and how in a way what they were doing was so anti–major music magazines, just in terms of how their writing was so different and the kinds of bands they were covering was so different.

Mark Redfern If we had been smarter, instead of starting a print magazine we would have started as a music website.

Josh Jackson We did print for years and years. We were an independent company. We didn't have big funding behind us. We did get some investors but we had a bit of a rocky relationship with them. By the time 2008 rolled around we had gotten control of the magazine back from them, but we owed them a lot of money. So everything was sort of going along great, then the advertising downturn happened and we just couldn't keep up. The magazine started losing money and we had no means by which to sustain it. We did a "Save *Paste*" campaign that kept things going for about a year longer than it would have otherwise, but even that wasn't enough ultimately to really save the print issue. The recession really is what killed us. We really relied on advertising, and when that went away we were one of the casualties in the magazine world.

Bonnie Stiernberg It was definitely weird. Nobody—Josh included—knew exactly what was going to happen, if it was going to completely go under or if we would be able to come back as it was. There was a point right after they laid off everyone [that] it was me and two or three other interns and Josh and Tim Regan-Porter and Nick Purdy—and that was it. We were writing news items to just sort of keep the website fresh every day.

Mark Redfern It's tough because it used to be that people would be accustomed to paying money for music journalism and printed content. Now everybody expects all of that stuff for free on the internet.

Jack Rabid For thirty-eight years I've been able to control a lot of things. I haven't had a major illness—knock on wood—or debilitation that would make it impossible for me to work. I worked on a pretty sane schedule of only two issues a year. So that gives me three, four months to put together an issue, and if I'm sick for a week, it's not going to kill me. And I can control the quality of the work because I have a standard I've set for myself without, again, being too crazy about it. If I make a few typos, well, I did my best. But there's things I can't control. And one of them is that I'm still working in a medium that is costly. The medium I do I've got to come up with like $25,000 every six months just to cover the basic cost of printing and shipping. And every year the printing cost goes up relative to inflation and the post office and UPS people, they're going up relative to inflation. So that doesn't help. And the market itself is constantly decreasing, which I can't do anything about, not just me personally or my magazine, but for all forms of printed media, because there is so much free stuff on the web. Why would you want to spend six dollars to read what we have to say? Just read all this free stuff on the net. The closing of stores all over the country has been a squeeze from the other end. When we were in Tower Records and Virgin Records we sold gigantic bundles of magazines because the people who go into those stores were interested in music. And now we even lost Borders. Ten years ago that was our biggest account by far. And they cared about our title more than Barnes & Noble does. But I'm glad that Barnes & Noble exists because they're the only ones just about left and they take me into most markets. All the more respected and loved cultural newsstands and small bookstores have been driven out of business in droves. And it's a double whammy effect because we've got a lot of new readers by people just encountering us in the store. It's gotten so bad that within the last few years we introduced crowdfunding. To a certain degree the subscribers and advertisers were the crowdfunding for the first thirty-five years. It's come down to that. It's like passing a hat after a free gig. I remember gigs I went to in the early '80s where they passed a hat around and I'd throw a buck in it. When the hat comes around you're like, "Yeah, the show is free, what's a dollar going to cost me. That was a good show. Maybe I'll throw in a fiver. Thanks for the great show. I hope you play again." Because if you don't actually fund these people why should they play again? It's the same thing for a magazine. If you want it to exist you have to ensure its survival.

Josh Jackson When we essentially went out of business—when the print magazine died—we had been doing pretty well on the web. In fact, our website had just started growing to be something more substantial before everything happened. So we got a new investor and came up with a plan for doing this all online.

Mark Redfern We really still depend on subscriptions and issue sales. We used to be making a lot more money from these newsstand sales, but people don't buy magazines quite as much as they used to. We still do okay, but we used to get bigger checks from our distribution company. Our subscriptions have always been pretty steady. That's never really gone down, but on the other hand our website traffic has grown over the last eighteen years, so there's that. We're one of the few print music magazines left. When we started *Paste, Filter* started the same year as us. There was a magazine called *Devil in the Woods*, one that was called the *Sentimentalist. MAGNET* was around then. Also *Harp*. A lot of those have gone away.

Josh Jackson We get seven million unique people coming to the site each month. Compared to the couple hundred thousand we'd reach with the print magazine, it's huge. It's neat to think about, that we're reaching out to that many people.

Bonnie Stiernberg I always will have a soft spot for print. I'm one of those old-fashioned people who likes holding a magazine in my hand. It's always something I will enjoy, but I also understand the business side of it and all the costs of printing a magazine and how it's not something that is necessarily worth the expense, particularly when most people are getting their entertainment news and content primarily online. And it's primarily because that's where everything is. All of the stories—everything is on the website—so that's just the one place everyone knows to go and I think that helps drive traffic. It's easier to convince someone to check out a website's pages and browse through it than it is to go to a newsstand and pay however much it costs to get it. I think I'll always have sort of a nostalgic place in my heart for print and will always be a consumer of print, but I also get a ton of my reading done online as well, and certainly understand that's what a majority of people do.

Josh Jackson I don't think print's antiquated at all. I think it's a totally different experience. I still love print. I still subscribe to magazines. The great thing about a print magazine is that you're able to curate an experience for your reader, whereas with online a lot of people are searching out specific stories. It's Facebook that serves as their curator. But I love magazines. I love being able to curate an experience that surprises and delights an audience, and help people to read stuff that they didn't know they wanted to read, as opposed to what they were already looking for.

Lindsay Zoladz I actually have a designated couch in my apartment that no electronics are allowed on. That's where I do a lot of my reading. It's my no-cell-phone zone. I really enjoy that. And because I spend so much of my day immersed in that digital sphere, I really like the nondistracted nature of sitting down with a magazine for an hour or two. It's also a good way to generate ideas and to not feel the pressure and pace of the internet.

J. Edward Keyes One thing I miss about print that I'm sure that you'll hear from a lot of people is you kind of had time to absorb things a little bit more. I once did a big story on Scott Walker for *MAGNET*—Scott Walker's one of my favorite artists—but it wasn't like "We have to rush to get this out with a clickable headline." I had months to listen to every Scott Walker record and absorb them and chase down his friends from when he was a teenager, and you could spend a lot more time with him. It's the same thing with album reviews too. You got an album and you just kind of lived with it. You learned all the intricacies of it and then when you finally wrote it hopefully would have just spent several weeks absorbing it. That doesn't always happen now.

Eric T. Miller When we stopped publishing in 2008, the letters that we got . . . I was just like, "Holy shit. These people are more upset than I am." I saved them someplace—some were actually handwritten. There were people who were just crushed. And that made me feel—I mean I felt bad—but it made me feel really good that we had an impact on at least some people's lives. They actually really cared about it. That outpouring was just was incredible. And then when we started publishing again, some people were just through the roof. They couldn't believe it. It was such a whirlwind for me.

Jack Rabid The people still buying ten thousand copies of the *Big Takeover* every six months are people that still see the value in it and don't mind parting with six dollars twice a year for it or twenty dollars for a four-issues subscription. It's a tiny amount, but a lot of people won't do anything now unless it's free. I try to foster a sense of community. It's very loose because it's not a local magazine. But to me it's always been a community of like-minded people.

Christopher R. Weingarten If you write something and put it on the internet there is an exponentially greater chance that more people are going to read it than if you put it in a print magazine. And yet there's still that part of me that thinks about when I was fifteen or sixteen and what it was like to look at a print magazine in the '90s and be like, "Wow!" And even with my current job I'm still out there trying to wrangle to get in a print magazine. It still really means something as a writer and it's not something that you can logically pinpoint a reason. It's just a feeling.

Mark Richardson A magazine cover still counts for a lot, and there's been nothing online that competes with a magazine cover in terms of its impact, in terms of how much an artist loves seeing themselves on a magazine cover. It's just this thing. It just doesn't have a digital equivalent.

Jack Rabid If I wanted I could be like everybody else and be a web-only magazine. It's very cheap and the writing still gets out there. But I don't like that. I do a fair amount of reading on the web, but it's very ephemeral to me. I read it once, I never read it again. I can't think of a single thing I've read on the web in the last several years that I've ever read twice, even really good writing.

Wendy Lynch Redfern Mark joked the other day that you're not going to find a webpage in your attic in fifty years.

Matt Fink I don't know what advantage print has besides just having a physical object in your hands at this point. As a reader I prefer online, but as a writer I love to have that actual piece of writing in my hands. That feels more substantive to me, whereas the online stuff is kind of like it's written in the wind.

Lizzy Goodman The problem with online journalism had always been that people had snottiness about it. It was less well edited, less good, and paid less as well. Those are all good reasons to be looking down your nose at it.

Maura Johnston Online media has always been devalued. It's always been seen as less than.

T. Cole Rachel When I first started writing professionally the goal was always still to get things in print, and people didn't really regard the internet as highly and magazines would ask you to write things for their website and then pay you literally nothing for it. I mean I sort of came of age as a writer at the same time people were really figuring out how to create good content for the internet. And now it's very different.

Ryan Dombal Some people still think of print as an upper-echelon or more prestigious—just because it's print. And even though I grew up reading print and worked in print, I just don't think that way anymore.

Ryan Leas When I started this whole thing I very much wanted to work in print and write big magazine features. I don't really feel that way anymore. I think at this point it's like, well, it's the world we live in.

J. Edward Keyes The internet has opened up so much. There's so many more bands and so many more people doing interesting things who have the ability to do it now because of the internet. And as someone who really loves new music, that's kind of the cool thing about it. I think the internet is also a leveling ground in a lot of ways, and creates more opportunities for people that the old print hierarchy might have shut out. It creates opportunities for voices that maybe used to be marginalized, which I think is incredibly valuable.

Hua Hsu Things that have only ever existed online do something a bit more interesting in that they can kind of engage with stuff as it's happening, but also step back and kind of meditate on what it is that's going on and be a bit more self-reflective. Whereas I think a lot of established magazines and newspapers just have a much harder time because they either have willfully chosen to not adapt or have embraced it too much where it obfuscates what their core values are.

Rob Sheffield They don't have to jump through hoops, to go through editors, to get their words and perspective and ideas out there. With the internet there are more places for a writer to write than ever and more ways for a writer to spread their ideas around. Also there's more music out there than ever. I mean it's an unbelievably rich and exciting time for writing about music. It's hard to overemphasize how utopian that looks to someone who came up in the '80s when you went to the coffee shop, you went to Kinko's and xeroxed your clips and cutouts of your pieces and put them into envelopes and sent them out to editors and you prayed that you would get a letter back from an editor through the mail or maybe even a call. You'd send out your clips hoping you would pick up places to write.

Joe Levy I think the opportunities are greater than the challenges. If you went back five to ten years there were fewer opportunities to do aspirational work. During a period of professionalization that lasted from some point in the early '90s until about twenty minutes after Craigslist was invented, there was not a lot of opportunity or encouragement to do long-form critical music essays. And I would say that there's much more opportunity now. The media disruption of the internet has made it difficult if not impossible to earn a living writing about this stuff, but it has opened up huge possibilities. And here is an important thing to remember: the original work that came from that first generation of music writers—doing things that were aspirational—comes from a time when it would have been ludicrous to say, "Oh I've decided what I'm going to do. I'm going to earn my living as a music journalist." Prior to that moment of professionalization there were plenty of people who had day jobs and wrote about music because they felt they had something to say, not because they thought they could earn a living at it.

Lizzy Goodman What is fun about doing music journalism in this era is that the whole infrastructure and all these rules and regulations about how you were supposed to do it have been just totally demolished by the disrupting force that has been online culture.

Ryan Leas You can be more creative. You can do weird pieces, you can do long pieces, all kinds of stuff.

Lizzy Goodman There are all these incredibly sophisticated, creative examples of the form that I don't think would have existed if things hadn't gotten so shaken up. There's a lot of stuff I get away with that I would never have gotten away with before. And I'm really excited about that. Also just your readership is more sophisticated. The argument I always made about why I don't want to spend an entire paragraph in this point in my piece describing the record to people has been kind of eliminated by the fact that everyone is just going to go hear it. There used to be all of this filler in copy in music journalism where you had to kind of quantify and qualify everything because it was more newsy. It was more informative. And now you don't have to say in a piece about Beyoncé—but I swear to god you used to do this—"born in Houston and blah blah blah year, she has a sister Solange and a mother Tina"— you don't have to do that anymore because there's this general level of awareness of the people who are reading everything about what you're writing about. And that part is really fun because I just don't want to write that shit. I want to get to the goods.

David Marchese I think for me there are only advantages. On a practical level I would never have the space for my pieces to be as long as they are in print where page considerations are a real thing. You can't run five-thousand-word Q&As all the time.

Andy Greene There's no space limit. I can go as long as I want on a story. When I report a story I always think at the very minimum I'm reporting two stories: the print version and the online version. The print version has a very set space limit that's overseen by a bunch of editors. I will have to possibly revise it. It's a whole process. For online I can do it my own way. I can do it as a Q&A. I could do it in an oral history. I could do four articles off the reporting. For me it's also very gratifying because there's a smaller barrier between my work and the audience. And it's seen immediately. I can write a story at 10 a.m. and it's up by lunchtime. And that's very gratifying. There are times where you do a print story and you'll lose the page or it's bumped back a month or it gets killed. It takes forever. With the internet it's instantaneous.

Ann Powers The one potential that the internet has that I think is super-valuable that I think media outlets aren't taking advantage of is that we are not tied to a schedule the way that we once were. There's absolutely zero reason why any online publication has to publish everything at the same time. And yet that's so ingrained in the symbiotic relationship between media outlets and the music industry that it keeps replicating itself and it's completely unnecessary. Artists and bands are going to have just as interesting things to say, more interesting things to say, six months after their record comes out than at the moment of its release. I really hope that that particular thing where everybody puts out a feature on the same thing falls away. I wish that there was more of an openness to stories that aren't tied to the production cycle of music.

Mark Richardson The one difference that really comes to mind is that before online, you never knew what section of the paper or magazine was being read. Publishers could do some market research and have an idea, but it was always just an idea. Typically you put together a magazine with short stories in the front of the book, big features in the middle, maybe some reviews at the end. There was this very clear format for how they were put together. And while some were really popular and some weren't, in terms of what the magazine was you didn't have a great sense of what each individual article was doing. And then in the digital era you got a precise measurement of everything you published and exactly how many people were looking at it. Having this precise data about exactly how many people are reading each piece and for how long, it's a good thing in one way because you get a sense of what resonates with people.

Maura Johnston Google Analytics is the exposing of the collective id, where it's just like, "This is what people want. Sorry you worked really hard on that thing you wrote, but nobody cares."

Chuck Klosterman There was much less creative anxiety prior to the advent of the internet. That was a period where you wrote something, you put it out into the world, and that was it. The experience was over. That was the end of the experience. You wrote it and you published it and then you would just wonder, "Did anyone care?" You never knew. Now publishing a piece—which used to be the end of the process—is the middle of the process. Now, any time you write something halfway interesting, there's this whole secondary experience where you sort of have to deal with people responding to the thing, very often in a context you didn't intend at all. A context that has nothing to do with you or what you wrote. That's the most anxiety-creating aspect, by far. It would be one thing if it was just people agreeing or disagreeing. That's totally fine. But now there's always a small chance your career might end.

Jayson Greene The feedback loop in a review or feature is nearly instantaneous. You have a deadline, you file it, and it's like being a cook during a brunch rush where there's plates just whizzing down the line. You've got your little prescribed time and then whatever has happened in that time doesn't matter. Now it's done, and you have to wing it out there. I've always found that to be energizing. I think some people find that stressful or unrewarding—and I get that completely—but for some reason I've found it to be gratifying.

Mark Richardson When I see reactions to something I might have written, that's probably when I get a sense of whether what I was trying to communicate came across or not. Because you never really know.

Sometimes you'll finish a piece and think, "Oh, I managed to say what I wanted there" and sometimes it's "Oh, I don't know if that was very good." And then you'll see it out there and see people picking up on things you said and you get a sense of, "Okay, that worked. People understood what I meant." That part didn't used to be there in the same way before the internet and social media.

Carl Wilson The thing I enjoy most is hearing and seeing reactions and responses after the piece comes out. That's the payoff.

Lindsay Zoladz I think part of it is the culture we're in now with social media. I think you're having more of a conversation with the people who are reading you than you might have thirty years ago or something, where it could feel easy to feel like you were writing into a void. I try to be wary of certain aspects of the internet and what it is doing to me as a writer.

Lizzy Goodman I think comments aren't for the people who wrote the thing. I have noticed that the most emotionally balanced, the most creatively prolific, and grounded people, the ones who can stay connected to what's great about them and continue to make amazing work, understand when it comes to the thing they make, how it is consumed is really none of their business. This is a hugely important element of the healthy creative ego in my mind. It's not for you. You're making a thing, you're doing your best. Writing and making records are actually quite similar in that you're in this dark hole by yourself or with your bandmates for a long period of time, having this huge relationship with this thing, and then by the time anyone else is hearing it you're done. You aren't having an active relationship with that thing anymore. It's true for everybody. You make this thing, and it's not for you.

Christian Hoard I think the demands of the job have become a little more all-encompassing. It used to be a little more defined when it was more about print. You'd make an issue and you could slow down for a couple days. But now there's always something to cover on the web. Everyone's always working, and that's not just at *Rolling Stone*. I mean everyone.

J. Edward Keyes The pace is insane now.

Matt Fink It's really difficult for print to even compete with online now because by the time the magazine gets in your hand the information is at least a week old, or in some cases a month old. With online you're basically getting it ten minutes after the news breaks.

Marc Hogan I'm a creature of deadlines. Actually I heard a cool quote from Brian Eno where he was saying if it weren't for deadlines he'd never put out any music. I feel like that's the same thing. You get used to doing these things on a certain day and juggle them.

Joe Levy It's not just that the coverage is immediate, it's that the window of interest has also dwindled. For commentary, for the people interested in commentary, and for the audience, the window of interest seems to have dwindled.

Mark Redfern I think what's hard for print magazines is that a lot of albums these days—or a lot of the big albums—are surprise released or they're released with only like a few weeks' or a month's notice. So that makes it hard when you plan three months ahead like we do with the magazine, and even once we go to press it's still three weeks or more before the issue is actually out in all the stores. So there are a lot of albums that we aren't able to cover in the print side of things. We used to do previews of the year in our print magazine, like our "Most Anticipated Albums of the Year," and it's harder to do because labels don't want any info out there on the internet. They'll say it's too early.

Ann Powers I think for music writers there's a challenge because we're expected to be an expert in everything. And we're particularly expected to respond to whatever little brush fire is happening at the moment.

Christopher R. Weingarten I hope I never have to be in a position where I have to start doing takes all the time. I've done that grind of "Come up with eight hundred words on this thing that has happened!" It's not for me. I find it very stressful. I see the race to get these things up. It consumes.

Liz Pelly The need for everything to happen so fast makes it challenging to look at the bigger picture. We're in this moment where we need to do some really big thinking about how things are changing, but that sort of thinking doesn't necessarily happen at the fast pace that the media economy currently requires.

Eric T. Miller I think the base hindrance for online is that it's always a rush to be first, not a rush to be right. We're not writing about North Korea's nuclear capabilities, but at the same time it's like everyone's always just trying to get stuff out there as quick as possible. Luckily, we're not even staffed to do that. If Jeff Tweedy has a bad bowel movement, we don't we don't need to be the first to get there, you know? I mean it's good mindless stuff to see when you're flipping through your phone on the subway or something. You want some little tidbit that you don't want to think about that much. But it's just instant information that you care about for half a day, and then you move on. Everything is down to little sound bites and stuff.

Christopher R. Weingarten Anyone who works online will share this, but whenever someone dies it is an absolute nightmare. It makes me sick. It really takes away a little part of my humanity in a way because when someone I love, such as a performer, when they die, I don't get to—like when Michael Jackson died I was freelancing. And it hit me really, really hard because I could just sit there and be sad, you know? But when Prince died, whom I love, I never got a chance to grieve. I sit down and I write and I assign and I edit, and you just go. And that's it. When MCA [Adam Yauch] died, I never got a chance to really let it sink in how much his music meant to me. It's just different. When Prince died I did nothing but edit Prince things for a week. And at home I was listening to Prince and it was like a combination of work anxiety and "Wow, this music is so good." It's sad that I don't really get an opportunity to feel that emotion. It makes me crazy. It makes me personally sad.

Ben Ratliff Writing about somebody who has just died an hour ago—oh my God. You better get on it and come correct and do the best job you can do and turn yourself inside out as if the rest of your career is going to depend on it. I'm describing an interior reaction, what's going on in my head, but the pressure around obituaries has become intense. At the end of my period working for the *Times*, I started to be fearful each night when I closed my eyes that somebody important would die. I seemed to need more time. If I review a concert, I don't know what I'm going to say about it when the show's over—I have to think about it a little bit. I prefer sleeping on it and writing in the morning. If somebody important has died, maybe even somebody who meant a lot to me, maybe even somebody I knew, in a sense I'm reviewing someone's life. I need more time than a couple of hours.

Carl Wilson There's a pressure that my editors and publishers are under just because of how the economy works and how the internet attention span works. They feel like they have to have a say on the big thing because they know that that's what everybody is going to be clicking on all day that day or that week. It's sort of a nonnegotiable demand.

Tom Breihan What I guess has stayed the same is that a strong personal voice will find an audience.

Lizzy Goodman I've learned when I have a bunch of ideas coming in the window of my brain, it's like, "Well this one would be good for print. This one would be good for online." And it's no longer a distinction between "This one's shittier and therefore good for online" and "This one's better and therefore good for print." It's more, "Where would this be better to read?"

Jayson Greene I'm kind of a platform agnostic when I come right down to it. I like seeing my name in print in very vain ways. I like the way things look and feel when I hold them. But those are not business decisions, and those are not the reasons that things live or die. I think that a lot of hoopla is made about the strength of digital and print, and I think that's people engaging in sloppy thinking. It's not in the format, it's what you brought to it, right? It's just a piece of blank paper until you put your work on there.

Christian Hoard You have to realize you're kind of making two different products in a lot of ways. A lot of it is realizing what works for one doesn't work for the other. It's like, "Okay, the web is the future but at the same time people really care about the magazine and being a part of it." People will still clamor for a print feature. The biggest names you can think of will clamor to be on the cover of the magazine. That's value. That means a lot. At the same time a long think piece might only work on the web. I mean these are questions we are constantly asking ourselves and it's not easy to figure out. But I feel like we've gotten better at working them together. Nobody who works in editorial works on just print anymore. Most of my focus on any given day is digital and I'm happy with that.

Jayson Greene I think there are certain qualities of good journalism that you have to work in different ways to achieve. Good journalism to me feels the same wherever it appears. There are lots of factors that go into making a good piece, but to me good journalism at its core feels the same—with different trappings—no matter where I encounter it.

Ryan Leas It feels better to me to be in the online era than the print era. But I mean, the whole thing is threatened. I think at a certain point the business model we have now isn't going to work in any kind of long-term way. It's a business model based on the way print magazines work—selling advertising. And especially because we don't have the circulation of subscriptions that print outlets have, it's purely these ad dollars monetizing traffic, which is a really weird, murky way of doing it. At a certain point we're going to hit a saturation point. It's not like all these outlets are picking up a million new readers every year. Something's got to give. I don't know what the solution is. Obviously that's the billion dollar question.

Lizzy Goodman The internet is very new in the grand scheme of things and we're still figuring out how to be good at it, and I mean that in the realm of music journalism, in the realm of journalism in general, and in the realm of being human, managing this insane thing that's been invented by us and how to not let Frankenstein's monster take over.

Jim DeRogatis I think this is a historical blip in time. If we look at Gutenberg inventing the printing press the 1690s, this notion of words on dead trees is only a couple of centuries old. And the idea of journalism as a profession is even younger, barely a century old. And I think the core concepts of storytelling and affecting people with the power of words and criticism, I think no matter how they are delivered—on dead trees or with bites or verbally or visually or some hybrid of them all—I think that those are really important.

CHAPTER SIX

As an Industry, As a Career

Though it's been a much longer process than many of those working in the industry would like, the profession of music journalism and the business of music journalism publishing is in a state of deep transition at the moment. "I think we're all just floating around in some sort of postsomething haze. I'm not really sure what it is," says Matt Fink. "I think the job description is shifting in a very real way that maybe we're not totally prepared for."

For those whose sole responsibility is on the content creation side of the equation, it's a little difficult to make sense of these economic nuances and monetary conundrums facing the business aspect of a publication's operation. Like the musicians we cover, music journalists didn't get into their profession as an expectant means of making tons of money and being part of an industry. They started writing about music because it was something they were passionate about and were compelled to do because it made them happy. Then through the course of developing a talent, you occasionally got lucky and started getting paid gigs. It wasn't reliable pay, and certainly wasn't your sole means of income, but you hoped with a little luck and timing attached to your talent, you might get yourself picked out of the mass of other eager individuals in the same position to turn what you love into an actual career. Whether you're writing music or writing about music, commerce has always had a bad habit of butting heads with anyone attempting to do something creative.

In today's environment there are reasons to be equally mournful and encouraged about the well-being of music journalism. Undoubtedly, it's incredibly disappointing as a music journalist to have to see so many publications struggle and have their financial ledgers run in the red. It's disheartening when any publication has to shutter its doors, because it may be an important source of someone's income, someone's rent or grocery money.

And yet despite the loss of these platforms, despite having fewer opportunities and outlets that are willing or able to pay their writers for their efforts, one needn't fear that music journalists are becoming an endangered species. While some of the industry's most notable and established publications may be shutting down or in dire straits, today's technology has made the hurdles of being published a complete nonfactor. If you want to write an essay and dissect the cultural implications of new record, if you want to interview an artist about their career, the internet allows anyone to build their own platform, their own digital DIY publication. You may not get paid, and you may not obtain the same larger-scale reach you might otherwise get with an established name publication, but you'll be able to get your work out into the world and build your voice and point of view, and hopefully in the process establish your own audience, your own band of loyal readers who value the content you're generating.

Amanda Petrusich It feels like a house of cards, like it's all going to sort of go away. I fear we're at a real nadir for this kind of work. It's gotta get better. It can't get worse. Everyone's so badly paid and the work is so undervalued. I think there's a lot of anxiety about how long this will continue being a profession.

Lizzy Goodman I came up in an era where music journalism and the music industry that supported it were flying high, but the iceberg has already hit the *Titanic*. I moved to New York in 2002. Napster emerged in 2000, and as soon as Napster happened it was over. The institutions of music, the music industry and the magazine journalism world that was adjacent to it, those two industries were never going to be the same again. It was a fundamental, industrial revolution–style shift.

Ilana Kaplan Well, I think that there's always an ebb and a flow in this industry, and I think that it's definitely gotten harder as media companies have lost money or cut their staff down. It's either they're just going through in-house writers and don't have a budget for freelance writers or they do have a budget for freelance writers but there are no staff positions.

Bonnie Stiernberg People can talk themselves blue in the face about traffic, page views, pivoting to video, whatever, but ultimately one of the biggest problems with the music journalism industry—and the journalism industry as a whole—is that so many publications and media companies are owned by these millionaire CEOs who don't know anything about journalism. They're just concerned with lining their pockets, so they latch on to whatever the current trendy idea is regardless of whether it's right for your publication or not. More often than not, it's a terrible idea that no one on staff wants to implement, and no matter how many times you try to tell them it's terrible, they'll force you to do it, and then when it inevitably fails, it's still you getting laid off instead of them.

Jillian Mapes Music is a fractured industry, and publishing is a fractured industry, and when you put them together...

Marc Hogan It's in a challenging spot. Between the music industry, which has suffered its problems over the past decade, and the journalism industry, which has suffered parallel problems, all of this drives home just how lucky I am, because they're both shrinking spaces.

Lizzy Goodman Those years were still incredibly profitable for the music industry. There was all this money in this business that was dying. We were running on battery basically.

Jayson Greene I can definitely say that the business is contracting, insofar as it ever was a business. Media as a business is its own sort of horror story, you know? I'm not sure the people in charge of media have ever known to how to actually make it a business. It's just been a series of explosions and bubbles and massive waves of success followed by equally massive waves of failure. There were many years where magazines seemed like a stable investment for people. Even twenty years ago, magazines were still a business where you could expect to be flown around and have expense accounts. But that was never a stable reality, and people are waking up from that. Some people lived inside a world where that was stable, or seemed stable to them. And I think that there's a lot of wailing and a lot of confusion and a lot of disorientation in sort of realizing that it wasn't. That's the mind frame that I have from it, anyway, because I came into this business just as all that was crumbling.

Craig Jenkins If the well dries up, I'm jumping headfirst into video game journalism.

Mark Richardson It's in a particularly tight spot right now in my opinion, partly because music journalism in general always exists relative to what's going on in music and technology. So, you know, in the past several years the rise of streaming and the ubiquity of Spotify and Apple Music, that has changed the landscape a lot because it's kind of turned music into like this utility that you pay a monthly fee and you can access it. I guess the easiest way for me to put it is that I think music journalism, in order for it to survive in the places where it is surviving now, is really geared toward hardcore fans rather than casual fans. If you look at twenty years ago and you picked up *Us Weekly*, *People* magazine, or some really large, mainstream entertainment magazine like that, they had a record review section. It was like a page or two in the magazine, and sometimes they had really good writers in there. And they paid well. But it's like the idea that *People* magazine in 1998 had to have a music editor who reviewed records, because it showed that there used to be this kind of broad informational system for alerting people to what was going on in music, and a lot of music journalism was defined around that. Every newspaper in every town had an arts editor or music editor and they were doing stories about shows that were coming to town or new albums that were coming out. There used to be this whole system of getting information out to people about music, and a lot of that has fallen away. One of the reasons for all of that kind of music journalism then was there was a hunger where people were like, "I want to find some good music to listen to." And whether it was *People* magazine or *Rolling Stone*, those were the outlets for saying, "Here's some good music." And now if you say "I want some good music to listen to," you're going to go to a streaming service's playlist and there's going to be music there and you'll listen for twenty minutes and you'll find some stuff you like. And that's it. You can do that without knowing anything about the artists or reading anything. There's algorithms that say "I know a little bit about your music taste. Well, here's some other music you might like." And those algorithms are probably going to get better over time. And for a lot of people that's all they need. And there's nothing wrong with that. It's just the way it is. But I think music journalism in general has had to do a lot of adjusting because of that. The idea of helping steer people and getting them information about what's going on in music, it's just not as significant as it once was. Now it's really more about serving more specialty audiences that really want a lot of detail and are really passionate about the stories and want to know as much as they can about music.

Jayson Greene Everyone's kind of on the same boat and it's a very fragile-feeling boat that's being buffeted by huge forces outside of it. Money is draining out of every single thing around it. Money is gone from ad-supported media.

Christian Hoard There's so many other ways for an artist to publicize themselves than talk to us, and we have to compete with all of the social media and all these other websites and it's like, how do you continue to do the kind of work that you've always valued while dealing with all of that and surviving? While attracting advertisers? While hitting the bottom line? How do you keep the work up in today's environment? It doesn't get any easier, but it's crucial to ask, how do you keep your standards? That's the question, and it gets harder and harder every day.

Chuck Klosterman It may be easy for me to say this, kind of being outside of what the media has become, but it seems like it is much easier to get into the business of music writing, yet much harder to make a living at it. That seems to be the primary evolution. If you aspire to write about music, it's pretty easy to do so. But what is very, very difficult is making enough money to have a house and buy food.

Lizzy Goodman If you work in music journalism or entertainment media or you're a journalist of any kind, you need to be paid for your work. We aren't in an academic institution. There isn't a benefactor system. There isn't some other construct supporting the creation of this art. It's a job.

Amanda Petrusich Writing for money is incredible, but also writing for money sucks. And it sucks even more now. The rates offered are so grim. My students will come up to me and say, "Oh I got offered this four-thousand-word thing and it pays thirty dollars." I mean, that's not even going to cover the cups of coffee you're going to buy to stay awake to write the piece. Writing has been so devalued by the marketplace.

Brittany Spanos Every single journalism professor that we had—in Gallatin there are so many professional journalists and writers who teach a lot of the music history courses and nonfiction writing courses—literally every single class, every time any student would mention they want to become a journalist they were like, "Good luck." It was just a very intense way to go through college. By the time I hit senior year I was already so anxious about finding a job. It was very, very stressful to hear that every single day. I mean, it's true. I was going to learn it eventually and it's good that they were very upfront. But for most of my senior year I was thinking that I would have to move back home and have to freelance from there in Chicago.

Maura Johnston Nobody gets paid enough. Freelancing also means you have to pay for your own insurance. I don't have someone to supplement my income. It can be very nerve-wracking at times.

J. Edward Keyes Honestly, a difficulty is staying employed and being able to pay your rent.

Matt Fink Right after I finished my master's degree I spent two years just writing. And basically just paying my rent and ordering off the dollar menu at McDonald's. That was my life. It was great in a way. My friends were all around. I had no nine-to-five job. I could kind of just schedule my life around writing. And that was really great, but you can't live like that forever. You want to be able to eventually get off the dollar menu and perhaps not live in a house with five other guys.

Ryan Leas When I was freelance I had a lot of freedom. It was a great time. But I was also broke all the time. Any given week could be thrown in upheaval because a piece got pushed back another month, and I'd be like, "Well, that was my rent money."

Bonnie Stiernberg Being a freelance writer is extremely tough. You're constantly wondering when your next paycheck is going to come. Sometimes you'll get paid in March for work the previous November. Sometimes you won't get paid at all until you threaten legal action. You get completely boned when tax season rolls along and you have to head over to H&R Block with your mountain of 1099 forms. Whenever an outlet folds, it hurts double—you sympathize for the journalists who got laid off, especially because you've been in that position and know how awful it is, but then you also get these thoughts like "Welp, that's one less outlet I can write for" or "The already-enormous pool of talented writers and editors competing for the tiny amount of work that's still available just got even bigger." Then, of course, you feel guilty for thinking like that. But it's important to remember that every time a publication shuts down, there's a batch of freelance writers who were relying on regular work there who now won't be able to, and they're not able to collect unemployment. Overall there's just a lot of stress and financial anxiety attached to the job.

Matt Fink It wouldn't have worked if I had to pay more than two hundred dollars for rent. But it was great. I look back at that as probably the happiest time of my life. But it couldn't last forever. If I was still in that position I wouldn't be getting much sleep at night. Even then if I wanted to I could have been writing every waking hour. And I kind of had it always hanging over me, too, to the point where my office was my bed. You have a difficulty drawing a line between when you're on the clock and when you're not. Should I really go to dinner with my friends? Should we really watch this movie? I've got five hundred words of an article I need to get done tonight. And what I would end up doing is watching the movie and then staying up until six or seven in the morning writing. But that lifestyle burns you out pretty quickly. That was the hardest thing. There's no office. There's no "I'm at work, now I'm not at work." I'm always at work—potentially anyway. I couldn't deal with not knowing where next month's rent was coming from. I couldn't handle it.

Ryan Leas When I had a regular, nonwriting day job, it was fucking exhausting. I would stay at the office late to write an article, or get there early. If I went out to a show that I had to write up the next day, I'd wake up and write and publish it and then go work a day at a job I didn't like.

Hannah Giorgis Just as an anxious person and an immigrant kid, I never wanted to depend on freelance checks. It makes me so anxious, the pitch. And I really respect people who can and do function that way. I can't. When I was freelancing I was also working full-time a lot. I'd finish the workday at 5:30 p.m. or whatever and then go home and work, write on the weekends, things like that. It's not sustainable, but it was fine at the time. I don't think I could do it again. I was also twenty-three. I'm not anymore.

Matt Fink I think at one point I was freelancing for maybe twenty different magazines or something while trying to be a full-time grad student. And it was very, very difficult. I probably wasn't able to fully do my best work in either of those settings because it was just way too much to keep up with.

Lindsay Zoladz When you don't really keep set hours you can be working all the time, especially when writing is a really difficult job to quantify. I hate when people ask "Have you ever broken down when you're writing a record review how many hours it took and how many hours you spent on the dollar?" And I'm like, "That would be depressing." I can't. It just sort of takes over your life. It's hard to put it in time because you're always subconsciously thinking about what you're working on too. I do think that is a particular struggle for people who write full-time. And also giving yourself the space to come up with new ideas and be okay. It can be really hard, especially when you're writing on deadline, to give yourself that space to go through that part of the process.

Laura Snapes When I was freelance, I was very bad at work/life balance. Sometimes I'd have a few weeks of having a normal life, but largely it was a lot of working evenings, weekends, and a lot of travel. I worked really hard to get good commissions, and so the financial realities were fairly positive, though not exactly lucrative—but it definitely took its toll on my sense of sanity. Even if you plan a holiday, you don't really get a break when you're freelance. I was extremely relieved to get a full-time job. I still sometimes go through periods of taking on far too much work—since I can freelance a bit as well, and there are too many things that I *want* to do—and working evenings and weekends and feeling a bit mad. But generally, I am lucky to have the rhythms of my work dictated by office hours, and the luxuries of paid holiday and colleagues to cover that come with it. I am not great at prioritizing life over work even now, but I enforce reading, exercise, and social time, where I felt like I couldn't afford to as a freelancer. However, if granted one wish, it would be to never have to read or reply to a fucking e-mail ever again.

Puja Patel Early on in my career I had secured enough regular writing gigs that obviously still did not pay enough. I think when I was at the *Voice* it was seventy-five dollars per piece. And so I would feel thrilled if I could get four in a week because that would mean three hundred dollars a week. And then I would supplement that with a couple of reviews at *SPIN*, and an MTV column that I think was one hundred and fifty dollars a week. I was piecing this stuff together. It was an extremely difficult time, hustling for what you believe is your art while also having an extreme imposter syndrome and extreme am-I-ever-going-to-land-the-big-gig anxiety. What I will say about that time, though, was that I think my relationship with music felt less—right now it can get clinical. Because we're reviewing five albums a day, there will be an urgency to listen to something. You have to listen to it before this particular review goes back to the writer so that we can come to a conclusion on X, Y, or Z, and it's just a different. It's a different way of living your life with music. When I was younger, I was living it by going to every show and going to the weirder venues. I would go to almost anything because that was the one thing a freelancer has, that writer cred, especially when you're an underground and indie writer. It gave me a lot of passes into a lot of places. I really felt like I was deeply ingrained in the New York scene in every way. I knew the bands; I knew the labels; I knew the record stores intimately. That part of my life with music felt almost like the dream way to live with music, to just be floating in and out of whatever you want whenever you feel like it with no expectation. It was difficult but it also felt like a real exploratory period.

Ann Powers I'm of two minds. On the one hand, of course, I share the general stress that content is becoming devalued, which in some ways makes it hard to be a professional writer. On the other hand, being a music journalist was always a pretty rare career. I hate to say it, but it's true.

Rob Sheffield This is really something to stress. Even in the '80s there couldn't have been more than three or four people in the country who were making their living writing about music. It was assumed that you had a day job, that everybody who wrote about music had a day job. You either worked at a magazine as an editor or a fact checker or something where you worked for a paper, or you were on staff at a daily newspaper just doing a column and reports on what band was in whatever town that night. There was no concept that as a freelancer you would make rent that way. That was absolutely unthinkable and not even something anyone aspired to until well into the '90s. The media boom of the '90s suddenly made it quite lucrative to be a freelancer for a while, and that's when it sort of began for the first time that people were actually making a living at it. But it wasn't something that anybody thought of as something that you would do without a day job.

Michael Azerrad It was always very difficult to make a decent living at this. Now it's even more difficult, and it's going to get even more difficult as time goes on.

Ilana Kaplan I've seen young people who are just out of school who after a couple of months are like, "I haven't been able to find a job. Maybe I shouldn't do this anymore." And I think the thing about this field is that you have to try and be resilient. And I'm a really sensitive person, so it's hard. But you have to be resilient. And you also have to be practical. I think a lot of people will work for pennies and struggle, but it's also important to not have your mental health suffer and to have health insurance if possible. If you need a steady income there's no shame in working a day job. At least that way you can support yourself and you can still do what you love.

Eric T. Miller Freelancing has gotten even harder than it was back in the day, and even then it was hard. People who freelance for us, I'd say 90 percent of them have jobs that have nothing to do with music. They do it because they love music.

Jessica Hopper I work in Chicago, where there's honestly maybe three or four people who are employed full-time, writing about music. It's not New York. My cohort here has usually been people who are freelance, people who probably don't even write anything full-time.

Carl Wilson There are lots of places where you have to chase them down after you've invoiced them—or in my case when you've forgotten to invoice them. I'm not great on the paperwork side of things.

Maura Johnston I wish I had a staff job somewhere. Staff critic jobs just don't exist anymore. When you're a freelancer you have to pick and choose your spots. As a staffer I could take more chances on stuff. I mean, I would have to run stuff by an editor, but at the same time I would be able to forge my own path. It's important to consider how a freelancer-reliant system affects what stories do and don't get told.

Jack Rabid I make the tiniest little eked-out living. The hours that I put in I probably make three dollars an hour or something like that. It's not much. I'm just glad to be doing it. I try not to make it into a big complain-a-thon about the grueling hours it sometimes takes or some of the thankless tasks, because I'm still here and I've sure had worse jobs that took up too much of my free time in the service of something I didn't believe in or felt unconnected to just to feed myself. I'm still doing it, so I feel darn lucky in that sense, and I really appreciate the readers and advertisers that make something like what we do exist let alone persevere. I did work for four years at New York Life Insurance in the late '80s and I didn't like it a bit. I wore the monkey suit and tabulated withheld taxes. That could have been my fate, but as soon as I paid off my NYU student loans I quit, and I haven't had a proper full-time job like that since, just a series of part-time jobs, like where I've worked for colleges and stuff. I should be grateful. I don't know how much longer I can be doing this, as it's not entirely in my hands, but the crowdfunding makes me ten times more grateful. All these people want me to continue—want us to continue. Thank you.

That's what I should say. Thank you! I want to keep providing this small service toward a better culture, including music. Music has always been part of every culture on earth, in every country, going back thousands of years, so I know it's a profound part of human life. So it's been good to have a small role in spreading some of the better stuff around.

Carvell Wallace You can't expect to be doing anything forever. Even if you have good quality in your work, that is not a guarantee that you'll get to do it forever. If you have an opportunity, you take it while it's happening because it can disappear from you at any point. The other thing is that everything reforms. Everything turns into something else. You have to view everything as a little bit of a hit-and-run job. You pull up, you spit out your piece, you go back into hiding, and then you have to pop up somewhere else because none of these structures are guaranteed. I think we have to have a little bit of a guerilla mindset around how we create this content.

Jessica Hopper Before I went to go work at *Pitchfork* one of my sources of income was doing recaps of *The Voice*. I also had three columns that I did on a weekly basis, was editing *Rookie* part-time, was taking up whatever make-longer work I could do, getting those two-buck-a-word Condé Nast checks for doing front-of-book stuff for *GQ*, which paid my rent. That's basically what I would have to be doing—really hustling full-time.

Mark Redfern We've still never raked in as much money as we deserve or would like, but we have managed to just about stay afloat with the ups and downs of the magazine industry and the music industry and the economy and all that.

Jayson Greene You can find yourself at work in any variety of incredibly unstable fields. It doesn't necessarily mean that you won't succeed or find your way to something. It just means it's incredibly hard and un-likely.

Jim DeRogatis I've always said if I lost every paying gig tomorrow, I would go work at Starbucks if I had to and keep doing what I do.

Eric T. Miller You know going into a deadline-based profession that it's not just nine-to-five.

Ilana Kaplan I set time aside. I'll be like, "Okay, I'm going to pitch stuff today," or "I'm going to write today," or "I'm going to do nothing."

Mark Richardson A lot of the stress comes just from just being accessible to work pretty much at all hours. I look at my phone and I see there's two e-mails. "Oh, now I'm going to look at it. One of them might be a work e-mail." It's not something that I'm going to deal with immediately, but now it's on my mind, you know? And I look at Twitter. Who do I follow on Twitter? It's mostly music writers. So it's partly just the all-pervasiveness of social media and the internet. And that's changed a lot over my life, writing about music. It's interesting now. It's pretty intense.

Stephen Deusner I don't have weekends. I have holidays and I travel with family occasionally, but there's always something going on in the background. Even when I'm spending time with my nieces and nephews, I'm always asking what their favorite songs are.

Ryan Dombal In my twenties there were a lot more sleepless nights writing reviews and trying to become more established. It took a lot of after-hours and weekend work, whereas at this point, I still work on the weekends sometimes, but I've been lucky that I don't have to do that as much. I can get most of my work done—at work.

Michael Azerrad My work-life balance is terrible. When I work, I go all in. During the time I was writing *Come as You Are: The Story of Nirvana*, I worked flat out for nine months without a break, constantly flying across the country to Seattle and back, then furiously transcribing and writing and editing when I got back. My father took a picture of me the day I turned in the manuscript, and I'm really pale and gaunt and I look at least ten years older than I actually was. I can't bear to look at that photo. And yet I didn't learn. When I was writing *Our Band Could Be Your Life*, I worked from the moment I woke up to the moment I couldn't keep my eyes open anymore. Then I'd wake up the next morning and do it all over again. And I did that every day for three years. Once again, I was a physical wreck at the end of it. I'm proud of the book, but sometimes I wonder what kind of toll it took.

Brandon Stosuy I talk to a lot of younger writers who are single and dating. I don't think they quite understand the whole family aspect of my life. It sets limits on time in a really wonderful, fulfilling way. I've never been busier, and I've also never been more efficient or productive. I love it.

Ilana Kaplan I look at my coworkers that have kids and work full-time and do other stuff, and I'm like, "When do you sleep?"

Chuck Klosterman I used to only write when I felt inspired, when I felt like "Now I have an idea." So as a consequence, I was intellectually working all the time. Any time I was doing anything at all, I was also unconsciously thinking about the writing work I was supposed to be doing. These days, I know I can only work from eleven till five, so that's it. That's the only time I think about it. For most of my life, writing was the single most important thing to me. It was my priority, always. It was my whole identity. But that's no longer true. And that's so great. Writing is a wonderful job, but it can never make you happy. It can't. It's a subjective art form where you're working in a field with countless other people, some of whom will inevitably be more critically and commercially successful than you. There's never going to be a point where you say, "I'm happy now," unless you're so goddamn arrogant and self-absorbed that you reread your own writing and somehow think it's great. It's a game you can't win. It's an interesting life that will never make you happy. But my kids make me happy. I did not think I would be good at this, being a father, but it turns out it's maybe the only thing I'm not terrible at. Writing is ultimately an external experience. The way you feel about your own work is inevitably affected by people outside of your life. There's just no way around that. However, your family life is internal. The outside world is almost irrelevant.

Hua Hsu I really think the main difference between having a kid and not having a kid is that nothing really matters anymore once you have a kid. There's just a lot of very base human things that begin to matter in ways that were only abstract to you before.

Tom Breihan Measuring yourself against your peers, you can always be like, "Oh if I only didn't have kids and still lived in New York I'd be an editor somewhere." But I'm very happy where I am and I feel like I've made the right decisions. There's always the road not taken thing that you get to thinking about.

Hua Hsu Perhaps one time my goal was to become a great writer. Now my goal is just to write in order to be able to continue writing. I said this to someone who does not have a child and I think they thought it was really sad. But I like this place, because it means that it's really just about the writing. A lot of the kind of anxiety and weird narcissism of being a writer is melted away.

Steven Hyden I feel pretty fortunate because I work from home. I have an office in my house and I'm in my office most of the day. But if I want to pop up and see my kids I can see them more than if I was driving to an office somewhere. I feel like I'm maybe more visible in my kids' lives than maybe a lot of dads are able to be. So I'm grateful for that.

Mark Redfern It's challenging because we work from home. We always have. Over the years we've considered getting office space but it's never really worked out. It's just made financial sense to not do it. Our staff and our writers are very scattered all across America and the globe, and we've never have a centralized office, so it would have just been a

waste of money, especially when the two publishers lived together anyway. At first our daughter was constantly coming up to us and saying,
"Will you play with me, Daddy? Will you play with me, Mommy?" For
the first few years of her life we lived in a country house in Virginia after
moving there from Los Angeles about a year before she was born, so we
were quite isolated, thirty minutes from our nearest town, which made
casual playdates challenging and made it harder to focus on work. But
now we live in town and she's in elementary school, so it's easier to balance work and family life. I take her to school and work from 8 a.m. to
2:45 p.m., then I pick her up from school and we play at the playground
after school for a bit, before I get back to work until dinner and her bedtime. Then when she goes to bed we have to continue working. Usually most nights on the weekdays—not so much the weekends—you will
find Wendy and I sitting in front of our TV with our laptops on our laps
on our couch finishing up work while we watch our favorite shows that
we taped or Netflix. I mean, it would be nice to just watch TV and not
do anything, but I would probably be on Facebook if I weren't working
or something. In this day and age it's harder to just focus on one thing.
I like getting stuff done. I like accomplishing things, and it's always too
much for two people to do. We are always doing the job of five people.
We really should have a much bigger staff of people to do stuff.

Wendy Lynch Redfern I think we've always done the live and work and be
together thing, so when we added our daughter into that it changed,
but it also just seemed normal on some level. So I guess the way we
work really didn't really change a tremendous amount when she came.
I mean, we had to figure out time a bit better, but I think she's better for
it. We're able to be with her. We may not be able to play with her all the
time but we're here. So that's important to us.

Josh Jackson Early on in *Paste*'s history I was a father to three young kids
and trying to start a magazine with no capital funding, no big staff, so
those first issues, the two or three weeks leading up to deadline I would
leave the office with the sun coming up and go home and sleep for a few

hours and then head back into the office. We worked ridiculous hours. It was a strain on my family, my marriage. I was not a great dad in those early years because I was too focused on work, and it took probably three years of really letting work define me as a person and the work/ life get really out of balance before it hit me all of the sudden that that was not sustainable, that it was not what I wanted and wasn't fair to my family. So I just sort of one day realized and started making sure I was trying to find a balance, that I was there for my family, that I was not getting caught up in my identity as the editor of *Paste*, because all of the sudden it was this cool thing that I got to be. It was a very interesting experience, as *Paste* was growing so fast and we were getting lots of attention. We were getting recognized among these national magazine awards. We kept getting nominated and going up to New York and rubbing shoulders with all these editors I had admired from afar and getting kind of swept up in it. I think that happens to a lot of bands too. You start out and all of the sudden this is who you are and that leads to all kinds of problems for people. So yeah, it was not easy to figure out how to do that. But once I figured that out, once I realized that I did not want to lose my family, that that was the most important thing for me, it helped me to get back in balance, and I feel like I have been for the past ten years. Work is work and it's only one facet of who I am as a person and it can't ever dominate the rest of it.

Jessica Hopper Those of us that are parents in this profession, I can tell you every successful music critic that has a kid, and I can tell you the three that have two kids. I can tell you the four women with children that still work. I literally don't know another woman that writes about music for a living that has more than two kids. I remember before I had kids reading in the Sontag journals that Sontag's son edited and put out. It was the first one that covered her teenage life. But there's this passage where she's really starting to come into serious renown and really wants to do this really heavy, intellectual pursuit, and her son is eight and she's sitting in a park with him writing in this notebook that the only way to really continue with this intellectual work is to give him up for adoption. And he was eight! And I remember thinking at the time, "God, that's fucking harsh." And now I'm like, "How else would anyone get anything done?" I mean, not really, but you have to compartmentalize all that stuff.

Carvell Wallace I think that there is a certain kind of ruthlessness that has to happen with your work time. You really have to use your work time to work. And I'm a terrible procrastinator. I'm probably the worst procrastinator on the face of the earth. It's insane. And yet I am 100 percent sure that I can never expect to get work done when I'm supposed to be with my kids. That time doesn't exist. And I also feel like I can't miss deadlines. And so things have to remain nonnegotiable in your mind. Trying to write when I'm with my kids—even if that were possible, which it isn't—even when they're doing homework and promising to be quiet between the two of them, someone's got something to say every forty-five seconds. And so you just can't get into a flow.

David Marchese If my wife is on deadline or something, I'll deal with the kids, and if I have to make a phone call in the middle of dinner or at bedtime, she deals with them. She's really good about being flexible in that way. But we also do try to proactively plan who'll need to be responsible for what and when. And then there's just a fair amount of discipline. Before I had kids, if I had a half hour to kill in the middle of the day I might fart around reading on the internet. But now it's like, no, I have to take that time to do research or work on a draft. I'm more particular and conscientious about how my time is being used.

Jessica Hopper When I was full-time freelance and my kids were really little, it was like, "Oh one of the kids is asleep, I need to write furiously for an hour and a half or forty-five minutes." Having kids will make you really learn how to not be precious with your time or your thoughts. So one of the things that I do is I just take notes constantly. I take notes in the car and have a notebook everywhere I go because it might be because of my kids' schedule or having other things that I do, it might

be seven hours, it might be two days before I can really sit down and go,
"All right, I've had my tea and I'm fed and I'm feeling coherent," and I can
sit down and kick this out really coherently.

Jayson Greene For me at least writing lends itself pretty well to a life being
an attentive parent. It depends on what kind of writer you are. I'm the
kind of writer who fits writing into the crevices of his life. I like having
lots of time, but I don't need lots of time to write. I like the way that writing and parenting slot into each other. I can be present, and if I have a
thought I can put it into my phone and put it away, and I'm still on the
scene. That's sort of true with some other jobs, but to me it's uniquely
true with writing.

Carvell Wallace A couple of months ago I was having lunch with my son
and he asked me what I was doing, and I was like, "Something something deadline blah blah blah," and then he just looked at me and he
said, "So you just write for a living. All day you just write." And I was like,
"Yeah, I do." And he was like, "That is so crazy." And I was like, "I know!
I feel that way every day." And he was like, "That is so cool that you can
just do that." And I'm like, "Yeah, it is."

J. Edward Keyes Here's what I think is true. I don't think anyone in the world
thinks music writing is as cool as music writers think it is. For real. And I
think that's the thing that people should keep in mind. What we get to do
is—it's insane that I get to do this for a living. That I should be so lucky is
insane. But I think it's helpful to have a sense of perspective.

Craig Jenkins I wouldn't necessarily recommend it to everyone, but for the
people who are interested, they need to be fearless and be constantly learning how to change. The best ones are doing that. I want to see
more people challenging themselves and challenging their subjects.

Steven Hyden Early on, 80 percent of the things I was writing about were
things that I would not have chosen to write about. But because I had to

write about it I had to learn that professionalism, where it's like, "Okay, this is your job." You have to find a way to be interested in it and find a little thing in it that you can care about. To me that's what being a professional writer is. It's not just doing cool stuff all the time. It's taking something that maybe you don't care about, finding a way to care about it, and then writing a story about it. Now I'm in a position where whatever I write about it's because I want to write about it. It's just cool stuff all the time. I still think about where I came from. When you have that kind of perspective it gives you a work ethic, and I think it also just gives you a sort of willingness to go the extra mile. So I'm really grateful for the experience. I'm really grateful for that experience now, but at the time it was tough. It was really tough.

T. Cole Rachel I think there are always going to be people who want to very superspecifically just write about music, and they love it, and really be into the sort of nerdy history of music journalism. They want to do that. They want to be a part of it. But I also tell my students it is to your benefit to be able to write about other stuff too. I could not have made a living if I only wrote about music. I mean, music was probably 80 percent of what I wrote about, but I also interviewed tons of actors about movies or wrote about books, wrote about fashion every once in a while. Being open to do lots of different things, it only makes your writing more interesting and better I think.

Mark Richardson I think in terms of people who want to be music writers, one of the biggest changes is that if you want to make your way into writing online these days, it's a little unwise to really focus exclusively on music, because there just aren't that many outlets that pay decent money for music writing anymore. I think more and more people are like, "I write about music, I write about games, I write about TV." And that seems like a really important part of being a cultural writer. And in certain ways that kind of mirrors something that's going on in culture, which is that music is not a separate thing the way it once was. It's part of the culture sphere. It's a thing on your phone among other things. It's that thing that's on in the background during a TV show. It used to be, "Here's a record store," and all they'd have is records. Now I think music is just part of this broader fabric of things that are consumed in culture. The writing in some ways mirrors that by being not just about music.

Craig Jenkins The more attention I've paid to fields outside of music, the more it has helped open up my depth perception in terms of what is happening in my main field.

J. Edward Keyes I think one of the problems is new writers can just get into a thing where it's like, "Oh I'm the 'this' writer and this is the genre that I write about and I only cover this." And I think it's kind of bad for a music writer to not at least have some kind of a generalist knowledge.

T. Cole Rachel A lot of my music writing early on was for nonmusic magazines. A lot of the big music stories I did were for fashion magazines. And that's a slightly different thing. You can't really nerd out writing about music in the same way if you're writing for a fashion magazine in the same way you would if you were writing about it for a music publication. You can't make the same kind of assumptions about your readers. You can't assume that they know what you're talking about, or you can't reference things the average magazine reader might not know. But you have to be adaptable. You have to be able to write about a lot of different kinds of things and not just specifically the things that you love, and being able to write for a lot of different kinds of places and sort of adapt to what their needs are. I was writing for a bunch of different fashion magazines, but I was also writing for Stereogum. I was writing band bios for record labels. I did a ton of work in the mid-2000s for a fashion company that wanted to do music promo tie-ins, and I was helping them find bands to work with and then writing the copy for them. I just kind of had to wing it, you know? I feel for a lot of these kids coming out of school, that's going to be more and more the case. You're really limiting yourself if you're only interested in talking or writing about certain kinds of things.

Maria Sherman I think a survival instinct is knowing that to do the writing that you want to do, you have to do a lot of writing that you're not going to enjoy at all. The survival instinct is simply knowing that you've got to do the grunt work. Everybody has their own path in this field, which is something I love and appreciate so much, but to be successful you have to do the work or else there's no growth, there's no improvement. How can you be the best if you're not really suffering for a while?

J. Edward Keyes A great experience was where when I was a stringer for *Rolling Stone* where they would just send me to all the summer festivals, and that was always a fun challenge. I also did live show reviews for *Newsday* for a long time, and I still think that's resulted in some of my best writing, because they'd send me to see Sleater Kinney and then also send me to go see fucking Staind and Rascal Flatts and Toby Keith. And it's like you go and you've got to write about it. How do you find an interesting way to talk about Toby Keith that isn't just "Courtesy of the Red, White and Blue" and isn't just a by-the-numbers Republican country thing? How do you say something different? More writers should have to do that.

T. Cole Rachel I'll just bring a bag of promo CDs and then have them [my students] draw one out blankly, and then they have to go research it, listen to it, and write something about it. And there are a lot of students who are just like, "Oh I just I really only care about hip-hop. That's all I want to write about." And I'm like, "Well that's not really how it works." Even if that becomes your sort of specialty. You can't be expected to know everything, but if this is the world that you want to operate in, the onus is on you to like do your homework and understand the context for the kind of music that you're writing about.

Michael Azerrad I would tell them to consider the ramifications of making a living by analyzing something you love. Ideally, we should all do what we love, but with music, it's a little different because music is a basic human pleasure, an amenity of life, only slightly less elemental than food, sex, or a nice nap on a quiet afternoon. Instead of listening purely for enjoyment like most people, you'll always be listening from a professional perspective too, anticipating what you'd say if someone should pay you to write about it, or even just having to come up with something interesting to say because your friends or even total strangers will expect it of you. For me, anyway, that taints the experience—I'd love to enjoy music without having to come up with a coherent reason why. So while everyone else in the crowd is just digging the music, which is what you're *supposed* to do, you're also thinking about it critically, *professionally.* Ironically, that takes you out of the experience, because while you're busy formulating your thoughts about that song you just heard, another one has started. But hey, for some people that actually heightens the experience of music, rather than diminishing it. All I'm saying is, consider that before diving in.

Lizzy Goodman The financial realities of music journalism are almost untenable. It's almost impossible to make a living doing this, and that is a real shame. It's true for the bands too. The marketplace has not stabilized enough to create the kind of financial support that allows these art forms—both the making of music and the writing about music—to breathe, to actually grow and have the space that they need. That is a genuine and sobering problem. So I don't in good conscience feel like I can tell kids who ask me, "Yeah you should really pursue your dream of being a music journalist." That seems like a really stupid thing to tell them to do. That's the downside. It's an impediment that almost eliminates the rest of the positives. Because if you can't make money doing this to support yourself, then it's not a career—and it is a career. It's important.

Matt Fink I basically tell them, do it if you really, really think you're going to love it. But I would say don't go into it expecting to make a living. Have a fallback plan for sure, because if you think this is going to pay the bills, I certainly wouldn't expect it to pay the bills right away, and maybe even ten years down the road you're going to be struggling still. I think to be successful in this line of work is not having a very high standard of living. You're probably going to work long hours for little pay, and your social life and other interests are going to get crowded out to some extent. If you can accept that and be good with it, then full speed ahead. I do know writers who do this full-time. They seem very happy about it, and they seem to not regret their choice. So if you can envision yourself being that person, then more power to you, but I don't think everyone's cut out for that. I think there are still romantic ideals about what this line of work is that pretty quickly dissipate once you're in it for a couple of years. I definitely had that experience.

Ryan Leas I don't know what to tell young people trying to start in web journalism. Staffs aren't big at these places, and a lot of people that make them up don't have a lot of incentive to move around. If you wind up with one of the, what, couple hundred staff jobs in New York? If that? It's a really small pool.

J. Edward Keyes Make sure you want to do it. Ask yourself if you can think of any other thing that you would be happier doing. And if you can think of something, do that. Seriously. Because it's really fucking hard and getting harder.

Carl Wilson I mostly tell them not to do it. I kind of feel this about writing in general, but the best advice is, only do this if this is the only thing you can do. If there's something else that you can do that will make you happy, it'll probably make you happier than doing this will. I've been lucky, but the odds are kind of against you. You have to be willing to feel like you're failing for a long time.

Lizzy Goodman I'm a fan of change. I really have very little emotional space for the kind of lamenting of how much shittier things are now. That's not really an attitude that I find to be very appealing or constructive.

Maura Johnston That's another thing I feel like we should talk about. The good old days—there were obviously some great pieces back then but most of it was also crap. There was just a lot of it that's just very poorly thought out or slapdash or racist or sexist because it was mostly white men writing back then.

Jenn Pelly The diversity of voices currently represented in music journalism is hugely exciting. This is true of journalism in general, and it also brings so much urgency to the immediate need for fair, sustainable funding models, and I think it's all of our responsibilities to push that conversation forward. The golden age of music journalism cannot be behind us. For my work, I spend a lot of time diving into archives and reading writing about women musicians from the '70s, '80s, '90s, and early 2000s, and the sexism is abhorrent. We are finally reaching a time where a lot of that no longer slides because the internet has pressed a magnifying glass up onto culture. So you could say that we're watching the economy of journalism crumble, or you could say that we're in a pivotal moment. I prefer the latter. It's up to all of us to consider what that means.

Michael Azerrad The thing that's changed the most since I started is who's writing about music. It used to be virtually all men, but starting around the early 2000s, more and more women started writing about music, and that really started rejuvenating the whole thing. And then other people who had previously not lent their voices to the music journalism/criticism chorus started getting in, and it got even more interesting.

Joe Levy The barriers for good work being done by diverse voices have decreased. They still exist but they have decreased and not because of anything other than the hard work of those with something to say.

Ann Powers For women in my field historically there was often one position for a woman, and it was never at the top. There was also a sense—and I'm not talking about my own personal experience, but just the general field—that women were good at certain things, especially writing about other women, and maybe not appropriate for other things.

Gabriela Tully Claymore There's always imposter syndrome. Whenever you're in the minority—especially for me when I started working full-time and I was twenty-one and was the only woman at the website and I felt like I didn't really know what I was doing—I now have interns that say similar things to me, that they feel like they don't have authority. Self-doubt is almost like a reflex when you work in an industry that traditionally favors the opinions of cisgendered, white men.

Ilana Kaplan I feel like I've had to work harder to get my ideas across or taken seriously. I've found that hard. I think that there are always guys that think they're smarter than you or use their position of power as an editor and basically will make you feel like your ideas don't have value. I think that happens to a lot of women. And in the reverse situation, female editors I know deal with male freelancers who are totally out of line.

Ann Powers One of the most exciting things about this moment is that it seems to really be changing. There's a genuine sea change. There's so many more women in positions of power as editors, as chief critics. That's fascinating and wonderful to me. I don't want to overly idealize. I don't believe in essentialism and I certainly don't believe that there is some kind of feminist her-land utopia out there that could exist. But I will say that that I'm very inspired by how women in music writing are helping each other and are dedicated to equity.

Liz Pelly I think we're in a period of time where outlets need to reckon with what resources they have and who they're giving them to, and to think hard about elevating the voices that have historically not been given platforms. That needs to be an ongoing commitment. And while visibility is important, it's also important for outlets to structurally uphold those commitments.

Clover Hope More and more it's important to make sure that that not just one voice is controlling or leading the conversation.

Brittany Spanos I definitely see more writers of color than I saw even when I first started. It's really incredible to see—especially young women of color—really rise up the ranks of journalism. That's my favorite thing to see.

Puja Patel It is incredibly meaningful to be in the position I'm in. Years ago I was counting all of the editors I have had and realized that I had only ever been edited by one person of color. What I will say about being in this position at *Pitchfork* is that it gives me the opportunity to raise up other voices and to be very purposeful about change. It gives me the privilege to forcefully say "I want to see this" and "I don't want to see this." Where before I felt privileged to even be asked for the assignment, I now feel privileged to be able to create the change, and that feels amazing.

Carvell Wallace In America music as a whole, as an entire entity across the cultural board, has to deal with blackness much more directly than all the other forms of media. It has to be positioned in terms of blackness. It's really hard to deny that in pop music, partially because at some point in the last however many years black music became everyone's pop music. Pop culture music critique provides a really good opportunity to talk about issues of race in a way that other mediums don't quite make it as easy to do. TV is still viewed—the stories, the ideas, the people, the narratives—are still viewed as white people. And then you might throw some black folks in there so that no one accuses you of not doing that. And movies are kind of the same way. But music is different in that regard.

Brittany Spanos I didn't really think too much of it and then I got into NYU and it was just so overwhelming how many white men were in all of my writing classes. It made me for the first time really uncomfortable. You know in high school everyone's sort of spread out and you don't really think about it, and I got to college and was like, "Why am I the only one that looks like myself?" And then I started to think more about the writers I was reading. I didn't really have a lot of background on the idea of race theory or gender theory or things like that and didn't really understand the discrepancy just because I never thought about it. And then you enter that world, and seeing it happen in college and seeing it happen in my college newspaper, where all the editors were white dudes, it was fascinating to feel that shift for myself.

Maria Sherman It wasn't until I got to college that I realized that all my favorite writers weren't women and there were no Latinos. And when I had that realization I was like, "Oh crap. I've really got to do this now."

Hannah Giorgis I think it is harder for, I think, writers of color, black writers, women writers, to sort of apply for gigs or to say, "I like music. I'm a critic." I think in the media landscape we're in, that's difficult. The barriers to entry for criticism, the barriers to entry for reporting—especially investigative reporting—are pretty high. But the way a lot of us have finagled our way into the industry has been through more personal essays or through commentary that's slightly political or social justice–oriented. A lot of my earlier stuff was in that vein, and in doing it I kind of got on people's radar. And then I said, "Take a chance on me to do this other thing." That was the purposeful and intentional effect after a while, because I really love criticism, I really love reporting, and sometimes you have to go in through a slightly different door. My whole life and my views are largely informed by the way that I walk around in the world, as a black woman, and the way that people treat me as a result of that. I don't know that I can ever divorce it. That being said, I also grew up having to be fluent in many different kinds of writing and kinds of speech to gain any sort of access in this industry. It's interesting to see how it feels like only just now in the last couple of years that that is shifting.

Brittany Spanos I'm glad that a lot of my mentors that I got right away, people like Jessica Hopper, and meeting someone like Ann Powers and reading Maura Johnston and doing stuff for *Rookie*, where all the editors are women, it helped to be in those environments very early on. I was very lucky to be in a community like *Rookie*, to have a lot of female journalists I immediately started seeking out and trying to consume as much of their writing as possible.

Jes Skolnik I do my best to bring in new freelancers and mentor them. I think that there is a problem when the industry stops hiring freelancers and does not build those people up into staff writers or editors. There's also a huge gap there where you see the exploitation of marginalized freelancers for their particular perspective, which to me is incredibly valuable. I think that opening up that field is huge. The next step is going to be opening up the staff rooms. The next step is opening up the mastheads.

Puja Patel It very frequently feels like women and people of color—and in my case women of color—are tasked with fixing systemic issues within their industries. There should be so many more women of color who are given the opportunities that I was given. And I've realized I was given an opportunity to grow and I took every advantage of every opportunity I had. That's why I'm here.

Hanif Abdurraqib I would like to see more black women. I would like to see more queer folk who could offer insights into music that speaks to their demographic. It is getting better. I of course would like more to change, but it's better than it was and I hope that it continues to be.

Gabriela Tully Claymore I'd like to see this be less of a fad and more just a changing of course, which I think it is. I think it's kind of course correcting.

Puja Patel I have to just remember that I can only represent myself. That's all I can speak for. I think the challenge is that sometimes the media, or people within your industry, or even people who work alongside you, hope that you can represent them, and when I can, I take full advantage of doing that. But there are other times where it is in no way my right to speak on behalf of other women or all people of color. So it's challenging but it's very exciting.

Christian Hoard It's really forced a lot of places to figure out exactly what it is they do well and do more of it. Back in the day *Rolling Stone* might be one of like only a couple of sources for music journalism for the average reader. Now you have literally thousands of websites out there. So we don't try and compete with *Pitchfork* and try to review every single record. What we're good at right now is reporting and long profiles and stuff like that. And so we've focused on that. And I think that people keep coming to us for that. Because the audience can go in any different direction, you've got to be among the best at what you do and really focus on what you do well.

Lizzy Goodman The benefit for me was that it forced me to ask a lot of questions earlier about how and what I really wanted to write about. I don't want to write straightforward profiles of rock bands. I don't care that much that X, Y, or Z band has an album coming out and therefore because of that record cycle we need to figure out something to say about them. I want to write culture pieces that often have to do with musicians because music is the lens through which I view the changing shape of culture. That's kind of how I approach it.

Puja Patel You just can't be everything to everyone as a publication, as a writer, as an editor. Finding your voice and your perspective and being levelheaded about that matters more than basically anything else. And I can't emphasize this enough: literally follow your own curiosity until it hits a dead end. That's the best gift you can give to yourself when trying to think critically about something. Follow your own rabbit holes and then wherever you end up, you've probably explored more than you ever thought you would.

Steven Hyden For me the future isn't about chasing some zeitgeist. It's about cutting my own path. I want to conduct my career in the way my favorite bands have conducted their own careers, where they're not in the mainstream. They're just doing their own thing, like Wilco or something. Wilco is just Wilco and they continue to be Wilco no matter what is happening on the outside. And that's the way I want to be in my career. I want people to come to me because they like what I'm doing and they feel like they can trust my voice. And it doesn't really matter what's happening outside of that.

Rob Sheffield Amanda [Petrusich] actually has a class at NYU on writing about music, and it's really funny whenever I'm there visiting and talking to her class, I just look at the room full of these writers and think there are more people in this classroom who are interested in writing about music than there were in the country when I was their age when I was doing it. It just was not as widely practiced, widely cared about, or a widely read genre of writing. Writing about music from any number of perspectives—whether that's journalistic or historical or personal or impressionistic—writing about music is something that has really come into its own as a form of creative writing and form of expression. And they have more to say and know more because there's no limitations on knowledge. They know the music deeper than we did. And they know each other's writing more broadly than we did. And I think it's no coincidence that the golden time for music writing is right now and most of my favorite writers ever are ones who are doing it now.

Marc Hogan I think we're going to be in a tough spot for a while. But the people working in music journalism are good people and good journalists and doing their best. So hopefully they'll continue to find situations to thrive wherever the pay comes from.

Larry Fitzmaurice As far as music writing, I'm going to keep doing it. I'm not going to not keep doing it. It's something that when I keep doing it I find people respond to it still, which is strange and funny to me. That's one thing that hasn't worn off. I'm always surprised whenever anybody reads what I write.

Stephen Deusner I like the fact that I got paid to listen to every single Tom Petty record. That seems silly or maybe that seems obvious, but when I'm going out and walking the dog and I've got the new Car Seat Headrest on or something like that, I do have those moments where it's like, "Oh. This is my job. This is what I do for a living. I get to do this."

Tom Breihan Most of the people I know who ten or fifteen years ago were doing this, if they still want to be doing this, they still are. Nobody's flunked out of the industry because they couldn't adapt with the times.

Eric T. Miller It's not writing about Watergate or the Pentagon Papers, but at same time it's a lot more serious than some of the shit that people write about that is of no consequence. It's never pretended to be important in the scheme of global events or anything, but sometimes you just want to read a music magazine. For some people, it's not even escapism. Music is their life.

Christopher R. Weingarten From the time I was out of college it really was the single-minded pursuit of what I was going to do with my life. I didn't know that there would be a recession. I didn't know that there would be another tech bubble. I didn't know. I mean, I graduated college in 2002 and I didn't know these things were on the horizon. I didn't know that print would be destroyed to the degree that it has been. I also I didn't know how expensive New York would be to live in. I just sort of had this fancy idea of what the job entailed, and over the next fifteen years that idea of what it meant to be a professional music critic, the job itself kind of slowly eroded for all but a very small number of people. And now all I can do is sort of hang on. I'm just like a barnacle. I'm just music journalism's barnacle.

Christian Hoard Hopefully people still see the value of having trained professionals write about music. I think it's really important. We as an industry have to make sure we're not ever just doing people's PR. That's not our job.

Lizzy Goodman I'm not doing this job because I learned how to be good at it. I just am this way, so I had to find a job that would allow me to profit from it. I don't know how to not be taking notes. I take notes all the time, so I might as well be taking notes for some purpose.

Ben Ratliff If you really want to write about music you're going to do it no matter what you get paid or even how much time and energy it takes. It's almost a biological need. And that's as it should be.

Larry Fitzmaurice I really can't get over chasing that thrill of hearing something I love and how it makes me feel. That's one of the best parts of my job. And that would exist even if I wasn't writing about music, which I think says a lot. I like writing about music because I love music. I don't care about how it's being used or what it says about the human condition or what people are advocating for. I think those are great. All those things are interesting and they're important to somebody, but for me it's just hearing the music and loving it.

Tom Breihan Because I've been doing it for so long I don't know how to do anything else. When whatever internet bubble that we're in pops and nobody wants to pay for words anymore, I don't know what I'm gonna fucking do. I have no other skill. It's an amazing ridiculous thing that I get to do.

Stephen Deusner That sense of purpose and that sense of determination when you find an album that you really love, that maybe a lot of people don't know about, and you've got to convince somebody to let you cover it. There's something really amazing about that.

Bonnie Stiernberg On a good day it doesn't even feel like a job, like I conned everyone into letting me make money doing this thing that I like doing, which is great because I don't really have any other skills that could be applied to a different type of job. I love that I'm fortunate enough to do something that I love and am passionate about, that makes me feel like I can take pride in what I'm doing.

Amanda Petrusich I do kind of wonder, "Am I going to age out of this? At a certain point am I not going to want to keep up with this stuff anymore? Am I just going to settle into the records I have and I love, and am I just going to lose the energy to keep up?" Pop culture moves so fast now. Everything here is the biggest deal on earth and then it's totally gone. There is a point at which I think, "When I'm sixty, is this not going to be undignified?" I worry about that. I worry about the longevity of it. But then you look at a writer like Greil Marcus, or Peter Guralnick, or Jon Pareles, or Simon Reynolds, these amazing lifers who have managed to do this work and managed to do it so well for so long. Maybe there's hope.

Ben Ratliff My assumption is that there will be some use and value for patient, clear, and discerning writing. That won't completely go away. The venues for it might change and the occasions for it might change, but I don't think it will go away.

Lizzy Goodman I think it's going to recover. It's already starting to recover a little bit. The bottom line is that so many more people are reading about music and so many more people are making music and so many more people are consuming music with a greater and deeper sophistication that you have to believe that that's good for music. But we just haven't figured out how to get the industry to scale up, develop a financial structure that can support that.

Amanda Petrusich There's a real appetite for music writing. Every once in a while I'll get sort of aggrieved and frustrated and think, "What am I doing? What is the point of this? I should be a real journalist and write about real things." But there is a real appetite for it. People are into it. They want to learn more about the songs and records that mean a lot to them.

Lizzy Goodman There were definitely points in my early career where I didn't feel that grateful for this, but I do now. It's like I got to see the last gasp of the most extreme versions of what it used to be like to be a music journalist, and then I also get to see the total collapse. And now I'm witnessing and participating in a kind of rebuilding of whatever music journalism is.

Jim DeRogatis I think that this stuff—journalism, criticism—are too important not to endure. And while I think where we're at is a period of historical disruption that has momentarily tossed up the whole model for getting paid or for organizations to make money to do this, I think that those things will work out. But even if they don't, I think the craft and the process and the product is far too important not to endure and we'll either figure out a way or we'll all have day jobs and do it anyway because, again, we can't not imagine doing it.

Ben Ratliff Having been in journalism for a while you see people make predictions about what the future is going to be and they end up being totally wrong.

CHAPTER SEVEN

What Music Does, and Why It Matters

Music has a pervasive existence in the life of a music journal- ist. We think about music a lot. And when we're not thinking about music, we're listening to it. And when we're not listen- ing to it, we're likely reading about it. And when we're not reading about it, we're writing about it. It is just a constant variable in our day-to-day. Not everyone shares this obsessiveness. Some people are completely happy and content to go through life without ever thinking twice about a song after hearing it. They don't care where the song came from, who wrote and performed it. They don't care what its lyrics could be possibly commenting on, what was happening in the artist's life when he or she wrote a particular line or what happy accident lead to the track's signa- ture hook or riff. The song is just a song. It fills the air as a substitute for silence.

The brain of a music journalist just can't seem to function this way. We need to know. We need to know the who, the what, the when, the where, the why, and the how of this disembodied thing that has somehow wormed its way into our ears and caused a very real, very emotional reaction. And yet even if we weren't afforded the opportunity and ability to answer these nagging questions through our chosen profession, the love and fascina- tion we have for the art form would not diminish.

One of the most incredible aspects of music stems from its immediacy, how it has the ability to say and do so much in such a short amount of time, leaving you just as elated, uplifted, overwhelmed, excited, exhausted, astonished, and ultimately satisfied as if you had watched a two-and-half-hour film or spent days reading a book. It's transporting, and moves under the influence of your own emotional compass. Whether you're in love, have just had your heart broken, feel lost, confused, confident, empowered, have deep questions pertaining to your identity, the world, and where you're supposed to fit in it, there's going to be a song that can successfully tap into and reflect what you're feeling in ways maybe you hadn't even thought about before.

Music does so many things. It accomplishes so much all while seemingly doing so little to affect your actual physical space. Its invisibility, its weightlessness, makes it all the more subversively powerful because it forces us to internalize it. We're forced to make it our own.

Amanda Petrusich There's a very visceral thing that happens for music fans when they hear a song or a record that they love. It's often an immediate, very uncontrolled, very intense response. I've talked about this with some of my colleagues at NYU, who teach in different creative disciplines. There's something unique to music simply because that reaction happens faster, and often in real time. It takes a while to read a book. It takes a while to see and understand a painting, or a play. With music, it's often so instantaneous. And I think because of that, there's a curiosity about the quickness of the reaction. Well, who made this thing? What does it mean? What is happening to me? Are other people feeling this way?

Matt Fink Music to me feels very subjective. These are the kinds of things I just love to mull over. What makes an album good? Was this the right choice for this artist to make? What were they thinking when they did this? I love to endlessly consider those sorts of things because really there's no answer—no right or wrong answer anyway. In a way that's very frustrating. I have friends who are very black-and-white thinkers and it frustrates them to no end to debate these sorts of ideas, but I'm the kind of person that just loves that. I can spend hours upon hours and years upon years just thinking about those little minute, probably inconsequential decisions that are very important to me. Music's perfect for that. You can think about things and never come to conclusions.

Josh Jackson There is something about music that is a very personal, a very intimate experience. We often listen to music when we're alone, whether that's in the car or on headphones or any number of ways. It is just this encounter with something with someone who's created it that's an intimate conversation.

Laura Snapes I've learned about the whole world from being a music journalist. I have no degree, I quit university, my general knowledge isn't amazing. But music has helped me make sense of at least twentieth-century history.

Ryan Dombal I still have a romantic idea of an album, of living inside of an artist's vision for forty-five minutes. For me, music has always been the art form that I react to most, emotionally.

T. Cole Rachel I know this is not specific to my generation—this is a thing that all teenagers have—but it felt very much in that time you were sort of a tribe and it was defined by the kind of music you like, and what band T-shirt you wore. Before there was social media or the internet I would go to the mall and if you saw someone else wearing a Depeche Mode T-shirt you sort of made eye contact, like, "We're on the same team." It was so much a part of my identity and how I like saw myself in relation to the world.

Clover Hope I enjoy that an artist who may have been born ten years before you, ten years after you, who is or was in a city that is thousands of miles away from you, who may have had a totally different upbringing, you can listen to their music and have an emotional connection to that person. That's a simple joy, but I like that this product, this song, this album, or whatever can contain so many multitudes and that ultimately it's an emotion behind it, whether it's sadness or happiness or anger or indifference. Good music makes you feel something.

Steven Hyden The thing about music is that it's invisible. It's not a tangible thing, so there is something kind of magical about it. It makes it really hard to write about. It's an elusive thing, music. It's also the only art form I think that people feel comfortable when it's totally abstract. People still don't really accept films or TV if it isn't plot-driven or linear. They have a hard time accepting that. But with songs few are linear or make any kind of literal sense if you really broke them down . . . The great abstract filmmakers are always trying to do what songs do instinctively. Songs are just about evoking a mood or an emotion through sound and imagery in lyrics, and we accept that in music. There's this sort of magical mystery aspect to music. Even when music is just like wallpaper. It can be so mundane or can be in your face. It's sort of a full spectrum in that. As a writer you're trying to figure out and unlock it and articulate it for people. You're never going to get to the bottom of it, but you still want to keep chasing it regardless.

Jayson Greene It's the most emotional of the art forms, I think. Movies are perhaps close in certain ways because they marry images to music, but the fact that sound exists only in your mind is incredibly powerful to me. That's only become more true with the increasing disappearance of physical artifacts. Music is entirely invisible. Its medium is the air. There's something very beautiful about that to me. The medium is not paint, the medium is not chemicals in film. It is the air. And if you are listening to a recorded piece of music, you're listening to someone else's dead air. It's already dead when it reaches you. You are listening to a recreation of life that happened somewhere else. Photography has some element to it as well, where you're capturing life, but something about the way that you spend time immersed in music has been very powerful to me. You can surround yourself in it in a way that it is hard to do with other art forms.

Jim DeRogatis I always had this fight with Roger Ebert. I said, "Look man, it's easy. You sit there for ninety minutes in the dark and you've got a million fucking things to write about. Right? You've got the dialogue, you've got the cinematography, you've got the direction, you've got the soundtrack, you have a million things. You try sitting here listening to an Aphex Twin album and review it. And of course he would tell me I was full of shit. But I think that there is an evanescent quality of music. Where is it? It's in the air. It's not something we can grab and hold and study necessarily, you know? Unless you're lucky enough to have synesthesia and you can visualize music as colors and shapes, it's this ineffable, magical essence that has a power beyond any other. Proust starts *Remembrance of Things Past* with walking down the street in Paris and the bakery doors open and the smell of that madeleine prompts him to recall his entire life. And okay, yeah, impressive. But what was the song playing when you got laid? Or when you found out your dad was dead? Oh boy. Now there's a rush of emotions, all the more powerful, forever ingrained. And you know you can't smell a madeleine and get inspired to climb a mountain or be so depressed you're going to bury yourself in a cave and not come out for a week. But music can do that.

Jes Skolnik The whole idea of popular music is that there is an emotional connection between the musician and the listener, if it succeeds. And what that means can look different depending on who you are. Other forms of art are not necessarily that intimate. Music you can carry with you in parts of your life that you can't with other forms of art. I love books very, very dearly, and I am a voracious reader and always will be, but I do not take literature with me in the same way that I take music with me. There are aspects of emotional connection obviously with, say, a book, but it's not like it's everywhere in your life, that it's not soundtracking your romantic relationships or just being there as you do the daily things that you do. Music is with you in parts of your life that other pieces of art don't get to be, and so that emotional connection is so strong. And I think that people relate to musicians in a really intense way because of that.

Mark Redfern I mean, when we started the magazine, you know, you had to go to the store to buy the albums, and we would often go to the Virgin megastore or Tower Records up on Sunset Boulevard—neither of which exists anymore—and you could go at midnight and you could buy albums and I remember being really romantic about it. Once, before I met Wendy and I was single, I went to buy Richard Ashcroft's first solo album—because I love The Verve. And you know back when we first started, indie rock in America was still very much not in the mainstream at all. Artists weren't hitting number one like, you know, Death Cab for Cutie or Arcade Fire and those kinds of bands have now. And I remember thinking, "I hope there's a really pretty girl here that is also here to buy the Richard Ashcroft album at midnight and our eyes are going to meet and we're going end up dating." Later that year I did meet Wendy, and it all fell into place. I wasn't buying the Richard Ashcroft album when it happened, but buying music was a big deal.

Christian Hoard I can still walk around the city and put on a track and have that feeling, that elation that I used to get as a kid. It was a source of strong and wonderful feelings when I was young and still is. It's also just a great way to learn about the world. In the same way I learned how to do math from being a young, obsessed baseball kid, I learned about culture from listening to music. It's just the thing that's opened up the world to me.

Marc Hogan I love music. That's the key thing. I mean, I've always been passionate about it for so long and kind of have always been drawn to it. It is this part of our culture. There's always different aspects of the culture, whether it's literature or visual arts or movies, and you know, I like all those things, but music has always just spoken to me the most powerfully. I was that music guy that was burning CDs for you or sharing songs with people, saying, "Oh, you know, if you like this like, then you'll like this." I think it matters and think it's something that even you don't consciously—you have to choose to watch something, you have to choose to look at a picture, but music if it's on it goes in your ears. You can't not hear it. It has so much meaning.

Maura Johnston Music is the most transformative I think of our forms be-cause it's the only one that has to be described with completely sub-jective language. You can say, "Oh there were two people in this movie shot." But with music it's all in your brain, and as a result it can summon and channel these deeply felt ideas and emotions that I think other art forms can but not to the same extent.

Ben Ratliff I often do think about sound as kind of a tactile thing, like an object that you might be able to see in front of you or walk around or even hold. It makes it easier for me to think about it that way—that the sound has some kind of form or shape.

Nitsuh Abebe When I was young there were two things that probably created the most interesting feelings in me, and one was music. The other was books, mostly fiction. Those two things would create real-ly interesting thoughts and sensations in me. With books I knew right away how to talk about that. It was like there was an existing language for how you would talk to people about what a narrative did or made you feel. But with music it's blocked off in a way. I would listen to it and have really intense feelings that attached to certain images that seemed very powerful, but if you're trying to explain why, there's not an easy avenue into words to say why this song seems like the coolest thing in the world when you're fourteen. So I think I was really interest-ed in how you try and capture what it is that you're getting out of that, to somehow replicate this extremely cool feeling that's in the music. How would you translate that into any other media?

Jack Rabid It transcends language. And I listen to bands that sing in Por-tuguese. I don't understand a word. You can still get into the vibe of the music even though you don't understand a word they're saying. The Cocteau Twins they just invent their own damn language. All those Cocteau Twins records, it's like, "What is she singing? Fuck if I know." But we listen to the records. People love music. Even people who just treat it as background wallpaper, which is the vast majority, you can see them humming to themselves sometimes. They don't even realize it. This is not something small, something pedantic or infinitesimal. The way I approach music even when we're talking about pedantic facts, to me they're not pedantic facts. They're very interesting facts that lead me into the creative process of the people who made it, the time in which it was made, the expression that's involved in it. There are so many fascinating backstories.

Hannah Giorgis I think music is one of the most powerful and uniting forms of expression and it defies so many boundaries and has been used to connect individuals more broadly speaking to political change, to woo people, to heal families. There's just so much power, and to play any small role in interpolating that or in bringing an artist's intent or vision to other people is really humbling and exciting and a fun challenge. Music has played much in how I relate to the world around me. When something happens it's like, "Oh this reminds me of this one lyric," or you send a song to somebody and that song often says so much more than saying the same thing in a written message. It's so weighty and one of the purest things that we have.

Eric T. Miller When I was younger, music was it. That's what we talked about. That was the determining factor of who in high school you would hang out with: what kind of music they listened to. I was always really obsessed with music and obsessed by artists' backstories and everything like that.

Tom Breihan At least for those of us in this business, we're all fifteen forever. I mean, I don't know how kids do it now, but I formed my identity and the way I thought of myself by the artists who I fell in love with. I saw myself reflected back in them and who I aspired to be like or dress like or whatever.

Liz Pelly A lot of teenagers get into music because it's a way to feel connected to something, or be part of a community, or be part of something that's more interesting than what they have around them in high school or what they see on TV. A lot of it goes back to this increasingly isolated culture that we live in. Against all odds I feel like music is something that still brings people together and still gets people out of the house and into a physical space on a regular basis to have a shared experience. It's something that people connect over in an increasingly disconnected, disengaged world and something that people still feel strongly and passionately about in a culture that's increasingly passive.

Gabriela Tully Claymore When I was growing up and was really angsty and having a hard time in a lot of ways, discovering new music could turn my whole day around. One song can elevate your mood or reflect it and make you feel less alone in whatever experience you're having.

Brittany Spanos I think something that I always loved about music was how intensely people can feel about certain artists and certain songs. A lot of my family, none of them are musicians. They all have very working-class, blue-collar jobs, but a lot of them have a really intense love for specific musicians. I always love how much my grandpa loved Elvis. I loved how much my mom loved Prince. It's just things like that always really got me. I love seeing that in my friends too. I believe there's something really interesting about trying to balance the idea of creating art yourself and creating art for these masses of people who have such ownership over your art. It kind of relates to the reason why I got so into music and music history, which is this idea of feeling this ownership over a song that doesn't necessarily belong to you—even though it feels like it does and it feels like it's connected to you. From the standpoint of the musician you have to create music that evokes that feeling for people but also still has personal meaning. I feel like it's such a complicated thing and I love trying to dissect that, this idea of how do you create for yourself but also create for these people who feel so much about all the work you make and feel like this is part of them?

Michael Azerrad Like a lot of people, I'll often say that music has gotten me through hard times of all kinds. But, truth be told, I would have gotten through them even if I lived in complete silence. Music just makes it a little easier, especially since—and I know this is true for a lot of people—music can articulate feelings that I can't articulate myself. I'm from a generation that defined itself by the music we listened to. And that still applies to some people—metal fans and hip-hop fans can be like that, for instance—but it was a much more profound and prevalent thing for people born between World War II and maybe the midseventies. Music had a lot of innate progressive social power, and that gave it a huge impact. But also, as far as youth culture was concerned, music was pretty much the only game in town. I look back at the music I was listening to at various periods of my life and connect it directly to who I was and what I was thinking at the time. But also I'm just kind of addicted to the progression of music. It's like a TV miniseries that ends in a cliffhanger every time—you have just *got* to see the next episode to see what comes next. Most of my generational cohort has stopped listening to new music and begun watching actual TV miniseries, but I go out to see music three or four nights a week and don't have a lot of interest in couch time. It's also really rewarding to wrap your head around new music. At first, it might not make sense, but then you suddenly—or gradually—get it, and there's nothing like that epiphany, you really feel like you've advanced as a person, and, like learning anything, it enhances your appreciation of the universe.

Ann Powers Music, like all art worlds, exists within an environment and an ecosystem that contains not just the artist but the fan, everyone in the industry who helps get the music out, the critic . . . everybody is working together to create work. Bruce Springsteen doesn't exist without his audience. He doesn't exist without his band. He never would have been Bruce Springsteen if not for the perfect combination of the players he played with. We can see this clearly. It took him three albums to kind of get the formula completely right. He kind of comes into existence in that moment. It's not that he doesn't exist as a human being, but he doesn't exist as an artist, as an icon, until that interaction with history and that interaction with a fan. I like the communities it creates. I like the way that I can have a dialogue with a work of music that feels like it speaks to me and I can speak back to it. There's something so intimate about music. The ear is the first sense that develops when you're just born. Your ear develops before your eyes, and I think music brings us back to our most unadorned selves. Rhythm has a relationship with the body. There's this phenomenon called entrainment where your autonomic nervous system in your body actually responds to rhythm. You kind of sync up with it. That's why you can kind of feel like you're in a trance when you're listening to music. I love those moments. I think that's one reason why I love live music maybe better than recordings, because I love to be in a room with people and have that experience happen and have that amazing mystical moment when total strangers are connected via this artist who's offering something and we are offering the artist something back. I still find that very profound. Whether it's a songwriter just sitting on a stage and the room is completely silent or it's a dance party and everyone is groovin', there's always that circular relationship and that's my fundamental reason I love it.

Rob Sheffield I was watching this band who were incredibly young kids, who are, you know, just out of school in front of a fairly young audience and I was thinking, "Wow this band is in the middle of the moment. They just made a fantastic album with all these great songs and the story can go anywhere from here. It can get incredibly heartbreaking. It could be just the beginning of an amazing, historic story." That element of the unknown is always there with music. You just can never tell. That romance of it, that's part of what makes it always a thrill for me.

Maria Sherman I remember reading in high school something Immanuel Kant said when I was a pretentious teenager, but he described music as being vulgar in a way that someone could put a handkerchief with a strong scent and wave it in front of your nose and you're kind of overwhelmed and disoriented. But essentially you can't shut off your nose. And music is the same way. You can close your eyes but you can't shut off your ears.

Hanif Abdurraqib I think the thing that interested me then is the same thing that interests me now about music, which is the way that music narrative's rests under these songs. I'm always trying to pick through those and unravel them. That's what's always interested me. I find that music is a driving force for a lot more, be it protest or love or fear or anger, all of these things condensed in a song that could be a few minutes long. That's really fascinating to me. I grew up really loving Bruce Springsteen, and the thing I love about Springsteen is that in these songs there were really long, stretched out emotions. I'm interested in how a small space can hold a lot. Music does that more than anywhere else.

Carvell Wallace I think there's something about the act of listening but not seeing that really opens up the pathway to emotion. So one morning a friend mine who I haven't talked to in a while texted me, "Oh thinking of you," and texted me the links to this Spotify track of "Nature Boy" by Nat King Cole, this vintage-ass song that's hella fucking morose and moody and melancholic, and when my son was getting up—he was lying in bed and I knew he was going to take forever to get out of bed—I just started playing the song on some little speakers in the kitchen, which you can hear in his bedroom. When the song was over it continued to play whatever else was on that Nat King Cole album. So, like, "Mona Lisa," "Unforgettable," so on and so forth. And at some point—I feel like it might have been during "Unforgettable"—my son was still in bed and I went into his room. His eyes were open and he was lying there and I was like, "Come on. We've got to get up." And he was like, "Dad you just ruined the moment." And I was like, "Okay, sorry," and I left. But he was having a moment. He was lying in bed, listening to Nat King Cole, and having a moment. And there's something about the fact that his emotions were being touched through auditory sensors but not through something visual. There was no other context. Something about that allowed him to experience a moment. I think that's what it is about music.

Jenn Pelly I always hope that music will surprise me. I would hope that the things I'm looking for are things that I don't yet know or can't anticipate.

Chuck Klosterman It really is intangible. I'm in my office right now, and I'm looking out the window, and I'm looking at a tree, and I'm thinking to myself, "Could I make this tree mean whatever I want? Could I look at this tree and decide, 'Oh this is actually a metaphor for how life works or how life changes or the passage of time or the conflict between nature and man? Or does it only mean something about me, because I'm the person looking at it? Does it actually mean nothing at all, to anyone?" I guess I could write any of those things. I could try to make looking at this tree into an emotional experience. But with music, that emotional experience just happens. I don't have to try. It just happens. I just hear the sound and I feel certain things and I think certain things. I don't use words like "magical" or "mystical," but it really kind of is that way. Why do I love mashed potatoes? I put them in my mouth and I love them. I just love them. And I guess I could describe all the details of what makes me love mashed potatoes, but the description might not be that different than the way I would describe how it feels to have a banana in my mouth. And I don't love bananas. I love mashed potatoes. So what's the difference? Well, it's something beyond my ability to write. This is why writing about music is fun. You are in some ways are trying to do the impossible. You are trying to describe something that is inherently indescribable.